# Observing and Recording the Behavior of Young Children

## FIFTH EDITION

# Observing and Recording the Behavior of Young Children

## FIFTH EDITION

DOROTHY H. COHEN,
VIRGINIA STERN,
NANCY BALABAN,
AND NANCY GROPPER

Teachers College
Columbia University
New York and London

Published by Teachers College Press, 1234 Amsterdam Avenue, New York, NY 10027

*Library of Congress Cataloging-in-Publication Data*

Observing and recording the behavior of young children / Dorothy H. Cohen . . . [et al.]. — 5th ed.
   p. cm.
  Includes bibliographical references and index.
  ISBN 978-0-8077-4882-4 (pbk. : alk. paper)
   1. Child psychology—Methodology. I. Cohen, Dorothy.
  BF722.C63  2008
  155.4072′3—dc22                        2008010255

ISBN 978-0-8077-4882-4 (paper)

Printed on acid-free paper
Manufactured in the United States of America

15  14  13  12             8  7  6  5  4  3

# Contents

# Preface to the Fifth Edition

At the time the first edition of this book was written in 1958, the practice of observing and recording the behavior of children as it was happening was pretty much confined to a small handful of early childhood teachers who were fortunate enough to have been trained in the tradition of child study. The tradition began in the 19th century, when some psychologists studied children, often their own, through recording their activities. The technique was applied to the study of children in educational settings just after World War I, when it was pioneered by early proponents of a developmental approach to curriculum. Although early childhood teachers accepted the principle of record-keeping based on observation, the practice failed to become widespread because the skills were not taught at most institutions preparing teachers. The original edition of *Observing and Recording the Behavior of Young Children* was a first effort at translating these skills into teacher terms.

In the years between the first, second, and third editions, interest in young children from birth to age 8 escalated, validating the new chapter by Nancy Balaban focused on infants and toddlers. Research constantly brought to our attention fresh information about how children think and learn, how their language develops, and how their families, their culture, and their environment influence and help to shape them. At the same time, there had been a resurgence of interest in ethnographic and natural observation. Could this be due in part because young children so stubbornly and persistently resist being captured by the commonly used standardized tests?

The fourth edition (Cohen, Stern, & Balaban, 1997) responded to innovations in the field of early childhood education stimulated by the passage of legislation requiring the inclusion of children with disabilities in general education settings. New knowledge about developments in social attitudes and roles that influence family life was also included without altering the basic approaches or premises of the former editions. The fourth edition also included the impact of culture, the influence of Vygotsky, and the significance of the environment.

Many colleagues at Bank Street College contributed their thinking and support to the fourth revision: Virginia Casper, Harriet K. Cuffaro, Kirsten DeBear, Eva Haberman, Marian Howard, Judith Leipzig, Linda Levine, the late Leah Levinger, Jean Mandelbaum, Miriam Pedraja, Karen Weiss, and the late Steven Schultz.

As we prepared the fifth edition, we took a fresh look at the book's relevance and focused on the diversity in early childhood classrooms. We thank our colleagues Nancy Nager, Lily Costa, Nilda Bayron-Resnick, and Sue Carbary for sharing insights that served to ensure the currency of this edition. We also acknowledge the many students at Bank Street College Graduate School of Education whose efforts at learning to observe and record appear in this volume and give it its contemporary validity.

We have tried faithfully to incorporate into this fifth revision the spirit and legacy of the two original authors and former colleagues: Dorothy Cohen, who initiated the idea for this book, and Virginia Stern, who collaborated with her on the first and second editions. This fifth edition is a new collaboration between two Bank Street College faculty members, Nancy Balaban and Nancy Gropper.

Our special thanks to Marie Ellen Larcada for her encouragement and support, and to Susan Liddicoat for her elegant editing.

—Nancy Balaban
Nancy Gropper

# Getting Started

Each of us has known at some time the glow of satisfaction that comes from reaching a child successfully. Having applied just the right touch at the right moment, we have warmed to the smile of pleasure and trust a child bestows on us when we have understood what she feels and thinks. And each of us has known, too, the frustration of using, to no avail, tested wiles and approaches, of being baffled and irritated because we have felt completely ineffective with some children. All teachers want to understand their students better. Many have tried to keep records of children's behavior in an effort to gain insight into why they do what they do. But all too often even records conscientiously kept seem to reveal very little, and we fall back on our hunches and our intuition as bases for judgment.

## WHY RECORDS?

This manual on record-taking describes recording techniques that will help teachers of young children work toward their goal of understanding children's behavior and enhancing their ongoing planning of curriculum related to children's interests and abilities. Observing and recording children's behavior is the wellspring that nourishes and integrates the dual elements of a teacher's role—"doing" and "reflecting." Using these techniques, teachers learn to rely on themselves as a potent source of information and to share what they've learned with colleagues and parents about the needs, interests, uniqueness, and diversity of the children they live with in the classroom. This manual does not tell how to interpret behavior, but it does suggest what to look for in explaining behavior. It also describes how to gather data and how to make the best use of the data. It discusses principles of observation rather than principles of diagnosis. If we could say that understanding a child is like unraveling a mystery, then taking records is the gathering of clues. Like experienced detectives, we must recognize the significant clues; we must develop special skills.

Teachers of young children do not get very far when they ask children to explain themselves. Nor can they use the personality tests and questionnaires that might help in understanding older children. For the present, our best technique seems to be the careful gathering of evidence via the on-the-spot record. To us, this means recording details that not only describe the action but reveal how a child feels about what he is doing: details on *how* he does something as well as what he is doing; the *quality* as well as the quantity of his interrelating with people and materials; and, of course, what he says.

The most complete recording of this kind, but not necessarily the best for our purposes, would be done by someone who knows shorthand and is not responsible for the life of the group. Obviously it is impossible for teachers to achieve near-perfect written records of all the details they actually see. Nevertheless, there is benefit to be gained from an awareness of what to look for in those odd moments when a teacher can whip out a small pad and let a pencil fly. Every teacher can get some records, and over the months even occasional jottings add up to something impressive. More important is the fact that knowing what is significant makes one generally more aware of the nuances of children's behavior, even if it is not always possible to write things down.

## A Teacher as One Part Scientist

In suggesting that teachers study children by careful observation and recording of behavior, we are borrowing a tool from scientific research that has sought to achieve the utmost objectivity and dispassion. For teachers observing the children with whom they work and live, absolute objectivity is impossible, and objectivity itself becomes a relative thing. One hopes that no teachers would ever try for so much objectivity that they would cease to be responsible and responsive adults to their children. It is far better for a child to have a warmly interested teacher who has kept no records than a meticulous observer with no warmth. But if we do not strive for the kind of absolute objectivity that eliminates all feeling, we do seek awareness on the part of teachers of the kinds of personal, subjective feelings that tend to skew records. The picture of a child that is influenced by such teacher involvement might not be a true picture of the child at all.

Suppose we look at a child with this in mind. Here is Johnny. He is 5. He lives on Third Street. He comes to school every day. To Teacher A he is a lovable roughneck, sturdy and full of fun. To Teacher B he is a sloppy child, wild and undisciplined. For Teacher C he hardly exists.

To Teacher D he is one big appeal for mothering. Which Johnny is the real Johnny? Does anyone know what Johnny thinks about himself?

Apparently people do not see children with unbiased eyes, or everybody would see the same Johnny. We need to examine these biases, or personal involvements, if we are to have some degree of accuracy in our record-taking.

## Our Conception of What Children Should Be Like

When we ourselves were the recipients of adult directions, we were told in definite terms what behavior would be tolerated and what would be punished. Within our families, within our communities, there were traditions and opinions, standards and values, set up as guides for our youthful consciences. To be clean was virtuous; to be dirty was naughty. To be polite was to merit love; to be rude brought on a spanking. But not all family goals were the same. Sobriety and thrift formed a code for some people, conviviality and relaxation as serious a code for others. To become a scholar was the goal for some, financial success for others.

When we are little, the teachings of the important adults are impressive—so impressive, in fact, that when we become adults and teach children in turn, we fall back with greater security and sense of rightness on what our parents taught us about how children *should* behave than on what research tells us about how they *do* behave. That is why Johnny's sloppiness stands out for Teacher B, and his good humor for Teacher A. Teacher C can hardly admit that such creatures as Johnny exist because to her way of thinking little boys are just not as nice as little girls! But Teacher D forgives all precisely because he is such a little boy.

We also form ideas about how children should act from the wider world of our particular cultures, the values espoused in our neighborhoods, and popular ideas from the media. If we are to see children as they are, our viewing lens must be anti-bias. By bias is meant "any attitude, belief, or feeling that results in, and helps to justify, unfair treatment of an individual because of his or her identity" (Derman-Sparks & the A.B.C. Task Force, 1989, p. 3). Bias has many sources. It may spring from one's experiences growing up in a specific family or community, from experiences with people different from oneself, from hidden messages in the media, or from unquestioned tenets of society.

Teachers often have feelings about children whose ethnic, racial, or cultural group differs from their own. Negative or fearful reactions may arise in teachers to children in wheelchairs or to children who cannot see or hear or have other disabilities, such as those resulting from Down syndrome, cerebral palsy, autism, or spina bifida. Disapproving opinions about gays and lesbians are sometimes projected onto children or children's parents. Teachers may ascribe particular behaviors as acceptable for boys but unacceptable for girls. Bias is at work when a teacher describes an inquisitive boy as "bright" and an inquisitive girl as a "chatterbox."

Biased attitudes can cause teachers to make incorrect decisions about children's capabilities and potential for learning, as indicated in the following:

> A teacher of 7-year-olds disliked the way Tim followed her and whined "teacher, teacher" many times during the day. The teacher was particularly repelled when Tim picked his nose and rolled the mucus into balls.
>
> One day the teacher brought in sand with fine, medium, and large mesh screens for the children to explore. She recorded a small group including Tim using the sand, as an exercise for a child development course. The record contained Tim's words: "Hey, the sand comes out faster when the holes are larger!" Reading the record aloud at the course, the teacher overlooked this statement until several members of the course called her attention to Tim's discovery. The teacher's prior judgment about Tim prevented her from seeing the child's achievement. (L. Levinger, personal communication, May 1994)

Embeddedness in one's own culture can also interfere with seeing children objectively. Familiar cultural customs, even the way we phrase what we say, can stand in the way of understanding or appreciating what others mean by their behavior. For example, an Asian-American author, writing about a Black boycott of Korean grocers in Brooklyn, New York, was shocked to hear a Black resident comment that "The Koreans are a very rude people. They don't understand you have to smile."

> Would she have reacted differently had she known smiling at strangers just isn't part of the Korean culture? . . . [That] they equate being solicitous to being insincere. The Korean demeanor is the absence of a demeanor. Koreans have a name for it: "mu-pyo-jung." It means "lack of expression." (Kang, 1990, p. 23)

Anglo teachers sometimes tell Latino children, "Look at me when I speak to you!" misunderstanding that in the child's culture looking down is a sign of respect. We need ways to step outside our own culture in order to be receptive to other meanings for familiar behaviors. Teachers can ask themselves, "Why did I do it that way? What did the child really mean?" For further clarification, if possible, share your observations with someone from the same culture as the child.

If we were to measure fluid milk in pounds and potatoes in quarts, we would be more accurate than if we measured children's behavior in terms of our own virtues and aspirations. While children will, when adult, take on adult ways of behavior, as children they are governed by somewhat different laws that are peculiar to this stage in the life of a human being. We know that a caterpillar is a stage in the life of a moth and it cannot fly. We know that a calf cannot give milk, although someday it will. But all too many people expect the human child to behave as adult as possible, and the sooner the better! In point of fact, we can be much more successful in guiding a child toward mature adulthood if we are clear about the nature of childhood.

Perhaps the thing that fools us about young children is the fact that they can speak. Because this special human ability is achieved so early in life, it is easy to assume that the thinking that lies behind the speech is surely the same as ours. By this reliance on children's speech as the key to understanding them, we close off meaningful avenues of communication between children and ourselves.

How many times do we say to a child, in anger or in sorrow, with insistence or with sweetness, "Why did you do it!" And in anger or in sorrow, belligerently or helplessly, the child answers, "I don't know." The truth of the matter is that children do not know, and cannot tell us why they do as they do. When we don't know either, that leaves us both confused.

### The Ways Children Reveal Themselves

There are reasons for a child's behavior, of course, plenty of them. Sometimes it is hard to decide which is the most likely of several possible reasons—for the same kind of behavior. But while each bit of behavior has a cause, we must sadly admit that the cause for a particular behavior is often a mystery. That is why as teachers we must gather good clues that will lead to understanding. Only by learning to see children as they are, and especially as *they see themselves*, will we get our clues. It is not as simple as it sounds.

Young children are still operating out of strong physical and emotional bases. Their bodies not only move into pretzel shapes with fluidity; body movement, body processes, and feelings loom large on the horizon of their existence. Young children *think* with their *hands* (they *touch* to find out) and *socialize* with their *feet* (stamping and kicking noisily are fine acts of comradeship). Or, they might think with their *feet* (what happens to a worm?) and socialize with their *hands* (what will happen if I touch him in the eye?). If we would record their growing and learning, we must record what they do with their bodies, even as we listen to what they say with their mouths. And we must listen without our grandmother, with her prejudices, peering over our shoulder!

Thus, even though the speech of a young child is a wonderful thing indeed when it occurs, it is far from complete for a long time. A young child's speech is not too good a tool for expressing feelings and thoughts, for example, although it fast becomes highly skilled at expressing a child's *wants*. (Even this is not true of all children.) Does a young child say, "I feel sad," or does she hang her head, cry, or stare into space (all *physical* expressions)? If we wait for her to grow to the stage where she is mature enough to pinpoint her emotions and tell us about them, we shall wait a long time indeed! We must learn, therefore, to recognize other behavior as clues to thought and feeling.

Children communicate with us through their eyes, the quality of their voices, their body postures, their gestures, their mannerisms, their smiles, their jumping up and down, their listlessness. They show us, by the way they do things as well as by what they do, what is going on inside them. When we are able to see the meaning of children's behavior as they do, *from the inside out,* we shall be well on our way to understanding them. Recording their various ways of communicating helps us to see them as they are.

## KEEPING RECORDS

There are many ways of keeping records of children's behavior to suit different purposes and situations. Some records are frankly *impressionistic*, and this is perfectly acceptable at times. When a new boy or girl enters school, a teacher cannot help but react and size up the child in her own terms. If she writes down her impressions, she will have a record to turn to later when she has developed another perspective on the child. How correct are her early impressions? To what extent are they borne out by more knowledge?

Some teachers keep a *log* or *diary* about their group. At the end of the day, or perhaps during nap time, they put down what stood out that day in as much detail as they have time and energy for. This is an excellent way of recording the activity of the group, its shifts in leadership, its ideas and interests, its accomplishments. It is an invaluable aid to planning. Some teachers do the same thing but with less regularity and only from time to time, spot-checking in a sense. There are charts and checklists that help a teacher remember which children have not used paints for a while, which should get a turn at the workbench, and which are taking a large share of social responsibility. And of course there are snapshots and drawings, video- and audiotape recordings. One can also keep track of the number of times a certain kind of behavior took place, like how many times Amy hit someone, and how many times she threatened to hit but didn't; or with whom and with what Orrin was playing at 10:30 every day during a 3-week period, or which new words have been added to Tammy's invented spelling. All these techniques are good and can be used profitably. The use of any recording technique, however, must be determined by our purposes.

**What Are We After?**

An important part of teachers' professional responsibility lies in their role as researchers in their own classrooms. This occurs when they enhance their day-to-day observations with record-taking techniques.

> Teachers need not wait for inquiries to be initiated by others. They can ask the questions that arise from their own classrooms, make their own records, collect their own data, and modify their teaching in accordance with what they find. (Martin, 1987, p. 23)

We are suggesting here a recording technique that will show a fairly full and realistic picture of one living, breathing child, responding to life in a unique way, interacting with people and materials, and functioning at his own stage of maturity and growth. It is hard to focus on a child as an individual in this manner when one has grown accustomed to planning for an entire group. But while a group has its own laws of interaction that are surely worth studying, the study of individuals in the group leads to greater awareness of what is significant in human growth and development. The technique of studying one child in detail leads to deeper understanding of the one child and broader knowledge of all children.

Although in the current climate, there is an increasing mandate to use standardized assessments in early childhood settings, many early childhood organizations take issue with formalized assessments of children under age 8 because the tests, which have often pressured teachers into using inappropriate classroom practices, are not valid measures of children's learning. The largest early childhood organization in the country, The National Association for the Education of Young Children (NAEYC), with the National Association of Early Childhood Specialists in State Departments of Education (NAECS/SDE)(2003), has issued guidelines for assessing young children. NAEYC views assessment as having "many components and purposes." The document continues

> Assessment methods include observation, documentation of children's work, checklists and rating scales, and portfolios, as well as norm-referenced tests. . . . High quality programs are "informed by ongoing systematic, formal, and informal assessment approaches to provide information on children's learning and development." (NAEYC Early Childhood Program Standards and Accreditation Criteria, 2003, n.p.). For young bilingual children, instructionally embedded assessments using observational methods and samples of children's performance can provide a much fuller and more accurate picture of children's abilities than other methods (p. 10). . . . Assessment practices in many preschools, kindergartens, and primary grade programs have become mismatched to children's cultures or languages, ages, or developmental capacities. In an increasingly diverse society, interpretations of assessment results may fail to take into account the unique cultural aspects of children's learning and relationships. (NAEYC & NAECS/SDE, 2003, p. 4)

Records, however, are not a panacea. They are no more than a means by which a busy teacher can take hold of a squirming, slippery, smiling, screeching, intriguing, and bewildering child and hold her still long enough to examine her carefully. This procedure, taking on-the-spot records of behavior as it is occurring, we call, for want of a better name, the *on-the-spot running record*.

## Recording Behavior as It Happens

It is comforting to know that there are practically no fixed rules in this job of record-taking. Although the technique has its origins in research, it has been used frequently in education as a way of getting to know children better and evaluating a teacher's own work. There have been modifications and changes as the technique has become more widely used. We are going to be suggestive for the most part, and the rest is up to you.

Since your primary responsibility is to be the teacher of the group, your times for recording will have to be snatched. Children's needs come first, and you may have to drop your pencil to race to someone's rescue. It helps to have pads, cards, or a small notebook in your pocket, on shelves around the room, and up your sleeve, too. Never miss out on a choice bit because no pencil is handy! Be casual and unobtrusive about it all. Get close enough to hear things, but not so close that you interfere with the play or the child's concentration on reading or writing. Notes can be rough and full of abbreviations, to be filled in and cleaned up later. Get the date and the time down and the child's name as well as where the action is set. To preserve confidentiality, always use a pseudonym because even the child's initial is a giveaway. Should the children ask you what you are doing, don't let them in on the secret because they may become self-conscious. Be nonchalant and say something noncommittal, like "It's teacher's work," or "It's writing I have to do." If you are observing 6-, 7-, or 8-year-old children, you will need to be even more discreet about record-taking because children this age may begin to feel "spied on." Perhaps you can observe carefully and then record a little later, out of the children's range.

Take records of a child at as many different periods of the day as possible, although not necessarily all in one day. You will want to record behavior at arrival and at dismissal, at toileting, and at music and movement, at wash-up and at story time, at free play and with creative materials, and in addition with primary children at math time, at writer's workshop, and at group discussion. You will want to see what a child does indoors and out, alone and with others. Recording in a variety of situations will show up all-pervasive behavior, such as relationships with children and adults, adjustment to school, feelings about routines, and position in the group.

Often it will seem that these everyday records are not getting anywhere, and it is easy to become discouraged. But when, after a period of time, details of similar character are grouped together, patterns of behavior emerge, and we begin to see what it is a child is really doing. Be patient and let the thing grow. Recording behavior is, after all, recording growth, and since children are in transition between stages much of the time, you will need many stills before you see the common movement running throughout.

## A Word of Caution

Never, never allow records to lie around in public view. Treat them the way a doctor treats data about patients. Even the most inconsequential information about a patient is kept confidential, and we must do the same. Unless there is a professional reason for doing so, tell your funny and delightful stories about children *without identifying the particular child or family.*

## LANGUAGE AS A TOOL IN RECORDING

The language of recording presents its own difficulties, especially for people unaccustomed to writing. It is easy to feel that the challenge is too great and to give the whole thing up as a bad job. Since the important nuances of behavior cannot be recorded adequately without some use of descriptive terminology, it is worth exploring this aspect of the recording technique. It is not at all impossible to grow in skill if you consider that almost everyone has a larger passive vocabulary than an active one. As a beginning, suppose we joggle our memories for verbs, adverbs, adjectives, and phrases that can be used descriptively.

### Verbs

Some of us could think of a dozen synonyms for the word *walk* in a matter of seconds:

amble, stroll, saunter, clomp, stomp, march, strut, ramble

Others are paralyzed at the challenge. Yet the distinction between one child's actions, or gross movements, and another's may depend on the correct synonym for the word *walk.*

Look at it this way: A turkey walks. A cat walks. Are they the same? A 1-year-old walks and an octogenarian walks. Their movements are obviously dissimilar. Johnny walks and Susie walks, and we must record the quality of each. To find the exactly characterizing word, we might say the turkey *struts*, the cat *slinks*, the baby *waddles*, the old man *totters*, Johnny *lopes*, and Susie *minces.* The word *walk* tells us *what a person does* but not *how he does it.* No two children walk across a playroom or over to a child or toward the teacher in exactly the same way. As teachers, we respond to the *quality* of the behavior as we watch the child. We respond to the child who walks frantically because we sense trouble, and we feel in our own muscles the swinging walk of a child who is full of joy.

Here are some synonyms as a starter for verbs commonly used in records. There are many more with which to become familiar.

Run—stampede, whirl, dash, dart, gallop, speed, shoot across, bolt, fly, hippety-hop, dash

Say—whisper, bellow, shout, scream, roar, lisp, whine, demand, tell, murmur

Cry—wail, howl, whimper, fuss, bawl, sob, mourn, lament, weep

## Adverbs

Adverbs are one means by which pedestrian verbs can be given character when the exact verb is elusive. They are somewhat interpretive in that we define the mood and feeling of the behavior when we use them. But they are not used to pass judgment on the child. They may describe an action. For example, we can say, "He tugged determinedly," "She looked at the teacher vacantly," and not in any way describe the child as stubborn or stupid. The descriptive word is a one-shot description of a single verb telling what the child was doing at a particular moment. Thus, going back to the verb *walk*, we can say walked *merrily, jauntily, heavily*, or the ordinary verb *talk* can be narrowed down meaningfully when we tack on *excitedly, pleasantly, sourly, resentfully, cheerfully, cheerily,* or *laughingly*.

At the same time, consistency in description becomes a safeguard against erroneous generalizations from a single gesture, smile, posture, or movement. For example, if a recorder writes that a child "whined" in describing the voice and "grinned" in describing the mouth, or walked "merrily" or with "tearful eyes," it is clear that that recorder is not really observing.

As we indicated earlier, teachers cannot be absolutely objective, since they themselves are part of the total situation in which the recording occurs. Yet in trying to capture the quality of *how* a child builds, sings, jumps, cries, fights, paints, speaks, or whatever, we may use the descriptive language of *how* a child does *what* without courting an unnecessary or biased interpretation of the child as a person.

## Adjectives

We need a good supply of adjectives, too. For example, is every smile a cheerful smile? Could a smile be joyous, tearful, wholehearted, toothless, toothsome, forced, heart-warming, wavering, fixed, reluctant? Could a child with a reluctant smile possibly be feeling the same way as a child with a tearful smile, or a timid one? Here are special shades of *happiness*:

jubilant, joyous, bubbling, bouncy, sparkling, effervescent, delighted, cheerful, contented

Here is *sadness* qualified:

mournful, wistful, downhearted, gloomy, heavyhearted, melancholy, downcast, sullen, dejected, discouraged

Be judicious about the use of adverbs and adjectives. Although the lack of such words produces records that are wooden and devoid of the child's special quality, it is important to remember that use of adverbs and adjectives tends to be subjective. Be sure that there is correspondence between the behavior recorded and the qualifier that you choose.

## Phrases of All Kinds

Still another descriptive tool is the little phrase that has the telling action in it. Although these have their place, one must be careful to avoid becoming too dependent on such phrases; sentences can be cumbersome when too many phrases weigh them down. Here are some phrases to give character to the verb *walk*:

| | |
|---|---|
| dragging his legs | with head turned to the sky |
| scuffing her toes | looking neither here nor there |
| swinging his arms | with a blank look on her face |
| hunched and bent | intently observing |
| hands in pockets | with an awful clatter |

In mentioning the language of the record, it seems as though we are adding more hurdles to the ones teachers already face while taking records. Certainly there are not enough good opportunities for recording, the speed at which one must work is frustrating, and sheer muscular endurance plays its part in the difficulties, too. Even though the challenge of using descriptively precise language may be still another hurdle, the problem of good use of language in recording is one we must acknowledge. We are not accustomed in our culture to being colorful and descriptive in our everyday speech, although we may enjoy such language when reading. Nevertheless, records that are truly pictorial are so in large part as a result of imaginative language. If you feel too discouraged, try looking in a thesaurus or the dictionary for synonyms for some of the most commonly used action words and feeling tones. You will be surprised at the number of descriptive words you actually know and can put into your active command with a little joggling. Just make sure that the descriptive word you use really characterizes the quality of the action.

## IMPORTANCE OF THE ENVIRONMENT

Our study of the child must include, in addition to the records, a thoughtful description of the *situation* in which she is being observed. Children do not exist in a vacuum. We must set them into their living environment in order to view them in *context* as fully as possible. This means that we must take note of the key aspects of the child's physical and social environments. It is no surprise that a child might behave differently in one environment as opposed to another. Think of a child, comfortable in his classroom on one day, and, on another day, waiting at a shopping center in a long line with his parent. He might seem a child you'd never seen before! Or consider the example of a child who had consistently been dubbed a "clown" in her classroom environment. When she moved to another community during the school year, she became a leader in the new classroom situation. We *must* take note of the impact of the environment.

In describing the environment, including the three following facets will provide a rich matrix for knowing the child more fully:

- The neighborhood in which the school, center, or family child care home is located
- The school, center, or (if family child care) the house/ apartment building itself
- The classroom, detailing the physical arrangement, the schedule, the manner in which the learning environment is constructed, the goals of the program

Physical space has a strong effect on both children and teachers and on the quality of the program. In a classic study of the physical environment (Kritchevsky, Prescott, & Walling, 1969), a clear relationship was seen between the quality of the classroom space and how teachers worked with children. In high-quality settings teachers were sensitive and encouraging, while in low-quality space teachers tended to be less involved with the children and more restrictive. This in turn affected the children's behavior. In addition to the impact of the space itself, we must be aware of the effect of children's culture on their *perception* of that space. We would assume that children crowded into a small space would fight a lot. Yet the same study observed a particular group of Mexican-American children age 2-and-a-half to 5 engrossed in conflict-free play in a cramped space that might have had the familiar ring of home.

Augmenting your records of the child's behavior with a description of the environment helps to reveal children in the context of their larger community. An example of one environmental description is found in Chapter 13.

# 2

# Recording a Child's Behavior During Routines

Since we need a starting point, let us start with observing a child at tasks and behavior that make up so much of her life—the routines. At school we generally think of these as cleanup, toileting, snack time, lunch, nap time, and lining up. These are the "uncreative" but necessary aspects of the program that are repeated day after day, the activities around which many a program revolves.

## ORGANIZING THE INFORMATION

Let us look at a child about to become involved in a routine—for example, getting dressed for outdoors. Although this seems to be a simple and obvious activity, let us look at a child with the following questions in mind.

### What Is the Stimulus for the Activity?

- Why is the child dressing now?
  - » Did the teacher ask her to?
  - » Did the teacher make an announcement to the class?
  - » Did the child notice others and follow suit?
  - » Did he just get an impulse and begin to dress himself?

In a word, we want to know what set the child off on the dressing process. We could call this spur to action the *stimulus*. It might come from within or outside the child. It might be obvious (the teacher told the child to get dressed) or not obvious at all (apparently an unexplained impulse).

## What Is the Setting?

- What's going on around the child while he is dressing?
  - » What is the physical setup affecting the activity? (near or far away from cubbies or lockers, chairs available to sit on, children crowded into a small space)
  - » Who are the significant people nearby and what are they doing? (adults important to the child, the child's friends and "enemies," a visitor about whom she is concerned)

This enveloping activity would be the *setting* in which the behavior takes place, since obviously nothing happens in a vacuum.

## What Seem to Be the Child's Reactions?

- If the activity was teacher-initiated, how does the child react?
  - » Does he accept the idea? (willingly, cheerfully, with annoyance, with complaints, silently)
  - » Does she resist the idea? (openly and directly, indirectly)
- If the action seems child-directed, how is it carried out? (eagerly, stealthily, hastily, calmly, dreamily)
- Does the child show any special attachment to his clothing? (clutches jacket tightly, fondles gloves lovingly, glares suspiciously at children who examine his hat)
- How seriously does she take the process? How much interest does she show?
- How does the child handle himself? (skillfully, clumsily, awkwardly, easily)
- Is her ability equal to the task?
- Does he have specific abilities? Are they age-appropriate? (can put on hat but not buckle it, can fasten buttons, can zipper jacket)

It sounds as though each of these questions requires an answer, as in a questionnaire. On the contrary, the questions are only reminders of things to be aware of as you are observing. One item may be far more important than another for a particular child. Some items may call for lengthy description and others for none. It all depends on how a child happens to approach the task.

With your two hands alone, you are undoubtedly "short-handed" as you attempt to help a group get dressed for outdoors, and it may be hard to get anything written down. On the chance that some occasions do arise when this is possible, a brief description of behavior that includes some of the above points might read as follows.

> As dressing time was announced, 3-year-old Ian shouted, "Cool!" and made a beeline for his locker. He plopped his hat on his head, scooped up his coat and snow pants, and shuffled over to where the teacher was sitting ready to help the children. "Yippee," he gloated. "Here's my pants. Put 'em down for me!" The teacher laid them out straight and Ian pretzeled into a sitting position, dropping his coat on the floor. With lightning speed he forced first one foot and then the other into the legs of the snow pants, then wiggled himself into a standing position. Still wiggling his torso, he hauled the straps over his shoulders and reached down for his coat. He looked at it speculatively for a moment and then handed it to the teacher. Turning his back to her, he waited for her to hold it in position. As he pulled it up, unmindful of the tucked-in collar, he fumbled with the zipper in an obvious effort to make haste.

There are still other reactions to be aware of in routine situations because they extend the implications of the action.

- Does the child seem to want to function independently?
  - » How do you know?
- How does he behave in relation to the group situation?
  - » Can he proceed in the midst of group activity?
  - » Does he withdraw?
  - » Does he get silly or otherwise disruptive?
- What are the external factors that may be influencing the child's reactions? (This is the dynamic aspect of the *setting* mentioned above.)
  - » Does the teacher sit in one spot and expect the children to come to her?
  - » Are the children expected to sit in their chairs and wait for the teacher's help?
  - » Are the children expected to do the job alone?
- How much individual attention is offered?
  - » As much as the child wants?
  - » As much as the teacher thinks the child needs?

We include these many details because everything children do is a response to *something*, whether it is to feelings within themselves or to situations and people *outside* themselves. To describe only the action, such as "child runs around the room," and not comment on the entire situation leaves us in the dark as to what the action means. Running around the room at music and movement is one thing, at lunch another, and at dressing or cleanup still another. A child responds to a total situation, and this includes people, things, the physical environment, the demands to be met, and so forth. A boy or girl responds as a total person, with thought, feeling, and physical activity.

Observing 6-and-a-half-year-old Hayien as she arrives at her 1st-grade classroom gives us some clues about her attitude about herself in the world.

> Hayien enters the classroom with a group of classmates and her teacher. While the others move toward the coat hooks, she walks purposely into the center of the meeting area and pushes off her coat hood. She walks over to the attendance chart and flips over her card. With a bounce to her walk, she finds her hook and unzips her backpack, then methodically removes her lunch bag and places it on the shelf above her hook. After pulling a piece of paper from her bag and reading it, she folds it and places it in the note box. She is focused and concentrating on this task. Now she returns to her hook and carefully hangs up her backpack, slides off her coat, and hangs it up as well. None of the activity around the room—other children entering and hanging up coats—diverts her attention. Hayien moves back to the center of the room and intently reads the morning message and the day's schedule posted on the chalkboard. She scans the room, then silently moves to her desk, sits down, alone, and begins working with a geoboard.

See how different another response to arriving at school is.

> Four-year-old Lisa goes to her cubby with her father. As he unbuttons her coat, she does not attempt to help, and her body is limp. Her eyes rove about the classroom. When her coat is off, she walks further into the room, still looking all around. She has completely ignored or forgotten about her father's presence, and he quickly leaves without saying goodbye.

### What Does the Child Do Immediately After?

When the dressing is over, we note what the child does then and thus complete the sequence of events from the first stimulus to the last, concluding act. Sometimes what a child does immediately after an episode we are observing tells us quite a bit. For example:

When Lisa's father left, the teacher offered her some chalk to draw with, but Lisa said decidedly, "I want play dough." She walked over to the play dough shelf, took some down, and put it on the table. She then found a seat with a good view of the entrance to the room. She began rolling balls very distractedly—she did not look at the dough but kept her eyes fixed on the door.

As we observe a routine, we ask:

- Does the child accept the group procedure that follows, such as sitting on a chair or on the floor, waiting at the door?
- Does she run out without waiting for the group or the teacher?
- Does he rush to get the first place at the door?
- Does she show the children what she has done?
- Does he cry? Does he sing? Does he chortle to himself?

This may seem like a lot of questioning about so simple a procedure as getting dressed and undressed. But there are important clues here for us to pick up, as we shall see when we examine the feelings with which a young child invests these selfsame routines.

## THE MEANING OF ROUTINES TO YOUNG CHILDREN

Do you ever wonder why some children stand patiently to be buttoned and belted but others scream with rage if you make a move to help them? Why some children are utterly confused by the dressing process and others use the occasion for mad dashing around the room? Why some children burst into tears if they cannot find a mitten and others reveal a fine carelessness about everything connected with their clothing?

Of course we know that individual children are different from one another. But *all* children are different from adults generally, especially in this matter of routines. For adults, routines are a means to an end. We wash for breakfast, we clean to get a place ready for work again, we dress quickly to get to work. But children understand time and schedule only hazily. Nor are these the criteria by which they guide their activities. For young children, routines are either an end in themselves or a deterrent to the important business of living. For example, washing hands does not necessarily have any connection with lunch at all—it might very well be an opportunity to explore and savor the properties of water, and perhaps of soap and paper towels too! It is an occupation in its own right, with its own enticements. Or it is a silly obstacle in the path of food when you're just too hungry. In the same way, cleanup may have nuisance value because it keeps one from having a last chance at the slide; conversely, it may be a cozy way of feeling closeness with peers under the warmth of your teacher's approval. In any case, the sense of responsibility that motivates adults is at its barest beginnings in early childhood and hardly a reliable ally for the teacher.

The pleasure principle is very, very strong in young children, so that "I want to" is as good a reason as any the teacher might think up, and "I don't feel like it" is a really compelling force. To children, routines have a meaning all their own, and it is not an "adult" meaning. In addition, individual children may add to the meaning a special flavor out of their own experience. Yet with all this, they want to, and will in time, learn to behave as we do.

### The Mechanics Come with Attitudes

Children learn how to behave at the table, the sink, or in any other routine from the adults in their lives. For some of us adults, efficiency per se is so important that adult standards are held up as a model with a certain amount of fretfulness and impatience. For others it becomes simpler and easier to do the job ourselves rather than wait for a child to bungle through it. But there are those among us who love to do things for children because we enjoy being good to them in that way. In some homes there isn't much time for children, and they must shift for themselves. Quite unconsciously, therefore, as children learn the mechanics of the routines, they absorb attitudes, too, not only toward the carrying out of the routine but toward *themselves* as functioning people. Willy-nilly, from the attitudes of the adults during their learning years, children build up conceptions concerning their level of achievement and their potential abilities, without the chance to compare themselves with other children of their own age and experience.

All this, children have under their belts by the time they get to school, and careful observation of their behavior at routines will reveal a good deal of it. In addition to their handling the mechanics of living, we may well see something of their feelings about being dependent on adults, or whether being independent of them means anything to them. Perhaps, too, their feeling of trust or suspicion of adults will appear. These general attitudes come through in relation to the specific tasks we call routines. Signs of stress due to such factors as inadequate housing, exposure to violence, uncertainty about living arrangements, hunger, inappropriate parental expectations, poor health, abuse or neglect, or an illness or death in the family may also become evident during routines. The different routines lend themselves to unique mannerisms and behavior reactions intrinsic to their function, and need to be looked at separately for this reason.

## RECORDING EATING BEHAVIOR

In observing an eating situation, let us bear in mind the intimacy of parent and child in the child's learning to handle food. In the back of our minds we might tuck away the observation of pediatricians that many eating difficulties stem from anxiety or pressure. Something of children's attitudes toward themselves is bound to come through as well as the degree of smoothness of functioning. It is certainly an indication of self-confidence and social strength, for example, if children take care of their own body needs when they are coordinated well enough to do so. Conversely, it may be an indication of stress when children cannot tolerate waiting for food, take more on their plate than they can possibly consume, or are unable to enjoy the social nature of eating with others.

**Details to Observe**

- What is the setting?
  - » Where is the food served—in the classroom, cafeteria, or another place?
  - » Who serves the food, teacher or children?
  - » Can children choose what they want or don't want?
  - » Is the environment quiet, relaxed, noisy, busy, frantic?
  - » Is there enough food? Is there too much? Can children get more?
- What is the child's reaction to the eating situation?
  - » Is she accepting, eager, resistant, choosy?
  - » How seriously or casually does he take eating?
  - » How does she approach the table? (fearfully, enthusiastically, aggressively, timidly)
- How much food does he eat? (rather little, two helpings, lots of meat, no vegetables, never gets enough, big portions in comparison with others)

- What is the manner of eating?
  - » How does she hold utensils? Does she eat with her hands?
  - » Does he play with food, throw food, hold food in his mouth?
  - » Is she systematic and well organized in her attack on food?
  - » Is he messy or fastidious?
  - » Is she concerned that she may not get enough? Does she hoard food?
  - » At the table is the child comfortable, restless, tense, able or unable to stay for the duration of the meal?
- Does he socialize, and how much?
  - » To whom does he speak?
  - » How else does he make contact with children?
  - » Is the socializing more meaningful to her than the eating?
  - » Does he manage both socializing and eating?
  - » Does she talk only to the teacher, to a special friend, to no one?
- Does the child show interest in food? In what way?
  - » Has he special likes and dislikes?
  - » What comments does she make about the food?
  - » What is his pace (speed or slowness) of eating?
- What is the adult's role?
  - » What group procedures are laid down?
  - » How much and what kind of individual attention is offered?
- What is the sequence of events?
  - » What does the child do and say?
  - » What does the adult do and say?
- How does the child leave the table? (talking eagerly, smacking lips, stonily, in tears; pushing the chair back easily, knocking it down)
- What does the child do then? (runs around the room, stands talking, stands and waits for the teacher, gets a book or toy, goes to the toilet, goes to the food wagon to help clean plates, looks into bowls for more food)

## How Selective Shall We Be?

Since young children are as likely as not to be unconcerned about table manners, we may find ourselves recording activity that is not socially acceptable, with the uneasy thought that putting it down on paper somehow carries our approval. Neither approval nor disapproval plays any part in recording technique, although they may influence what we do or say as we respond to children. To guide children on the long road to maturity, we must start with them where they are, which means, first of all, noting accurately what they do without moral bias or judgment. To deny the reality of their behavior because it is displeasing to us or because we are showing them better techniques is to limit ourselves unduly as teachers. It is only human to be subjectively selective about what we observe and record; therefore we must take pains to incorporate a little of the scientific approach into our professional selves. Whatever a child does is part of that child and should be recorded. How we deal with the behavior is another matter.

## Eating Records

The following records, one of a 3-year-old and the other of a 6-year-old, reveal how much more than simple ingestion of food is involved in an eating situation. We see something of Erin's competence and her ability to abide by the social requirements of the classroom. We see that for Simon lunch is an occasion for an intriguing investigation.

> Erin is sitting at the table with a napkin in front of her, waiting for juice and crackers. When the juice pitcher is passed to her, she holds the handle in one hand and the bottom of the pitcher with the other hand. She pours the juice very carefully into her cup, her tongue licking her top lip. She puts the pitcher down gently and takes the basket with crackers, which has just been passed to her. She knocks the basket against the cup and spills her juice. She looks at the teacher with concern.
>
> The teacher suggests that she get a sponge. She goes to the sink where the sponges are, reaches for the paper-towel dispenser, and struggles to get a towel out. The assistant asks her if she wants any help, but she finally gets the towel out. She is holding a cracker in her mouth the entire time. She starts wiping up the juice but spreads it all over the table. Her napkin has gotten wet and she states matter-of-factly, "I need a new napkin." The teacher gives her one and she starts shredding the old one. She crumples it into a ball and puts it on a shelf. The teacher asks her to throw it in the garbage and she does this without question.

> Simon makes his way towards his class's lunch tables holding his Styrofoam lunch tray with one hand. It looks semi-stable; it could tip over at any moment if someone bumped into him. About halfway to the tables he supports his tray with both hands. On his tray he has four chicken nuggets, a small pile of vegetables, three cheese cubes, and a carton of milk.

He does not immediately select his seat. Simon seems to be looking for something or someone. Peter joins him. They smile at each other. They both sit down next to each other at the lunch table.

Peter takes a dollar bill out of his pocket and says, "Look what my aunt gave me." Peter and Simon examine the back of the dollar bill. They point to the pyramid and Simon says, "Look at the treasure!" He then asks the teacher who is sitting nearby, "What does this mean?" pointing to the small numbers to the left of the serial number on the bill.

## RECORDING TOILETING BEHAVIOR

As in eating, the toileting routine has its specifically important aspects, such as a child's attitude toward his own body and the important question of whether the child sees body functioning and control as a source of pride in achievement or a bond to babyhood. Unusually fearful behavior, age-inappropriate lack of or overly cautious control of bodily functions, or uncommon interest in or knowledge about sex might be a sign of stress.

### Details to Observe

- What is the stimulus? (child's own need, imitation of a friend, response to group practice, request by the teacher, wet pants)
- What is the child's reaction—acceptance or resistance? (might obviously need to go to the toilet but refuses to use the school toilet; might not go when the group goes; might go cheerfully, absentmindedly, hurriedly, casually)
- Are there signs of tensions or fears? (stiffness of body, clutching at genitals, whimperings)
- How interested does the child seem to be?
- How seriously or casually does the child take the toileting procedure?
- How does he handle himself? Are his coordination and skill up to the task?
  » Is he competent? Awkward? Smooth? Clumsy? Slow? Fast?
- What is the child's manner like?
  » Is she casual? Excessively modest? Exhibitionistic?
  » Does she show awareness of sex differences? Does she show interest in sex differences or similarities?
  » What kinds of interactions does she engage in with other children, if any?

» Does she use language or act in a manner that indicates exceptional sexual knowledge?

Of course, the behavior has to be seen against the background of the group procedures and teacher role to which the child is reacting at the moment. As in other episodes, we record the sequence of events from beginning to end, and if possible, we include the exact language of the child (or note its absence in everything we record). These illustrations may make this clearer.

## Toileting Records

The following records of 3- and 4-year-olds show how different children's attitudes are about body functions.

Riding on a seesaw with Priscilla, Lorna (age 4-and-a-half) hops off and says, "I almost wet my pants." She runs inside, with Priscilla following. Both pull down their clothing and sit on toilets, singing, "Skit, scoot, skit, scoot." Lorna flushes the toilet, pulls up her underwear and pants. "I think I'll wash my hands." She removes her jacket. "See I have two shirts, isn't that funny? Are you going to wash your hands too, Priscilla?" She washes quickly. "Now I'll go into the dressing room and see how I look."

Four-year-old Robert is not so casual:

Robert is in the play yard, standing on top of the packing case, holding his pants and jiggling up and down. He sees the teacher and says, "I want to go into the building." "All right," replies the teacher. "Do you want to go to the toilet?" "Yes." He climbs down hastily, saying, "I don't want you to watch." As they go into the building, the teacher promises, "I'll close the door. Do you want the seat up?" Robert frowns for a moment. "No, I don't know yet what I'm going to do. I want the door all the way closed."

The teacher closes the door and waits. Robert calls out twice, "I'm not through yet." After several minutes, he shouts, "I'm finished now," flings open the door, and struts out. "Do you want to wash your hands?" asks the teacher. Robert's brows go up in surprise. "No, 'cause then I'd be ready for juice and crackers, and it isn't time." He skips out to the play yard; plays in the water tub, splashing hands madly; then holds up his hands, fingers spread wide. "Look at my hands—clean!"

Another view, this time of some 3-year-olds. This record demonstrates a teacher's sensitivity to one child's natural curiosity about another's body.

> At the end of the story, the teacher reminded the children to go to the toilet if they had to, before washing up for snack. Martin got up slowly, dreamily, curiously watching the others as they clamored, "I did. I didn't." He says nothing and suddenly walks over to the bathroom, by which time three girls were already in it. Lois and Paula are on the seats and Wendy is standing waiting. Martin edges past Wendy into a tight little corner between the sink and the wall. He is completely absorbed in watching Lois, who is now wiping herself. She wiggles off the toilet. "Wendy, I'm finished," she says and begins to pull up her underwear. Martin comes out of the corner just then and kneels down in front of her. Without saying a word, he holds down her slacks and panties with one hand, and pulls up her shirt with the other. She watches him. He has a look of innocent wonder as he carefully, with one finger, pokes her navel. She is as absorbed as he. They say nothing. The other children are by now watching him. The teacher says to Lois, "You had better move out of there, Lois, because these children are waiting." Martin and Lois both look up at her, and Lois pulls up her pants as Martin walks out to wash. He did not go to the toilet.

## RECORDING BEHAVIOR AT NAP TIME

Nap as a routine has its own particular responses, too. Along with such reactions as showing trust in adults and acceptance of group patterns is the matter of body tensions and ability to relax. This is especially significant for the child who is new to the school or child care situation. Nap time may be especially stressful for a child who comes from a shelter or another situation where there is no regular bedtime or where the bedtime setting is frightening or unpredictable. This routine may also be trying for a child who divides her time between divorced parents' homes, who has experienced recent hospitalization or the illness or death of a parent or relative, or who has just moved from one home to another.

Even after adjusting to school or child care, however, some children continue to need comfort and support during nap time, while others have their most successful social experiences then, and still others just drop right off to sound slumber. It may help to see the meaning of nap time to a child in the following terms.

**Details to Observe**

- How does the child happen to be napping? (What is the stimulus?)
  - » Did he sprawl out by himself, or is there a prescribed time?
  - » Did the teacher decide the child was tired?
  - » Does nap automatically follow lunch hour?
  - » Does the child seem to understand what is expected of her?
- What is the child's reaction?
  - » Accepts? (in matter-of-fact fashion, with pleasure)
  - » Resists? (dawdles, talks, does not respond, frequently asks to go to the toilet, frequently requests water)
  - » Refuses? (cries, runs around the room, runs out of the room)
- Does the child require special attention from the adult? (patting, sitting nearby, taking her to a separate room)
- Are there any signs of tension while resting?
  - » Body tensions? (amount of movement, restlessness)
  - » Comforting devices? (thumb-sucking, masturbation, ear-pulling)
  - » Acting in an overtly sexual manner with another child?
  - » Special attachments? (dolls, animals, handkerchiefs, blankets, pillow, diaper)
  - » Leaving cot frequently on one pretext or another?
- What seem to be the child's bodily requirements for rest?
  - » Is there evidence of fatigue? (yawning, red eyes, peevishness, frequent falling)
  - » Does he sleep? For how long? Is sleep itself peaceful or fretful?
  - » Does she need something to play with? (book, doll)
  - » If he does not sleep, does he seem relaxed?
- What is the child's reaction to the group during rest?
  - » Is it disturbing and disrupting? (shouts, sings loudly, runs about, crawls under children's cots, pulls up blinds, annoys children)
  - » Is there social activity? (talks to neighbor, signals)
  - » Is she conscious of other children's needs? (whispers, walks quietly)
- How does the nap end?
  - » How does he wake? (smiling, talking, whimpering, crying, tired, refreshed)

>> What does she do when she wakes? (lies quietly, calls the teachers, rushes to the bathroom, starts to play)

**Nap Time Record**

Nap time might look like this:

The teacher is seated near a group of five 4-year-olds who are lying quietly on their cots. Eli is having a little difficulty getting comfortable. He tosses restlessly about, occasionally playing with his hands and feet. Near his head is a teddy bear, which he tosses up into the air from time to time and tries to catch, unsuccessfully, with one hand. With a jerk and a grumble, he is under his blanket and out again. He stretches onto his side, with a finger in his mouth and looking tired. All of a sudden he is hidden again under the blanket, whispering barely audibly to himself. At times one of the other teachers walks through the room to the coat closet. Eli raises his head long enough to watch her get her purse and leave. Then he drops back onto the cot, repeating his starting performance— playing with his hands and feet, as well as the fringe on the edge of his blanket. He stares dreamily at the chairs and beds around the room, all the while playing with his hands, feet, or blanket fringe. Suddenly he starts to clap loudly. Teacher cautions him about this, explaining that this is nap time and children are sleeping. He stares at the teacher for a moment and then lies back without so much as a sound until the end of nap time.

## RECORDING BEHAVIOR DURING TRANSITIONS

Transitions are often difficult parts of the day for many children. They require children to reorganize themselves in terms of activity and time. Because young children are not adept at seeing the structure of the whole day, their agenda, once they are engaged in a particular activity, is quite different from the agenda of the teacher. It is hard for young children to stop building, or playing with water, or working on a storybook project. In some cases, a transition might act as an emotional disorganizer causing the child to fly off, unable to center without adult help. How children handle the transition time itself gives us clues about their temperament, their relative maturity, their sense of time, and their internal ability to organize their experience, and may reveal indications of stress.

## Details to Observe

- How did the transition begin? (abruptly, with subtlety, or with a few minutes' warning of its approach)
- What is the structure of the transition—consistent or changeable from day to day?
  - » Does the child have an assigned job?
  - » Does the teacher tell him what to do?
- What does the child do when the transition begins?
  - » Is she eager, tentative, confused, resistant, out of control, weepy, argumentative, casual?
- Is he able to complete the task as required?

## Transition Record

The following record of a 7-year-old reveals her ease in dealing with the transition.

Narissa has finished some paperwork at her desk as the teacher announces time to line up for lunch. Narissa pushes back in her chair and wiggles her feet into her sandals without using her hands. Stealthily she removes a small package of candy from the desk and stuffs it deep into her pocket. Then she rises and saunters toward the door. Her eyes are wide open as she scans the room casually. As she passes the teacher's desk, the teacher begins scolding another child. Narissa stops and watches their interaction matter-of-factly. Her face is smooth and expressionless. After watching the confrontation for about a minute, she turns and skates toward the door, her arms swinging freely. She does not look in the direction she is going; instead she takes in other activities in the room. When she reaches the door, she finds a place in line. While standing, she shifts her weight frequently, swinging her hips loosely. She begins playing idly with the ponytail of the girl in front of her, and keeps this up for several minutes until the group is ready to go to the lunchroom.

## PATTERNS OF BEHAVIOR

Observations of children's behavior during the daily routines at school reveal behavior at any given moment in a child's life. Many such on-the-spot observations, added up over a period of time, reveal that which is consistent and repetitive in a child's responses to similar situations. We can then see the particular patterns of response, which may be similar to or different from other children's, but, in any case, are true of that child. A pattern of behavior may be fixed and steady, even to rigidity, or it may be shifting and changing, even to the point of utter unpredictability. Over a really long period of time (6 months to a year), the records may reveal sharply changing patterns as the child learns to handle routines differently, with increasing maturity and experience. The importance of the on-the-spot record taken over time is the evidence that is accumulated to support or dispute the generalizations we usually feel able to make after we have known a child for a while. This is a basic reason for attempting frequent recording, even though admittedly it does not come easily in the life of a teacher.

This is one child's pattern of behavior at nap time:

> Tony's face always puckered up when he saw the shades drawn, although the distress never developed into tears. Not until the teacher came to sit with him did he relax, and then noticeably. He never asked for anything to comfort himself, like a toy or a cracker, and never said anything. But when the teacher sat quietly near his cot, he would fall asleep in 5 minutes.

A *changing pattern* is revealed in this end-of-the-year generalization about a child's behavior at dressing time:

> At the beginning of the year Tanya would rush to get to the door the minute her outdoor clothes were on. She would lean against it stiffly with arms and legs outstretched and look like a formidable opponent for anyone who might challenge her. Many times she fought verbally with Ralph and John, the only ones in the group who dared question her right to be "first" all the time. As her friendship with Maya and Kate grew, she began to urge them to hurry and be first with her. Since Maya and Kate enjoy conversation too much to be hurried, she got nowhere with this. She would look anxiously at the door as she prodded them and eventually run off to her coveted spot. But one day Tanya stayed and waited for Maya and Kate. Triumphantly she confided to them, "We don't care if we're not first, do we, huh?" This was a great day for Tanya!

The patterns do not always reveal themselves immediately. We may have to hunt for them deliberately. It helps to go back, say after 2 or 3 months, and tease out the items in the records pertaining to the aspect of behavior we are trying to check. Listing the highlights of the individual episodes helps make the pattern become clear. For example, a teacher might note these highlights of Barry's napping behavior:

9/23    Barry cried when he woke from nap.
9/30    Barry clung to teacher as he woke.
10/6    Barry would not fall asleep without teacher sitting next to him.

The consistency of behavior is rather obvious. Barry's nap time at school is fraught with feelings of uncertainty at this point.

## Summary of a Child's Behavior During Routines

A child is all of one piece, but different situations may cause any child to react in different ways. In finding the pattern of reaction to different routines, we might find similarity in all or positive or negative reactions to different ones. For example, a child might be cheerfully cooperative in all school routines, or silently withdrawn; or she might be a fine group member until toileting, or eating, or nap time. A child's reactions in any case are uniquely his, and the record tells us about these unique responses to the life situations at school. In gathering evidence bit by bit and then seeing the patterns emerge, we really begin to see the child as she actually is. These persistent or changing patterns of behavior can be grouped under broad generalizations. The following are useful in understanding a child's behavior during routines:

1. Usual attitudes at beginning, throughout, and at end of routine
   » Accepts easily, complies, resists directly or indirectly, shows signs of tensions, fears
   » Degree of interest
2. Dependence or independence as evidenced in routines
   » Has to be reminded or told; acts on own responsibility and initiative
   » Accepts or rejects assistance
3. Consistent emotional reactions to routines
   » Excitement, silliness, relaxation, self-confidence
4. Coordination and abilities, tempo and time length
5. Effect of child's behavior on group functioning
6. Routines as social experience
7. Adult participation and child response
   » To group procedures established by adults
   » To individual attention

8. Expression of physical functioning
   » Amount of food eaten
   » Length of sleep
   » Frequency of urination
   » Ability to relax
   » Need for rest
9. Awareness of and interest in own sex and sex differences revealed through routines
10. Special problems (excesses)
   » Excessive modesty or exhibitionism at toileting, dressing, and undressing
   » Attachment to clothes
   » Extreme choosiness at eating time, retaining food, not eating, inability to eat solid foods
   » Dreaminess
   » Excessive physical tension and inability to relax
   » Fetishes
   » Excessive need for attention from teacher
   » Special ways in which teacher handles this child, and why
   » Wetting, soiling (in relation to age and frequency)

## Generalizations About Behavior During Routines

The following are illustrations of patterns that have emerged from teachers' records of routines, taken over time. These patterns present an overall picture of the child's participation in routines that would be incorporated into a final study, as described in Chapter 13.

On entering school, Leo resisted vigorously any and all routines, gradually accepting them one by one. He has never had a toilet accident at school, but called for the utmost privacy in toileting and usually postponed the process until he reached home. It was not until December that he went willingly without signs of stress. I was delighted last week to have him come to me and say, "You know, I went to the bathroom twice already." He knows when we wash hands and washes his in methodical fashion. He eats his snack matter-of-factly, placing cup and napkin in wastebasket when finished. He rests quietly after settling down on his cot. He dresses and undresses himself, asking for help only when necessary. He knows where to hang his clothes, and is careful to hang them up correctly.

Ebony is fully independent now in dressing and undressing and no longer asks for help. She handles toileting entirely by herself and even our presence is not required. Nap time is still a time for socializing but for the most part without too much giggling. If she has been playing hard, she usually stops periodically to sit and look at a book or just watch what is going on around her as she sits. The rest period sometimes lasts for 10 minutes, then off she goes again.

The generalizations based on what we see happening tell us something about matters that are of vital importance to young children. Adults, who developed social acceptability in these areas long ago and perform correctly with ease and without thought, are likely to overlook their significance in children's growing concepts of themselves as people in a social environment.

# 3

# Recording a Child's Use of Materials

We turn now to another area of functioning in the life of a child—experiences with materials. Play materials are as integral a part of young children's school life as routines, but their function in the development of personality is somewhat different. If we tend to see play materials as a means of keeping idle hands busy, or if we evaluate their use in terms of work, we are likely to miss the special role they do play.

## THE MEANING OF MATERIALS TO YOUNG CHILDREN

A good part of the role of play materials is supporting children's cognitive growth, specifically in symbolization. *Symbolization* refers to the human capacity to make one thing represent something else. The following brief record shows the beginning of this role. The small rolling pins, in this case, are "nonverbal symbols" for birthday candles while the play dough studded with rolling pins represents (is a symbol for) the birthday cake:

> Three-year-old Suzanne and Jamila are sitting next to each other working with the play dough. Both have small rolling pins stuck straight up out of the dough. Jamila starts singing, "Happy birthday to you . . .," and they both stand up and fall back into their chairs giggling and laughing in high-pitched voices. Suzanne puts a blob of play dough on the end of an ice cream stick, and Jamila watches her with her index finger inside her mouth. Suzanne offers the stick to Jamila, and Jamila pretends to lick the play dough off the stick. They again break into laughter, kicking their feet under the table.

Most people tend to interpret symbolic activities quite narrowly as the ability to write and to read the writing of others. While reading and writing are symbolic processes, they reflect only half of our symbolizing capacities. They are part of the more common, *verbal* half. The *nonverbal* half gives us our art—painting, sculpture, dance, mime, music, and drama (which combines both verbal and nonverbal). Nonverbal symbolization is an important way of communicating, even if it is not the most common, because many experiences, feelings, and thoughts either cannot be or are too difficult to be put into words.

Few people become artists, yet nonverbal symbolizing activities are a necessary aspect of the learning process in childhood. Experience in nonverbalizing activities, such as dramatic play and the use of materials, is the basis for children's ultimate use of the more abstract forms of symbolization, such as letters and numbers. The reason for this is that young children use language primarily for social purposes and considerably less for intellectual conceptualization than we would like to believe. Until about the age of 7 (give or take a year for individual differences), children's understanding is markedly limited by what their senses feed back to them, and their language is a reflection of that. They can and do make simple comparisons as they approach 4 and 5, but on a concrete level and in a personal way. "My painting is better than yours," they say. "Yours is yukky." "That truck is bigger than the old one we had." It is too hard for them to be objective or analytical because they are still so egocentric. They find it almost impossible to deal with concepts that are not somehow related to their experience. As a result, what they can express or uncover through language is also limited. This does not mean that children do not talk about real, important, and valid experiences. It is rather that their thinking, and therefore their talking, is tied to concreteness, to physical reality.

Nevertheless, children do begin to have an awareness of abstractions, even if they cannot fully grasp or explain their half-formed, shadowy understanding in words. They gain an intuitive sense about abstract concepts from the relationships and transformations they themselves cause in the materials they use in their play. In the following record it is apparent that two 4-year-olds are confronting the abstract concepts of time, birth, and adoption in their typically personal, physically involved ways. They are using clay.

> In the following record, one 4-year-old uses her work with clay as a stimulus for imagining a predatory world. Another child, who had been adopted by her parents, uses it to imagine what happened to her birth mother.
>
> Christina rolls out a log of clay, then uses her finger to hollow it out so that it is a tube. As she moves the tube across the board it is on, she says to the other children at the table, "This is the children's tunnel, so

they can crawl through to the other side. This is the river with the piranhas." When another child asks what piranhas are, she explains in an
authoritative voice, "They are fish that eat people." The children con-
verse about piranhas and then start talking about saber-toothed tigers
that lived long ago. Isabelle tells a story about someone she calls her
first mother who lived in the time of the saber-toothed tigers and got
eaten. When the teacher asked her what she meant by "first mother,"
she said "the mother that borned me but got eaten." Christina then
adds, "A first mother is someone who has a baby and dies or gets hurt.
But that doesn't happen a lot. I don't have a first mother. I have my
mom at home."

Thus, as children use materials to replicate experience, they are
spurred on to increasingly subtle levels of symbolization without being handicapped by their as yet inadequate verbal power. This in no
way downgrades the role of language. It merely recognizes the reality
of how children learn, which is through their senses, with language a
secondary reinforcer that helps define and extend their learning rather than initiate it. Not until they are well past their early childhood
and near the end of middle childhood can they learn about concepts
primarily through words (Piaget, 1962a). For this reason, nonverbal
forms of symbolizing activity can and should be well advanced before
a child is asked to deal with the more abstract forms of symbols such
as letters, words, and numbers.

Here are two children learning a variety of concepts through their
use of materials:

Larissa is a 2-and-a-half-year-old at an infant-toddler center who is finishing what she calls "stick-down," collage work with two-inch, precut
pieces of paper. Her concluding efforts involve getting more glue out
of the squeeze bottle. She does this by turning the bottle upside down,
grasping it with both hands, and pressing very hard with her thumbs.
The top of the bottle appears to be clogged because she applies a
great deal of pressure for a long moment, accompanying the force
with a quiet but determined grunt and a strained facial expression—
jaw set, teeth clenched, head averted slightly as if anticipating that
she might be squirted. A drop finally plops out onto the paper. Larissa
looks satisfied and puts the glue bottle down, relaxing her face and her
previously tensed shoulders. She then picks up a piece of wallpaper
carefully with the thumb and index finger of her left hand and places it
down with the fingertips of both hands. She turns to the teacher and
says, "I finish now."

Could she have understood through a verbal explanation about the flow of glue what she learned intuitively by using it? See what 5-year-old Lin is learning in the sandbox without a word on her part or her teacher's. She is working by herself, not joining the conversation of the other children:

> Lin pours sand through a large funnel and observes the running sand from the top, putting her head almost into the mouth of the funnel, and then lifts the funnel to see the sand run out of the bottom. Then she fills a large bucket and shakes it, watching the action of the dry sand. She pushes down hard with her hands on the sand in the bucket. She pours the sand through a sand mill the other children are using, steps back from the box, smiles broadly, and says, "All right, I've got the baby food."
>
> The other children continue pouring sand through the mill and announce that it is a volcano machine. Lin pours sand into the machine with a small shovel and remarks to no one in particular, "We're going to build the biggest volcano in the world." She pours sand into the machine from the bucket and then the funnel. Edwardo takes the funnel from her and removes the machine from the pile of sand. Lin does not object but takes a bottle and fills it with a scoop, then pours the sand from the bottle onto the pile. She fills the bottle from a jug, pouring from different heights. She empties the bottle by shaking it backward and forward in an arc, watching the patterns of the falling sand.
>
> The teacher announces cleanup. Lin starts to level the sand with a cardboard comb. The other children leave, and Lin levels the sand again with wide movements of her whole arms reaching for more space. She nips the sand to and fro with flicking motions of the wrist of one arm and sweeps through it with both arms describing a semicircle before she leaves to join the group.

At the same time that children use materials for learning, they use them to express and cope with feelings of all kinds. Their bodies can exert more or less pressure, can express gentleness or anger; their nails can scratch, their muscles can pound; their fingers can manipulate with care and composure or with awkwardness and distress.

Materials, ordinary play materials, are a bridge between children's inner selves and the outside world. They are the means by which children capture impressions of the world outside themselves and translate them into forms they can understand; they are the means of pulling out of themselves what they feel and giving it concrete expression. Materials (toys, blocks, sand, paint, clay, wood, paper, crayons, pencils) help children to:

- Transform feelings into action:
  - » Anger or high spirits get pounded into clay.
  - » The desire to be big and strong goes into building "the tallest building in the world."
  - » The mood of spring sunshine is gently painted in pinks, yellows, and pale greens.
- Translate ideas into forms, concepts into shapes:
  - » A house of blocks, like a real house, has to be closed in.
  - » A road of blocks rambles on and on.
  - » A bridge is high up and across.
- Turn impressions into products:
  - » A cookie of clay must be round and flat.
  - » A crayoned grownup has long legs and a big smile.

Even if their impressions of a tree, a cow, or Daddy all come out looking like a blob of red paint, children feel they have made a good try! Through their use of materials, children externalize impressions and feelings, develop muscles and skills, grow in powers of reasoning and logic. They gain in inner strength as they clarify hazy, incomplete understandings of the real world of objects, phenomena, and people.

Children approach materials as they approach life itself, with directness or shyness, with attack or withdrawal, with fear and hesitancy, or with courage and self-confidence. Do all children plunge into soapsuds with the same zest? Do all children build daring block towers? Do all children sprawl paints across every inch of paper? Don't we all know the tidy child who handles clay and paint almost daintily? Or the cheerful little person who is never willing to stop playing and put toys away, who makes the most mess at the clay table, carries the mess over into an orgy of soap and water in the bathroom, then disappears just when it's time to clean up? And what of the many others who confine themselves to a limited few of the materials we offer them, as though starving themselves in the midst of plenty? Or the occasional child who does not play with anything? There is a consistency of style and approach to materials that reveals much about children's responses.

Children will take any material, shape, or form and breathe a bit of themselves into it. The more shapable, or "unstructured," the material is, the better it serves for them to project feelings and ideas. At first contact, a material is something outside oneself, and a curiosity for that reason. It has to be explored as an item of the world outside of self. Then there is experimentation with it for its own sake: What are its properties and possibilities? Does it stick, stretch, break, fall, crush, smear? Eventually the material becomes a medium for expression and projection, and it is *used* for the child's own purposes.

When a child is fairly well able to break down the details that pertain to objects and people, and has the physical coordination for detailed work, materials are used representationally to crystallize that clarity. If a child is confused about some details, the confusion is set down, too. In this record, two 1st-graders represent their ideas with blocks as well as words. Lorenzo helps Daisy confront some of her confusions:

> Daisy places two long blocks on the floor. Adding smaller blocks, she systematically builds up walls along the foundation. She moves around her growing building with ease, taking care not to knock into any build-ings. Lorenzo joins her, saying, "Let's make a huge house!" Daisy agrees, "Let's make a house building!" They begin to work together. "I'll make a window," Daisy states as she positions two blocks to create an opening. Then she places two arches on the roof of the building. "That can't be on top," cries Lorenzo, feigning annoyance. They both burst into laugh-ter. Daisy places two unit blocks on the roof saying, "This will be the door." "Okay," agrees Lorenzo, "but how will they [the wooden family now inside] get out? They need stairs. You make the stairs. I'll make everything else. This will really be a great house!"
>
> After Daisy works on the stairs, she announces, "I'm making an el-evator." Lorenzo asks, "How will you make an elevator?" "Well, you do like this," explains Daisy. She knocks down her stairs and begins working on a tunnel-like structure that stretches in the direction of their house/ building. "This is one of your stupid ideas!" exclaims Lorenzo. "It won't be attached to the house." "It won't?" Daisy asks. Then she knocks down her "elevator" and says, "Let's make stairs. Oh, I have a better idea. The bottom can be the house." (The building by this time is now two levels.) "I know the bottom is the house," responds Lorenzo. "Then what's the top?" puzzles Daisy. "The terrace," answers Lorenzo. Daisy returns to the location of her original staircase and places a ramp against the building. "See," she says, "you can just walk down." "Yeah, that's a good idea," agrees Lorenzo. Daisy brings a box that contains a name tag for every student. Both children locate their tags and place them prominently on the corner of the building. They step back, regarding their work, smiling with satisfaction and pride.

Interestingly enough, if feelings are stronger than intellectual curi-osity or creativity, a child may seem to misuse the material, as when a boy or girl makes mud out of clay or uses a doll for poking and throwing, or deliberately breaks block buildings. At such a point, children may need materials that are especially suited to their individual needs.

Materials that have a specific use and function, like dolls and bikes, are *structured* materials. Children use these for the implied purpose, but they will also project feelings onto them. (The doll is naughty and rebellious or is crying and upset.) Or children use them as a means for carrying out ideas, desires, or fantasies. (The bike is a plane, the doll is a traffic officer, the lotto cards are tickets.) Semi-structured materials, like blocks (not as fluid as paint or clay, or as finally formed as a toy car), give the satisfaction of construction and three-dimensional solidity.

But beyond this description of the characteristics of materials, there remains the wonder of children's imagination. If they need a plane, a car or a stick can become one. If they want to make a person, they will struggle with the material until the essence of *person* is there. In short, materials are used by children in the way children themselves need and want to use them. The manner and style, however, are unique to each child.

## WHAT TO OBSERVE

There are many aspects of how a particular child approaches and uses materials that reveal otherwise unseen thoughts and feelings. Taking note of the setting and the stimulus will place the child in context.

### The Setting

- Who are the nearby significant people and activities?
- Is there a variety of materials? Are supplies accessible to children?
- What is the amount and kind of adult supervision?

### The Stimulus

- How does the child come to use the material? (teacher-suggested, group procedure, imitation of another child, self-initiated, suggested by another child)

#### Response to Paint

- What colors does the child use?
- Does she mix colors? (in jars, in coasters, or on the paper)
- Are the colors separated on paper?

- Does she paint one color over another?
- Is he able to control the drips?
- Does he try to control the drips? Does he deliberately drip?
- Does she confine herself to one small spot or bit of space, or does she spread out? Does she paint off the paper?
- What forms, if any, are used? (vertical lines, curves, circles, fill-ins, letters, dots, numbers, blotches of color, representation)
- Does the child paint over the forms?
- What kind of brushstrokes? (scrubbing, dotting, gliding)
- How many paintings?
- Does he paint quickly? Does he work for a long time on one painting?
- Does she name the painting? (in detail, in general)

Response to Clay

- How does the child handle the clay physically? (pounding, rolling, pulling apart; squeezing, poking, making mush; making balls or snakes; slapping it, stamping on it; patting, stroking, scraping)
- Does she use supplementary tools? (tongue depressors, sticks, toothpicks, scissors, beads)
- Is there representation? (naming, size of products, accuracy of detail)
- How does he use materials in the space available? Does he work in his own area or does he spread out? (off the board, over the table)

Response to Blocks

- What blocks does the child select? (size and type of blocks; supplementary materials—dolls, small blocks, cars, wooden figures)
- What forms does she construct? (up in the air, crisscross, along the floor, piling, enclosures, recognizable structures)
- How does he use space? (confined or spread out, close to shelves, aware of obstacles)
- How flexible is the child in solving problems? Does she try different approaches? Repeat the same ineffectual ones? Repeat a successful approach again and again?
- Does the child verbalize while working?
- Is the structure named? Is it used in dramatic play? Is the child interested primarily in the process of building?

- Is there a repeated theme? Are themes changeable and varied?
- Does any kind of imaginative play develop while the building is going on? After it is finished?

### Length of Time Spent with Materials

The length of time spent can reflect concentration span, interest, distractibility, disinterest, feelings of inadequacy, tolerance for struggle, tolerance for challenge, response to something new, age.

## RECORDS OF USE OF MATERIALS

The following two children are getting something very different out of their use of materials. Seven-year-old Zeke uses clay to express and resolve emotions that he might not reveal in another situation, whereas 5-year-old Clover retains a sense of purpose in her own work within a social context. In each record we glimpse an aspect of the relationship between child and teacher.

All children in Ms. Diaz's 2nd-grade classroom are sitting in groups of two and three rolling, pounding, and squeezing clay except Zeke, who is working alone at his table. As Ms. Diaz stops at one table to answer questions from several children, Zeke calls out to her, "Ms. Diaz! Come here!" "Just a minute, Zeke!" she answers. Zeke, frowning, seems very annoyed and begins to pound very heavily on his ball of clay. He pauses a moment, looks briefly in Ms. Diaz's direction and yells out again, "Ms. Diaz, will you please come over here!" He continues to pound the clay with his fists. He begins to work furiously, rolling the clay and squeezing it frantically. At the same time, he stares coldly at the clay and speaks to it in a soft, but vicious, voice, "You have *got* to make me a dog." He begins to pound again. Then, in a low commanding tone, he says, "If you don't make me a dog, I will burst you open." He stands up, takes the clay in his hands and begins gently shaping it into a form. He sits down and calmly begins rolling the clay on the table. After a few minutes, Ms. Diaz comes over. Zeke gives her a wide smile, holds up his shape, and says, "See my dog. How do you like him?" Ms. Diaz smiles her approval, and all seems right with Zeke.

The teacher has deliberately put out new materials on the drawing and writing shelf—hole punches, colored tape, yarn, a ring binder with familiar words like "Mommy" and "cat." Clover is working with white paper in which she has punched eight evenly spaced holes at the bottom. The hole puncher is close by. She then takes a pair of scissors in her right hand and cuts a piece of the red tape, but it gets stuck to itself. When Lara, who is sitting next to her, says, "I need the hole puncher," Clover passes it to her while continuing to hold the scissors in her other hand. She then shifts her focus to the stuck piece of tape, using two hands to try and pull it apart. She uses the piece to attach a cut piece of paper to the whole sheet, then willingly passes the roll of tape to another child who says, "Clover, I need some tape right now." Clover then retrieves the roll, cuts more tape and attaches another piece of paper to her sheet. As she finishes cutting, Lara says in a slightly annoyed voice, "You know you almost cut my finger. Did you know you almost did that?" In a carefree tone, Clover says, "No."

## *HOW* THE CHILD DOES *WHAT*

Thus far we have recorded children's use of materials in such a way as to get a fairly inclusive picture of *what* they are doing. But we must also note what the special meaning of the experience is to an individual child. We must get down *how* a child does what he is doing. We must consciously and deliberately include, along with the actual action itself, the signs that show feeling. When we record *gross* movement, such as "she reached for a block," "he lifts the brush," "she grabbed the sponge," we are recording actions completely objectively, but without their life-pulse, or even our own response to their meaning. A child might be reaching for that block stealthily, hesitantly, or victoriously; perhaps she grabbed the sponge angrily, defiantly, efficiently, or just quickly; and he could lift the brush suspiciously, hastily, or absentmindedly. In the above descriptions, the meaning of each activity is different with each qualifying word. The descriptive adverb indicates the unique character of the gross action.

As we live and work with people, we react spontaneously to their range of feelings without ever thinking about how we know they feel as they do. We just sense it. With children, we certainly sense when they are delighted with themselves, when they are unhappy, when they are tense, when they are completely at ease. Actually, we take into our mind's eye a wide variety of cues that the other person sends out and get a composite picture that we then interpret according to our own experience and associations. Often we jump to conclusions before we get all the clues. It helps, therefore, to break down the nuances of behavior so that we are able to include them in the record.

Even though something of our own interpretation will be there, the evidence to support us will be there, too.

As indicated in the discussion of the language of recording, there is a difference between the subjective interpretation that *labels the child*—"He is hostile," "She is stubborn," "He is anxious," "She is greedy"—and the interpretation of one small piece of the total behavior—"He gave the teacher a *hostile look*," "She *replied stubbornly*," "He showed an *anxious smile*," "She reached *greedily* for the cookies." The difference is more than semantic. Labeling children defines them and confines them within a total appraisal. Interpreting a piece of the whole, such as a gesture, a smile, a posture, or a voice quality, leaves room for the gathering of many such expressions of feeling within a variety of situations. One can have hostile feelings under certain conditions and not be a hostile person. One can be stubborn about certain convictions and not be a generally stubborn person. One can feel anxiety about particular occurrences and not be an anxious person. One can even be greedy about one or two things and yet not be totally greedy at all.

### Reactions to Materials

Describing *how* a child does *what* adds up in time to clues we seek in order to understand children's motivations and feelings. These clues to feeling are the involuntary, noncontrolled, nondirected movements and gestures that accompany any gross action and give it its character. They are unique to every child and every action, for no child works at materials, or is involved in any form of play, without a variety of accompanying behaviors. Thus, as we pick up the child's action and at what or to whom it is directed, we note other things as well.

- We include the sounds a child makes and the language a child speaks.
  - » If the voice is being used, what is it like? (Loud, soft, ringing, well-modulated, high-pitched are descriptions of the physical quality of the voice. Jubilant, wavering, whining, reassuring, hesitant, gleeful, nonchalant, casual, fretful, smug describe the feeling tone of the child's voice.)
  - » What does the child say? (Pick up direct quotes if possible.)
  - » Does the child chant, sing, use nonsense syllables or phrases, tell stories while working?
- We note the movements of the body as a child uses materials.
  - » What is the posture like? (erect, rigid, hunched, floppy, straight, curled, squat)

» What is the rhythm of the body movements? (jerky, smooth, easy, jumpy, staccato-like, flowing)
» What is the tempo of the body movement? (rapid, sluggish, measured, slow, swift, leisurely, deliberate, speedy, hasty, moderate, unhurried)
» How much and what kind of effort does the child expend? (a great deal, excessive, very little, moderate, strained, laborious, easy, vigorous, forceful, feeble)
» What kind of freedom does the child show in his body movement? (sweeping movements; cramped, tiny movements; free-flowing; restrained, tight, restricted)
• We identify the details of facial expression.
» What describes the eyes? (glint, dullness, brightness, shine, teariness, blinking)
» What describes the mouth? (grin, quiver, pucker, tongue between lips, biting lips, smiling, wide open, drawn tight)

From these details we can surmise the child's emotional response to the materials, for example, excitement, contentment, frustration, self-criticalness, confidence, squeamishness, stimulation, overstimulation, taking in stride, intense interest, preoccupation. Feelings come through clearly in this next episode.

> Angelita, 4-and-a-half, was sitting next to the teacher, playing with Tinkertoys. One of the other children held the box. In an annoyed voice, Angelita blurted out, "I want to use that." She had a look of strong concentration on her face as she took each piece and pushed it forcefully into place. She took time choosing which piece to use next. The teacher got up and walked away, but Angelita did not seem to notice. She kept on working in the same way, thoughtfully and forcefully, without talking to any of the other children at the table. Her construction was large and intricate. When the teacher told her it was cleanup time, Angelita said, "No!" and continued working. Later, when the teacher told her that she could keep her finished work on a shelf, Angelita very carefully carried it there. When she noticed a child going toward the piece, she screamed, "Don't touch that!"

### Reactions to People While Working

The feelings that children reveal may be reactions to more than the materials they are using. We include in the record, therefore, what we see of their reactions to the people around them.

- Is there any socializing with children as the child uses materials?
  - » How does the child show awareness of children nearby? (talking, showing materials and products, touching others; using products in dramatic play; helping others, criticizing; calling for attention to what she is doing)
  - » Does the child work alone or with others?
- What are the child's relations to adults while using materials?
  - » Does he call for help, approval, supplies?
  - » Is she suggestible, defiant, indifferent, heedless, mindful of adult offers of help, adult participation, reminders of rules and limitations, offers of suggestions?
- How does the experience end?
  - » What events and feelings follow immediately after? (puts things away, puts work on the storage shelf, destroys own work, shows things to the children or teachers, leaves everything and goes to another activity, dances around the room)

## RECORDS ILLUSTRATING DETAIL

The following records all show attention to detail and nuance. The first, of Yvonne, age 5, is primarily a recording of gross movements and sequence of events:

> Yvonne comes directly to the outdoor table on which the teacher has placed a basket containing scissors, crayons, and glue. There is a stack of paper and two aluminum plates filled with materials for collage such as string, paper, and cloth of various shapes. "I wanna glue, I wanna glue, I wanna glue," shouts Yvonne.
>
> The teacher, busy with another child, replies, "Yes, Yvonne. It's Tony's turn now. . . . It will be yours next. Help yourself, Yvonne." Standing in the same place, and not looking at the teacher, Yvonne says in a babyish, whiny tone, "I wanna glue, I wanna glue." She looks along the table at the others who are cutting, crayoning, pasting. She moves around a child, and helps herself to the entire basket of crayons, placing it in front of her seat. She helps herself to paper, sits down, and makes a few crayon marks. As though realizing that this was not what she had planned to do, she calls, "Mrs. Chang?"
>
> "Yes?"
>
> "I wanna glue."
>
> "The glue is down at the end of the table, Yvonne."

Yvonne goes for the glue and gives herself some. Back at her seat she pastes a piece of collage material on her paper, helps herself to another piece, and pastes that. She works intently, lips parted. She spends more time than needed pushing her finger around and around in the glue on the paper, as though enjoying the feel of it. She pastes wool, lace, paper, and cloth. A piece of string sticks to her fingers. The teacher approaches.

"May I help you?"

"Yes," responds Yvonne, whiny and a little pouty. The teacher puts a short line of glue on the paper and lays the string on it.

"Now you show me how you want your string to go and we will put some glue there." Yvonne accepts this idea.

"Now you put the glue where you want the string to be." She does.

"I'm finished!"

"Okay."

She smears the glue around on her hands. "I wanna wash."

"There's water and towels on the tree stump," says the teacher.

Yvonne washes and runs off to the bikes. She had not spoken to any child while she worked.

The second record, of 4-and-a-half year old Carlos, has more "qualifying" details, and reveals the mood of the child more successfully:

Carlos points to the window and with a radiant face calls in delight, "It's snowing cherry blossoms! First they are white, then green, then red, red, red! I want to paint!" He goes to the easel and quickly snatches up a smock. Sliding in beside Isaac, he whispers to him caressingly and persuasively, "Isaac, you want blue? I give it to you, okay? You give me red because I'm going to make cherries, lots of red cherries!"

After the boys exchange paint jars, Carlos sits erect, and with a sigh of contentment starts quickly but with clean strokes to ease his brush against the edge of the jar. He makes dots all around the outer part of the paper. His tongue licks his upper lip, his eyes shine, his body is quiet but intense. The red dots are big, well-rounded, full of color, and clearly separated. While working, Carlos sings to himself, "Red cherries, big, round, red cherries!" The first picture completed, he calls the teacher to hang it up to dry. The next picture starts as the first did, with dots at the outside edge that soon filled the whole paper. He uses green, too, but the colors do not overlap.

Still singing his little phrase, Carlos paints a third and a fourth picture, concentrating intently on his work.

The other children pick up his song and Isaac starts to paint blue dots on his paper. Waving his brush, Carlos asks, "Isaac, want to try my cherries?" Swiftly and jubilantly he swishes his brush across Isaac's chin. Laughing, he paints dots on his own hands. "My hands are full of cherries," he shouts. He runs into the adjoining room, calling excitedly to the children, "My hands are full of cherries!" He strides into the bathroom to wash his hands. Nellie follows him in, calling, "Let's see, Carlos." "Ha, I ate them all," he gloats as he shows his washed hands with a sweeping movement.

The following record of 6-year-old Sam shows us something of a child's need to relate to others while working and the flexibility of his symbolic thinking:

> After hanging up his jacket, Sam edged into a chair at the end of a table where no one else sat, his eyes dreamily watching in an unfocused manner the actions of others at two other tables as they rolled, punched, and pounded the clay they were using. Moving like a sleepwalker, he accepted a hunk of clay and in an absent manner rolled it under the palm of his right hand, his head turned to the side, eyes directed toward the 10 or 12 children in the room.
>
> A few minutes passed thus. Then he picked up the hunk of clay and let it fall "kerplunk" on the table. Instantly his mood changed, like pressing a button and changing a still picture into an animated one. "Boom!" he shouted, "I got a ball! Look at my ball, teacher! Bounce! Bounce!" He banged it down a few times. Then he started rolling it into a long thin piece. "Here's a snake. I'm making a rattlesnake. Are you making a rattlesnake, Donna?" he asked the child nearest him at the other table.
>
> To Angel, who had a moment before entered the room and started to work at the table, Sam exclaimed, "That's a snowman, Angel. Now I'm making a snowman. . . . Now I'm making a snake big as Edward's." Sam held it up and chortled with glee. "Hee-hee-hee."
>
> "Look what I made. I twist it here." He dropped it on the table and began pounding it.
>
> "Now I'm making a pancake. Look at my pancake. Taste my pancake, teacher."
>
> Flop! He dropped it on the table again, rolling it over and over, faster, faster, his motions in keeping with his words. Head and shoulders were hunched over the table, his lips and tongue stumbled over each other in an effort to increase the speed of his words. "Chee—ee—ee—eeeeeeeee . . ."
>
> Everything slowed down. He was quiet, absorbedly working for a moment. Then in a sharp staccato and prideful tone: "Look what I made, teacher. . . . Look what I made, Donna. . . . Look at my wristwatch."

At this point it was necessary for the teacher to help another child, and she was in a stooping position, with her back to Sam. He poked her insistently in the back to add emphasis to his exhortation. "Look at me, teacher!"

She turned to find the clay covering Sam's upper lip. His head was tilted back to prevent its slipping off. "It's a mustache. Ha-ha-ha [he laughed uproariously]. Now it's a hat." He quickly transferred the clay to his head. "Teacher, look at my hat."

## INTERPRETATION—THE LAST DIMENSION

Even though we spot the separate, small parts of an action, we actually respond to the whole, integrated behavior of a child, such as his anger, joy, surprise. Our response follows a spontaneous, unspoken assessment of the child's feeling, which is drawn from our personal experience and understanding. To some extent we must rely on this subjectivity to define or interpret a child's behavior. We are dependent, however, on correct descriptive words about significant details to place that feeling on record. The value of a record that includes details such as those suggested in the preceding sections is that our interpretation (he is happy, she is sad) is bolstered by objective evidence. We are therefore less likely to be assuming that a feeling is present in a child because we happen to be identifying with him as the underdog or victim, or because we are reacting with subjective antagonism to an aggressive or uncouth person, or because for any other reason we are putting ourselves into the situation irrationally. Interpretation represents the sum total of our background of understanding. Professionally valuable interpretation relies heavily on objective data.

Yet it is impossible to get everything into every record. No child ever does everything possible in human behavior at any one time, nor could a teacher get it all down if a child did. Don't try to use the suggestions for details to record as a checklist! While the teacher is busily checking off what seems important to look for, the child may be doing something we never thought of at all, and that would be missed. Keep your eyes on the youngster, not on the printed page! It is not *how much* you record, but *what* and *how,* that makes a record valuable.

## PATTERNS OF BEHAVIOR

The review of on-the-spot records of children's use of materials over a period of time will be a mirror of their growth in this area and lead to supported generalizations. We will get to know many things about them that we might have missed without these concentrated observations of their activity. We will see a profile of their tastes and ideas and learn how much confidence they have in their own imagination and capacity. We will note their dependency on adults and other children, their concern for standards or indifference to them, their pleasure in doing things or their anxiety about doing things wrong. These responses are evaluated best when seen against the backdrop of a child's general coordination, maturity, experience, and age, as well as against the usual behavior of children of the same age group.

## Summary of a Child's Use of Materials

As with the summary on routines, we look for patterns of behavior—overall patterns that indicate a general approach to materials and specific patterns relating to different materials. Here are suggestions for what to include in such a summary:

1. How the child uses the various materials—paint, clay, blocks— over a period of time, in persistent or changing ways
   » How the child comes to use the material generally (on his own initiative, on the suggestion of the teacher or another child, through imitation of other children)
   » Coordination (physical ability to carry out techniques)
   » Techniques (the stage of development—manipulative, exploratory, representational—in relation to the child's age and background of experience; for example, painting dots, rolling clay, or piling cubes are techniques that can be early steps in the use of new materials, typical techniques of an age group, or excessively simple usage of material by a child who has the age and background for more complex approaches)
   » How the child works (concentration and care used; exploratory; competently, skillfully, intensively, carelessly, tentatively; distractibility; in different ways)
   » Language or sound accompaniments
   » Mannerisms
   » Products (creativity, imagination, originality shown)
   » Attention span (in general, and in relation to specific materials and activities)
   » Materials chosen by the child for dramatic play and how they are used

» Whether the child completes what she starts
» Adult role and child's response (indicate rules, limitations, participation, what is permitted, and how child accepts all these)

2. How the child seems to feel about the materials
   » Number, variety, frequency of materials and activities enjoyed, used, and avoided (include changing and static interest)
   » General attitudes—enthusiastic, eager, confident, matter-of-fact, cautious (include attitude toward new as well as familiar materials)
   » Importance of given areas to the child—interest, intensity of pleasure, preoccupation, fears, avoidance, resistance
   » Specific materials in relation to which the child apparently feels satisfaction, frustration, self-confidence, inadequacy
   » How the child reacts to failure, to success (include what constitutes failure or success, the level of aspiration)

3. How the child's use of line, color, and form changes over time (saving first and later paintings and drawings can be a data source.)

4. Child-adult relationship revealed via materials (independence–dependence)

5. Special problems
   » Distress over breakage
   » Avoidance of messiness
   » Concentration on only one material or idea
   » Inability to concentrate and enjoy

## Records of Overall Response to Materials

The following are examples of two children's overall use of materials. The various items from the records, when brought together in a summary of persistent or changing patterns, are easily written up as a sketch of a youngster's use of materials. In time, this sketch becomes part of the end-of-the-year record of the child. The first sketch is of 4-year-old Julio:

Julio's work with creative materials has been largely teacher-initiated. Before he begins any activity, he usually spends some time watching the other children. Then, when he apparently feels sure of himself, he begins. His attention span is adequate to complete the activity. He works deliberately and quietly, absorbed and interested in the task at hand.

It is quite evident that this is real work. His work is neat and carefully done. When he abandons this approach to materials, he seems worried and seeks reassurance from the teacher that this untidiness is accepted comfortably by her. He verbalizes as he works, a running commentary to teacher, children, or no one. He shows pride in accomplishment and again often seeks approval from the teacher. His work with clay is delightful and imaginative, and he seems to feel more freedom here than in the use of other media.

Materials most used by 3-year-old Ling are sand, mud, crayons, easel paints, finger paints, and water. Just recently she has begun to use the clay to make cakes with cookie cutters or to make imprints with any article handy. At first her attitude toward materials was one of indifference, but now she is interested in what she is making and comes to show it to the teachers or children. Paste on her hands at first annoyed her so that she did not want to use it. Today she was pasting, and I was delighted to see a paste smear in her hair and concentrating intently on her creation.

When a new material was introduced, she looked at it but did not attempt to play with it. Recently we received a train and track, musical bells, and new dishes, and started a new project of covering our rug chest. She wanted to be part of each group playing with the new materials, except the dishes, and went from one thing to another as fast as she could. This was so unusual that we almost gasped in surprise. The part that gave us the biggest thrill was this morning when two children were taken upstairs to cover the chest. Ling went to the toilet and on the way back noticed what was going on. Going up to a big 5-year-old she said, "Give me hammer" in a demanding voice. Teacher said she could have a turn next. Stamping her foot, trying to pull the hammer from Lucy's hand, she replied, "Now, I want it right now." Not receiving it instantly, she came down to tell the other teacher her trouble. She did get a turn and then went to the musical bells. While there are still materials she has not touched, such as blocks, dishes, and cars, she is adding to her play more materials each day.

From the beginning, she has used the playground equipment without fear of falling. Every piece of equipment has been used by her, and with good control of muscles, expression, and movement of body indicating extreme satisfaction. The swing is one place where she often hums and sings.

# 4

# Recording Children's
# Behavior with One Another

It is perhaps hard to believe, but nevertheless true, that young children at first look at one another as they do at objects and materials—as something to touch, to smell, and maybe to taste! Watch a toddler pour sand on another child's head and then stare in amazement at his distress, or calmly push someone down the stairs if she is in the way, or poke a finger into a youngster's eye to see what makes it shine. This sounds like the cruelest savagery, but it is really nothing more than evidence for the fact that there is a time in the life of human beings when they do not fully understand that other people have feelings like their own. As a matter of fact, there is even a time when human beings do not fully understand that they themselves are separate, individual people, capable of independent feeling and action. The consciousness of self, of being somebody, comes gradually. Paradoxically, one must have awareness of this selfness, this being, before one can even suspect that other living creatures feel pain and pleasure.

## HOW CHILDREN LEARN TO SOCIALIZE

The early years are the time when attitudes toward people are laid down in the character structure of the child, and the techniques for getting along in our culture are more or less painfully learned. As teachers, we have to be aware of three aspects of children's social development:

- A child's attitudes toward people (affection, love, trust, suspicion, hate)
- The strength of a child's feelings (deep, casual, indifferent)
- The amount and kind of know-how a child has in getting along with others (getting a doll by asking for it, stealing it, or grabbing it)

In this sense, a child may feel warm and loving to all humanity, but show it crudely, perhaps by hugging those who do not want hugging at the moment. Or a child may be jealous or resentful, but knowing that hugging is approved by adults but hitting is not, may hug to hurt. By the time children come to elementary school at age 5 or 6, there has already been a complex background of experience shaping their attitudes and techniques. They are, however, still very much in the process of learning (as we are too) and quite receptive to our efforts to help them develop wholesome attitudes and to practice constructive techniques.

### Becoming Aware of Self

Infants become conscious of others in relation to the fulfillment of their own needs and wants, which means, quite naturally, from a self-centered point of view. This is neither wrong nor unnatural. It is, however, the base from which future behavior will develop, sooner for some, later for others.

At the time that children start to speak of themselves as "I" instead of in the third person ("Baby wants a drink"), they are still examining other children with curiosity and interest but with limited comprehension. Not until children feel themselves persons (know their names, their gender, their likes and dislikes, and something of where they belong) can they look at others and know, "They feel even as I feel." It is natural to the growth of a young child, therefore, to be in a state of progression from nonidentification with others toward increasing capacity for sympathy and understanding. Before one can guide a child in social relationships, one must know how far along that child is on the road to maturity.

### Relating to Others

A brief look at a pair of 2-year-olds and a pair of 3-year-olds reveals clear differences in their social maturity:

> Two-year-old Natasha and the teacher have been playing together with a clown jack-in-the-box on the floor. Cory has been playing hide-and-seek in a nearby closet with some of the other children. Suddenly Cory's attention is caught by Natasha saying, happily, "Bye-bye, clownie," as she pushes the toy back into the box, and he reaches out to grab the toy with a look of envy in his eyes. Natasha, startled, whines, "No." Hesitantly, she reaches out toward the toy while gazing pleadingly at the teacher. The teacher explains to Cory that Natasha does not want

to share the toy just now, maybe later. Cory looks angrily at the teacher and then leans viciously against Natasha, attempting to bite her but biting the jack-in-the-box instead. He breaks into a frustrated sob, then, after some comforting by the teacher, wanders off to find another toy to play with.

A group of 3-year-olds are sitting on the floor while the music teacher plays her guitar and sings "There was a farmer, had a dog . . ." The children had been instructed to clap their hands and sing along if they know the song. Melissa and Jonas are sitting next to one another, each focused on the music teacher. Both of them clap and join in singing many times. At one point Melissa sings words that are different from the teacher's and Jonas's. Jonas quickly switches his focus to Melissa and stops clapping and singing. He leans over, looks squarely into Melissa's face, and announces matter-of-factly, "Stupid!" Melissa stops singing and clapping and looks at Jonas quizzically but says nothing. Jonas once more proclaims Melissa "stupid," but not before he is almost on top of her. By this time, neither one is focused on anything but each other's eyes, waiting to see who will make the first move. Suddenly Melissa smiles, happily repeats "Stupid!" to Jonas, and falls on the floor laughing. Jonas catches her infectious laugh as he falls on the floor, having fun with the word *stupid*. Very soon they are both just laughing together and the word *stupid* is no longer heard. By the time the music teacher finishes the song, both children are sitting up and clapping along with one another and with the teacher.

When teachers first see young children at school, they have not had too much time as yet for maturing. They behave with one another only as they know how within their limits. They may long to please but still do unto one another only as they know how rather than as we think they should. Even as we show them better techniques for getting along with one another, we must accept without condemnation the inadequate techniques they already have. This does not mean that all and any behavior is permitted to go on without an effort to direct it. To do that would be a real disservice to children because they are dependent on us for cues to what is socially acceptable. It does mean, however, that we may not expect of children behavior they neither know about nor are capable of performing. So often what we judge to be naughty is due to sheer ignorance.

By the time we reach adulthood we have already incorporated into our personalities the morality and ethics of our culture. Young children, however, are still somewhat uninitiated, and much of what they do is meaningful to them only in the purely personal terms of how they feel about what's happening and not in the objective sense of what is right or wrong. Understanding and accepting children's anger, jealousy, rivalry, fear, ambition, and anxiety establish an atmosphere of acceptance in which they can grow into socially necessary and morally desirable behavior without losing their self-respect and dignity as human beings.

We cannot close the gap between adulthood and childhood by trying to behave like children ourselves. But we can use our imagination and feel with children so we see what is important to them from the limits of their experience as well as from the breadth of ours.

### Children's Social Reactions Differ

Some children follow a consistent pattern toward all other children. They are pleasant and sweet-tempered with all comers, welcoming and accepting and equally gracious with everyone. An opposite kind of consistency is present in the child who is often suspicious or hostile, a "lone wolf." How many such completely one-dimensional personalities are there in the group? Not many. We might say that such people, big or little, seem to have something inside them that keeps them one way all the time, regardless of what is happening outside themselves. But most children, like most adults, react to a number of things. One might be the behavior and expectations of another person. A second might be the irritability of coming down with mumps or measles. A third might be the abundance or scarcity of something a child wants. And so on.

Many situations can affect children's reactions to one another. The presence or absence of certain teachers or children, or a long spell indoors with no chance for physical activity, would be such situations. Or, on occasion, normally unaggressive children can become aggressive under the cover of group protection or when they feel unjustly deprived. Some children learn quite early whom they can push with impunity and whom to follow with regard. Most children seem to have a sixth sense about the children who are unable to defend themselves.

In other words, reactions to people are many-sided, especially while children are still learning the techniques of getting along with others, as is true in the early years. It is no surprise, therefore, that the healthy, normal youngster may show contradictory reactions. If we are to guide children to good, successful interpersonal adjustment, we have to be sure that we know what their reactions to others actually are.

## DO WE REALLY SEE WHAT IS GOING ON?

It is inevitable that teachers will apply their own yardsticks of social right and wrong to children's behavior, and it is good for children to learn from people who have convictions. But we adults have to be reasonably certain that our expectations fit the capacities of the children. We feel sure about what is right and wrong because we learned our lessons well in childhood. It may happen, however, that our "intuitive" knowledge is contradicted by thoughtful child study, because what we learned as children we learned uncritically and without understanding. Many of the attitudes we consider "natural" and "right" as adults were learned this way. In Chapter 1, biases and prejudices that influence interpretations of behavior were discussed. They influence what we see, too, as anyone who has listened to the conflicting testimony of eyewitnesses to an accident realizes. But observation and, it follows, interpretations of children's behavior are more likely to be accurate when we know what our particular biases are.

Seeing a child rejected by his peers is for some of us clearly a call to come to the child's defense, and in we move to demand humane behavior from a little tyrant. Others among us find a physical tussle between youngsters unnerving and perhaps a little frightening. Again we hear the call to action and with feelings of righteousness mete out justice "impartially." For still others, the "show-off," the "bossy type," the "hog," the "poor sport," the "sneak" are children whose behavior does something to us, impelling us to stop them somehow. And stop them we do, not always because it is necessarily right or in the children's best interests, but because we need to quiet the disturbance inside ourselves. We have feelings, too. And when children's behavior makes us uncomfortable, we do something to ease the discomfort if we possibly can.

How sure can we be that our techniques for handling antisocial or asocial behavior are the most helpful ones when we ourselves feel personally involved in this way? How sure are we that we are seeing all there is in a situation, and not only the obvious, the dramatic, or that which is personally important?

Do we assume that all smiles mean pleasure and all tears pain? That boisterous, noisy fighting can hurt more than quiet, calculated avoidance? Do we really see what is going on? What, for example, is happening to the two who are smiling at each other on the swings? Is this a budding friendship of two shy ones or a budding plot of two rascally ones? Just what is going on between the two who hog a corner and engage in endless conversations? Are they seeking each other out for support or for stimulation? Can we always be sure what and who started a fight? Is every fight bad?

We need to ask ourselves whether every child in the group has a friend and whether all the friendships are profitable to those concerned. Do some children need special help from adults in getting along with others? Are there some for whom the best adult guidance is a "hands-off" policy?

We must learn to look at children without preconceptions of what they "ought" to be doing, if we want to see what they *are* doing. The following observation records a scene that is quite commonplace among 6- and 7-year-olds. It shows behavior that can be very upsetting to some teachers. Yet the recorder does not reveal a single bit of her own attitudes. She just describes what she has seen and heard, quite objectively:

> Seven little girls sit busily drawing at a round table, the center of activity in the empty room. Spying the group, Eva scampers over and seats herself comfortably on a chair. Meanwhile, Koko has been displaying the contents of a plastic doctor's bag that she has brought to school. She hovers about the circle speaking and gesticulating importantly. Calling out in a stentorian voice meant to arrest all activity, she offers, "Who wants some gum?" Eva asks politely and cajolingly, "Can I have some?" Koko answers in a stern, firm manner, "Only my best friends." Instantly a chorus of voices pledge in unison eternal friendship with Koko, Eva among them with her lilting, "I'm your best friend."
>
> Koko then commands, "Just raise your hands, and you'll get some." All obey unquestioningly, enjoying the game, as Koko walks around distributing wads of white tissue, which serve as gum. Eva's eyes sparkle with excitement as she rocks in her chair from side to side. "Now everybody close their eyes." Eva sits upright, her eyes barely closed as if in a trance, eyelashes trembling slightly. She claps both hands over her eyes, opens her mouth slightly, and waits expectantly. Disappointed, she opens her eyes and begins to mold a bit of clay, declaring in a confident, conspiratorial tone of voice to Koko, "Anyway, I don't have to close them because I already know, right? I don't have to because I already know it, right? Right, Koko? I don't have to. Yeah, because I already know the trick, right?"
>
> Koko whispers to Alexis. Interjecting, Eva says, "But I'm going to your birthday, Alexis." Koko turns to Eva and says, "Don't go to her birthday. You can hold my baby brother Leo." Completely persuaded, Eva croons, "Oh, Leo's so cute." Koko, looking satisfied, strolls off.

We can assume that any good teacher would make a note to herself to watch Koko and Eva more closely and to find the appropriate time and place when she could be helpful to each in a more effective way than if she had interfered at this point. The teacher *as a teacher* is given to action; the teacher *as an observer* must record as though not involved. These are separate parts of a teacher's task, both necessary and not to be confused with each other!

## WHAT TO OBSERVE

Every teacher picks up a lot of useful information out of the corner of her eye as she goes about her busy day. She knows that a combination of Safia and Naomi is sure to end up in mischief; that once started on cowboy play, Juan, Sean, and Evan will keep at it for the whole outdoor period; that Akira will probably wander again today as she has since coming to school; and so on. Is that enough?

### How Is the Contact Made?

*Who approached whom* in the Safia-Naomi combination? Who started the cowboy idea? Who leads? Who follows? How do the children make contact with one another? Is it that way all the time? Are there some children who typically have to be asked and some who always ask? Are children different with different members of the group, asking some and not others, accepting some and not others?

Some children approach others with certainty and sure-footedness. "Let's play," they say forthrightly, and play it is. Others come along with less assurance. "May I play?" they ask timidly, or hesitantly, or uncertainly. Some children walk up to others and stand speechless, waiting for acceptance and admission to the golden realm. And some wait for no introduction, but direct the activity immediately. "You be my passenger. I'm the driver."

- What was the child's attitude when he initiated the contact?
  - » Was he bold and demanding?
  - » Was she friendly and assuring?
  - » Was he frightened and expectant of rebuff?
- How was the approach made?
  - » Did she touch or push?
  - » Did he caress the other child?
  - » Did she gesture at the other child in some way?
- Or did the teacher get the whole thing started?

As children approach one another, they may be casual, relaxed, and at ease; they may be friendly or hostile, confident or afraid. They may have the right words or still be relying on body contact. *Their approach will show both their attitude and their know-how.*

## How Does the Child Do What He Does?

We get the quality of a child's approach to other children by the quality of the voice, the rhythm and tempo of the speech, the facial expression, and the body movements. They are all there in one integrated response. We react to this total response, of course, but in recording it is necessary to articulate quite consciously the nonverbal clues that will eventually help us determine a child's feelings. We have talked before of the difference between *what* a child does and *how* he does it. It is perhaps more important to see how children behave socially than how they use materials, because adults are far likelier to take sides and do something when children are working out their social relationships than when they are exploring materials. To see the meaning of the experience to the child, we must be sure to see *how* that child does what he actually does. The action alone is not enough.

*Body Positions and Movement.* Perhaps it is hard for us to pin down and record significant body positions and movements in children because as adults we have become so circumscribed in our own movements that we cannot feel the meaning of theirs in their own bodies. We do not sprawl on the floor spontaneously anymore; we don't give way to laughter by flinging our legs over our heads; we don't fall easily; we prefer sitting to running. In short, we have ceased to use our own bodies with the freedom and abandon of children. Consequently, we do not look at jumping or climbing youngsters and tingle in our own muscles with their exhilaration in stretching limbs. Yet body expression is personality expression. One's body is oneself. One uses one's body as one feels.

Even if 5-year-old Janine, in the next record, had not said a word to her father, we would know how uncertain she was about getting into the swing of things from her body movement and gestures.

> Janine arrived, holding her father's hand tightly, her thin body curved in an S-shape, her hand gently rubbing her father's sleeve. In a soft, anxious voice, she whispered, "I don't want you to go." Then she put her index finger into her mouth and sucked on it wistfully, while her father

put his arm on her shoulder and urged her to take several steps forward. Janine dragged both feet forward hesitantly, still sucking her finger, and put one hand up, resting it on the door frame. Her father rubbed his hands together cheerfully and said gaily, "Well, I'm off," and left Janine still leaning indecisively on the door frame. Mousily she moved to the chair next to Andrew only four steps from the door and stood with both hands resting on the back of the chair, watching him write his name. Abruptly, she plopped into the chair and a moment later stood up again. With a sudden burst of energy she stepped over to the crayon box. She picked up a crayon and purposefully and quickly wrote her name, her tongue sticking out between her lips. Still no greeting passed between the children, Andrew being involved in decorating his sign.

Just as quickly as she had started, Janine finished her name, did not decorate it, and slunk over to the rug by the book stand, shoulders drooping, head slightly hanging down. She flopped loosely onto the rug, reached casually for a book, and gazed absently at it, methodically turning page after page. She looked up as another child sat down with a book. She stared at the child. Except for her eyes, she was motionless, with her big toe occasionally wiggling in her sandal.

In the process of relating to one another, children so often strike first and ask later, or grow rigid with fear but say nothing, or stand with head low and voice mute. The tilt of the head, the use of the hands, body stances, amount of body activity, bodily contacts (touch, shove, push, pat, buck), all are means of communicating. Trust and fear, self-confidence and inadequacy, all find expression in bodily posture. So do restlessness, irritability, composure, and serenity. We know this to be true from experience. We must include the details of body movement in our records.

*Quality of Voice.* This is an integral part of communication. As children speak, their emotional state will be revealed in the voice.

- Is it strident, soft, querulous, screechy, flat, pleading?
- Is it lilting, whining, demanding, loud, strained, forceful, quivery?

"'Give it to me,' he growled" is hardly the same expression of feeling as, "'Give it to me,' he whined petulantly." "I want that" can be said angrily, hungrily, wistfully, urgently, teasingly, or happily. It makes a difference to know with which kind of voice a child makes a comment or asks a question.

*Tempo and Rhythm.* These qualities of a child's speech tell us something about the tempo and rhythm of that child. He may drawl and move in unhurried fashion; or her words may tumble in unending floods of ideas and feeling. Slowness or speed may simply be the result of the organization of the child's nervous system (as it usually is), but it may be the result of anxiety, too. Children slow up when they are afraid of saying the "wrong" thing. They hurry when they are afraid they won't be listened to.

Fast, slow, moderate—these refer to *tempo. Rhythm* is something else again. Rhythm is smoothness, jerkiness, or hesitancy. The rhythm of speech can be staccato, cadenced, flowing. Combining tempo and rhythm, we find that a child's speech can be fast and smooth or fast and jerky, slow and even or slow and hesitant. Rhythm and tempo together characterize the quality of the speech.

*Facial Expression.* This accompanies "quality" in speech. We expect smiling eyes with laughter, a droopy mouth with tears. Here are some of the descriptive terms we can use:

*Eyes* can be solemn, glaring, flashing, tearful, smiling, sleepy,
    bright, shiny, dull, sparkling.
*Mouth* can be drooping, smiling, pouting, quivering, laughing,
    puckered, drawn, lips curled over teeth.
*Smile* can be wholehearted, uncertain, full, wistful, furtive,
    reluctant, shy, open, dimpled, and half.

Of course, not all details appear in every record. For one thing, children do not use their entire battery of possible shades of expression every time they react to life. For another, no human recorder could see enough or write fast enough to get everything onto a piece of paper. But the more details you can record that point to what is happening inside a child as she makes contact, the more accurate and expressive will be the picture that emerges.

> Vanessa shaded her eyes with her hands, frowned, and stared across the yard at Khadijah. Her under lip jutted forward in a pout and her brows furrowed deeper than ever. Suddenly she swung her hands into fists at her side, stamped her foot, and exploded. "Hey!" She ran across the yard and grabbed Khadijah by the arm. Her head punctuated every word as she screamed into Khadijah's face, "Who told you to take my umbrella out of my locker?"

> Elisa slithered silently against the wall, slowly edging her way from the clothing lockers to the clay table. She stood still some two feet away, sober and unsmiling, eyes darting from side to side as she followed the conversation being tossed around the table. Norman looked up and saw Elisa. "Hi," he grinned. "Hi, Lisey." Still standing immobile, Elisa crinkled her face into a warm, open smile. Her eyes alive, shining, she chirped, "Hi, Normie."

Approaching someone is only part of the relationship. After that, the other person's response or lack of response determines further action. What does the other child do and say? How does that child do it? The record above about Elisa, though short, is a clear-cut illustration of how behavior is affected by other persons' responses.

## What Does the Child Say? How Does the Other Child Respond?

Speech may not reveal everything, but it tells a good deal. Record the actual words as far as possible and not just the sense of what a child says.

> "Hey, Pete, let's put the big one here."
> "Naw, it'll fall off."
> "No it won't, no it won't."
> "Okay" (good-naturedly).
> "Push that one back a little."
> No answer.
> "Hey!" (sharply) "Push that one back."

Does it take longer to write the actual dialogue than to write a paragraph about dialogue? The conversation above could be written about as follows:

> Lucas told Pete where to put the blocks. Pete was pretty agreeable. When Pete didn't answer, Lucas shouted at him.

The first is raw material. It is flavorful and authentic and, more important, uninterpreted. The second may be accurate as to interpretation, but it involves the teacher's appraisal of the situation. Should he be wrong, there is no going back to check. In the following record, both the dialogue and the quality of the voice comprise an important part of the children's interaction.

Four-year-old Pilar and Ann are building together. Pilar puts a large cardboard cylinder in the house.

*Pilar*: We need this. (She accidentally knocks over the blocks of another nearby structure.)

*Ann*: Why are you doing that? That's not our house.

*Pilar* (has begun using the knocked-over blocks, switches gears, and starts rebuilding the toppled building): I'm fixing it up.

*Ann*: How was it? Do you know?

*Pilar* (matter-of-factly): We'll just put it back. (She finishes and stands up. She has previously been sitting on her haunches in a scrunched-up but apparently comfortable position in which she moved about easily. She watches the goings-on in the dramatic play area inquisitively and then stoops down again. She speaks to the wooden doll in a chastising tone.) How did you get out of here? (She puts the doll on the bed, speaking firmly.) You go to bed. (She begins talking in a stream-of-consciousness style while Ann sits nearby.) And the woman (meaning the little doll, which she is holding) is the "figura," right? . . . You know what a "figura" is? (Ann does not respond so Pilar continues.) The woman goes out to a "figura" and dances now. (She sings.) Doodoo-doo-doo-doo-doo. (She moves the doll to make it dance, going up and down a clear aisle in the block area, walking on haunches as before.)

*Ann* (bringing over a male doll): Man's gonna dance too.

*Pilar* (with furrowed brow, her eyes bright, and a hint of authority in her voice): Wait, I'm gonna tell you something. We're gonna sing together. (And they do, making up words to their songs.)

## What Happens Next?

After a contact is made, what does a child do? Is there a sigh of relief and a quiet settling down to blissful submission? Is there a staccato-like bidding for supremacy of ideas and position? Or is there a purr of contentment as alternatives are weighed with other children? Do the children carry on conversation? Play the same thing separately? If the contact ends without going on into dramatic play, tell how it ends and what the child does immediately after. Subsequent behavior may reflect feelings about the contact.

Here are two boys reacting very differently to an event that was disturbing:

It was the middle of writing time in the 1st grade, and the children were working on their stories. Hank, however, was very upset, having just been involved in a very emotional, yelling, fist-swinging altercation that was broken up by the teacher. Seething, Hank stomped away from the table where he was writing, but on his way he accidentally brushed against Takeru's arm, causing a long pencil line to go across Takeru's paper. Takeru became upset, and his face started to wrinkle as if he might cry. Then, as if having second thoughts, he raised his head and hurried over to Hank, shaking his fist menacingly in front of Hank's face, but not too closely. Hank was by now sitting in a chair in the meeting area, his face tense, silently fuming and staring in the direction of the blackboard. He was obviously still troubled by his previous altercation and could only blankly acknowledge Takeru's anger. Takeru looked into Hank's face, saw how upset he was, then turned and edged his way back to the writing table and began to erase the pencil line.

## PATTERNS OF BEHAVIOR:
## SUMMARY OF A CHILD'S RESPONSE TO OTHER CHILDREN

Out of such details as those above, perceived in many episodes, there will emerge *patterns of behavior*, or the characteristic way in which a child is likely to respond in the daily relations with other children. Over a period of a school year, *changing* patterns indicate growth or regression. We can organize these patterns of behavior by clustering items from the single episodes around such categories as the following:

1. Evidence of interest in children
   » *Direct evidence* would be the number of children played with; or a child's request for help in entering play situations; or positive approaches to children.
   » *Indirect evidence* would be staring at others or watching them; imitating; attempting to attract attention from children by various means.
2. How contacts are made
   » Does the child move toward others or against them? (initially or always)
   » How does he move? (confidently, tentatively, pleadingly, timidly, aggressively)
   » Do others move toward him, away from him, or against him? (initially or always)
   » How does she react to the behavior of others? (to their affection, invitation to play, criticism, suggestions and ideas, aggressions)

» *What* does she do? (withdraws, enters play, rejects, tolerates, defies, aggresses, complains to adults)
» *How* does she do it? (shyly, confidently, eagerly, with curiosity and interest, crying, angrily, happily, fearfully)
» What methods does he use in making contacts? (speech, attacks, with ideas or things, enters situation directly, threatens, bribes, uses others to gang up, asks adults for help)

3. His behavior with other children
   » To what extent can he make his wishes, desires, irritations, annoyances, ideas understood?
   » To what extent is she able to share equipment, props, materials?
   » To what extent is he able to await his turn?
   » What are the more usual causes of clashes with others? (possessions, ideas, unprovoked attacks)
   » How does she handle conflicts?
   » *What* does she do? (runs to teacher, cries, fights back, reasons, jokes)
   » How does he do it? (tearfully, righteously, sobbing, angrily, indignantly)
   » To what extent is she aware of others' rights and needs?
   » How realistic are his demands for his own rights?
   » How does she protect her rights?
   » To what extent does he seek help from other children? (how, under what circumstances, from whom)
   » To what extent is she able to help others? (how, when, and whom)
   » To what extent does he contribute ideas, suggestions?
   » Does she accept other people's ideas, suggestions?
   » What seem to be the child's defense mechanisms?

4. The child's feelings about other children (likes, fears, envies)
   » Does she have special friends? (how many and who, nature of interrelationships)

5. Special problems or trends (impatience with others; allowing or encouraging exploitation by others; excessive hitting, temper, or withdrawal; lack of speech; excessive dependence on teacher)

6. Evidence of growth (comparison of earlier and later behavior indicating more mature level)

## GROUP MEMBERSHIP

If children learn to get along with one another within a school situation, they inevitably begin to develop a sense of the meaning of the large group along with their more intimate excursions into twosomes. But becoming a member of a group is a challenging task.

Every group develops a dynamic of its own, and groups of young children do the same. Once the children's first period of adjustment is over, they begin not only to seek their own place within the group's emerging structure but to recognize the places held by others as well. See, for example, how Paul, a 6-year-old, was already wise to the hierarchy within his group:

> Ricardo and Larry were playing a board game at table 3 as Paul and Alex stood by watching, when George, the acknowledged leader among the boys, arrived late. George sat down at table 2. Ricardo, with no outward sign that he was aware of George's arrival, said to Alex (who had just joined the crowd watching the game), "Alex, how would you like to play my man in the game? It's a very lucky seat."
>
> "All the boys like George and all the girls like Heather," said Paul to the teacher.
>
> "What makes you think so?" replied the teacher.
>
> "Look. See how all the boys stay near George?" Paul then decided he would take Ricardo's place, at which Ricardo announced, to no one in particular, "I have to do something."
>
> Larry, his erstwhile partner in the game, remembered he had something to do too and stood up, saying to the teacher, "I'm very sorry."
>
> Both Ricardo and Larry then made a "casual" beeline for table 2. Paul gave the teacher a significant look and declared, "See, I told you so."

### Details to Observe

In addition, then, to observing a child in relation to individual others, one would want to know how the child is faring within the larger, total group.

- Where does the child fit in relation to the entire group?
- Does she play with any children, one, or many, of both sexes?
  - » Is he an established member of the group? Is he making his way? Is he a lone player?
  - » How does she act toward new children entering the group?

- What is the child's position within the group? (leader, follower, instigator, disrupter, clown, uses group to hide)
- What status does the child have?
  - » Is the child chosen by others? (e.g., in games)
  - » How frequently is the child chosen by others? Repulsed by others?
- Is the child accepted? A "fringer"? A scapegoat?

The older the children, the more important the group is in their lives. Although Ben, a 3rd grader in a boys' school, figures out a way to become a group member, it is doomed to fail.

> Ben is a large, stout boy. At snack time, when all the boys took out their snacks, Ben looked on hungrily. He pleaded with each child to give him some of their snack, for he didn't have one (his parents had put him on a diet). Although a few children did give him a bit, Ben complained that it wasn't enough.
>
> The next day Ben came to school with an enormous writing pad. When the others asked him about it, Ben smiled and said, "It's for my club." "What kind of a club is it?" they begged. "Can we join?" Haughtily, Ben said, "It's a private club. Only special people who donate some snack to the club can join." Almost every student in the class ran over to Ben to donate some snack to the club. Ben grinned broadly as he wrote each child's name onto his pad, placing a check or a star on receipt of the snack. Then he sneaked off and greedily ate it all up.
>
> After a couple of days of this, the boys caught on and one by one stopped their contributions. The only member left was Ben, who sat as before, alone and hungry, begging each child for a crumb.

## Records of Group Membership

Summing up the generalizations that seem reasonable in light of the patterns that emerge out of the wealth of detail, we bring into focus an image of how a very much alive, vibrant child reacts in one important area of living. On the basis of such evidence we shall eventually be able to form hypotheses and plan for action. Judgment will have been based on objective data. Generalizations about two children's relationships with others follow:

> With his peers, Ari (age 5) shows a pattern of caution, observing them closely before he joins them. It has just been during the past few weeks that he has taken part in singing and rhythmic group activities. He seems to derive great satisfaction from this type of activity, asking, "Are

we going to play the Jingle Bell game today?" If sufficiently absorbed in a certain task, he ignores others in his immediate vicinity completely. He is friendly with most children, but tends to seek out one particular child to play with. This child changes on a day-to-day or week-to-week basis. When a third child enters (it always seems to be Michael), he feels very insecure, covering his feelings of hostility with a sulky withdrawal, seldom with an overt act of aggression. (This week I did see him pounce unexpectedly on Michael's back and wrestle him to the floor with much triumphant laughter on his part and complete bewilderment on Michael's.) Although Ari talks a great deal, he seems to be talking at the children most times, not with them. They all delight in listening to his tall stories. He has a good sense of humor and his hearty laugh can be heard throughout the room. He often uses laughter as a release from tension.

Just lately Ari has shown signs of approaching readiness to take aggressive action (e.g., wrestling Michael and Greg). His mother reported that he has told her proudly at home, "I had a big fight, and I made that kid almost cry." Actually, it was a very little fight, but its importance to Ari in his self-picture is very evident.

The issue of self-control seems to play a role in 6-year-old Quinn's difficulty with her peers. Repeatedly, Quinn does not respond to questions or comments of other children. Even when she works effectively with Cam during problem solving, Quinn speaks only toward the end of the activity (perhaps when she is certain she is on the right track or has the right answer). Is she so focused on the activity that she shuts down her communication with others? However, in the yard, at snack, and while "freely" investigating the crocuses, Quinn's conversation is engaged and animated. I wonder if Quinn's seeming inconsistency in interacting with peers prevents her from forging more friendships with her classmates.

In recent weeks, her budding friendship with Seth has fallen apart. Seth began treating Quinn in a mean manner—taunting her, hitting her, and telling others not to be her friend. I have no idea what caused this falling-out, but in its aftermath, Quinn hasn't been able to establish another link with a classmate. Quinn doesn't seem to be a loner—she looks to others for guidance and ideas—she just seldom communicates verbally. Nearly all the children seem able to work with her, and she is paired with a range of students during partner work. She gladly cooperates, though silently, with her partners. It seems that she is well liked (with the current exception of Seth), so it is curious that some stronger bond with a peer hasn't developed.

# 5

# Recording Children's Behavior in Dramatic Play

Dramatic (or symbolic) play often springs from children's contacts with one another, but it also occurs when children play alone. Whether the child plays alone or with others, there are many aspects to be considered. These can best be understood if we recognize that children project themselves into their play and work out problems both of intellectual comprehension ("Is steering a bus different from steering a plane?") and of emotional complexity ("I want what I want now, but if I say so, Rashid may not play with me"). Mostly, dramatic play is fun, and deeply satisfying fun at that. But it is also the children's way of exploring the meaning of activities and relationships in the grown-up world. It is, of course, learning to get along with other children, to share and bargain, to compare and evaluate, to compete and cooperate, to give and take. At the same time, the magic of make-believe allows children to work out their wishes, aspirations, fears, and fantasies. All this they do by playing a part, a role, or by making objects—real or imaginary—act as if they were animals, persons, or superheroes. Both the roles they take and the content of the play with these symbolic objects are composed of bits from the real world and pieces from inside themselves. Bits and pieces do not always make a logical whole in the eyes of an adult, and that is perhaps why children's play often seems inconsequential, irrational, or delightfully fluid and without boundaries to adult perceptions.

But play has logic to children, and the strongest evidence of this is the amount of symbolic play that goes on all through childhood. Even children who hardly know each other slip into the world of imagination together, understanding each other hardly at all in our sense, but speaking the language of dramatic play. Finding purpose in play, children commit themselves to it wholeheartedly. Not only is play purposeful, according to Vygotsky (1933/1976), but it is the "source of development" in which "a child is always above his average age" (p. 552).

Listen to these two children, Willie and Tracy, age 4-and-a-half, working things out individually and together as their imaginations meet, diverge, meet, and develop together:

Willie was building with the large cardboard blocks and using one of the child-size trucks in his construction. As he carefully placed the blocks in rectangular formation around the truck, he began howling with a high-pitched "Oh-ooh!" that sounded like the siren of a police car. Tracy came over and got on the truck, and she and Willie rode over to the nearby playhouse and went in.

Willie began tapping a rhythm on a drum, with a stick in each hand. "Give me one," Tracy said playfully, pointing to the sticks.

"I have to practice somethin'," Willie replied in a spirit of concentration. After a few more taps, he gave the sticks to Tracy and announced with an air of having come to a conclusion, "I'm finished." He got up to leave and stepped out of the house.

Tracy poked her head out and caught Willie's eye. "I have to go to do my work. How should I go?" she asked expectantly. Willie was busy pushing the truck over a mat that prevented its movement and didn't answer. They both then got on the truck, and Willie drove it over to the area where he had been building with the cardboard blocks.

"At last we have a new garage," he declared proudly as the truck rolled into the enclosure he had constructed earlier.

"This is my *house*," Tracy cried gleefully.

"This is the *garage*," Willie countered.

"So where can I sleep then?" queried Tracy with a note of concern in her voice.

"In my room. You'll sleep with me," Willie replied firmly. "We must go," he commanded.

Tracy walked quickly over to the housekeeping corner. "Honey, don't leave," Willie urged in a manly voice. Then he drove the truck around to the library corner, where he picked up two pillows, and drove back to the playhouse.

Tracy returned to the housekeeping corner carrying a small blanket and pillow. "I got the blanket," she said cheerfully.

"You can lie on it if you want to," said Willie with an air of unconcern. They both went into the house.

"Let me sleep this way," Tracy said lying down on the pillow.

"I have to practice somethin'," said Willie as he tapped the drum with two rhythm sticks.

"Who's wakin' me up?" Tracy complained, sounding annoyed.

"I'm practicin' somethin'," said Willie, defending his activity.

"Honey, could you sleep?" pleaded Tracy.

Willie put down the drum and sticks, and, sounding tired and weary, said, "I'll do this tomorrow." He lay down next to Tracy with his head on the pillow too.

Suddenly he shouted angrily, "Who' wakin' me up?" He popped his head out the door to observe some other children who were playing on the climber nearby. "They are big boys. They can stay up," he said in a tone of responsibility. "Just ignore them. Go to sleep," he said to Tracy fondly. For a moment they just looked at each other as they lay quietly together.

Tracy and Willie are joined in a symbolic representation of some aspect of each of their lives. Even though their individual experiences have been different, they are bound together by their common interest in play itself.

## CAPACITY FOR SYMBOLIC REPRESENTATION

Symbolic representation—making one thing stand for another—is a capacity with which all humans are endowed. Its development proceeds in a fairly sequential fashion, and it becomes the base for continued learning, since it makes it possible to learn from the experience of others, thus leading to a broadening of one's horizons. The presence of symbolic representation in a child's repertoire of activity is one indication of intellectual functioning; yet its most likely appearance in early childhood is not in writing or reading but in dramatic play and in the use of materials. Although research (Vygotsky, 1931/1976) indicates a link between play and language development, speech—which is a form of symbolic behavior—serves in a secondary way to reinforce young children's learning rather than as a primary, instigating vehicle of thought.

Symbolic representation may take many forms. It appears at two basic levels:

- The ability to *recognize* that one thing, for example, a picture of a cup, stands for another, the cup itself; or a doll stands for a baby and a toy car for a real one.
- The ability to *create* symbols—to *make* one thing stand for another. Children create symbols in dramatic play (the child himself represents a father; a stick is used as a pretend hammer), in block building (a line of blocks represents a road,

a line of chairs a train), and in painting, drawing, and work with clay.

The capacity first to recognize the role of symbols and then to create one's own is the essential underpinning for the use of *social symbol systems*, such as words, numbers, letters of the alphabet, and the innumerable symbols we have to learn, such as traffic lights and signs, mathematical and scientific symbols. Children who do not develop symbolic representation in their play and use of materials may have difficulty learning to read because the basic awareness of the function of symbols is likely to be missing. Pellegrini (cited in Monighan Nourot & Van Hoorn, 1991) found a significant relationship between the complexity of symbolic play and achievement in reading and writing for 5- and 6-year-olds.

Here is 5-year-old Tricia using symbols, one after the other, with the greatest ease and competence.

> Tricia is slowly pushing Holly in the carriage around the play yard. She seems to be a mother pushing her baby. She stops the carriage and bends down to pick up a small wooden wheel. She hands it to Holly and says, "Here's a doughnut." She continues to push the carriage and occasionally stops to supply her baby with more doughnuts and cookies. She pulls the carriage backward, using two steady hands, and controls the movement of the carriage competently. Hanging onto the carriage, she keeps an eye on all of the play on the terrace. Ayesha and Joy walk up to her and ask, "May I play?" "No," says Tricia. "We're going shopping and then we're going home."
>
> Tricia pulls the carriage behind her with one hand, leaning forward against the strain of the load. She reaches into Mario's wagon and snatches an imaginary ice cream cone (much to Mario's surprise), licks it, and tosses him a pretend coin in payment. She continues to push the carriage until she gets to the climber. She lets go of the handle, reaches for the rope on the climber, and starts to climb up. Holly screams, "I want my mommy." Tricia acknowledges her by looking down at her. "Wait, baby. I'm right here."

In this record of dramatic play, because Tricia *recognizes that one thing stands for another*, she is able to *create symbols* (the little wooden wheel stands for a doughnut, she herself represents a mother). She also creates symbols by her actions (licking an imaginary ice cream cone, tossing an imaginary coin to Mario).

Here is an example of the *creation of symbols* in a child's painting:

Raoul and Jeremy (age 6) are painting. Raoul begins to paint from the bottom of his paper in slow, steady, upward strokes. He uses green on his figure, slowly adding more lines. Finally he says, "I made a cactus," and he points to his picture, which does look like a cactus. He then dips his brush in the yellow. He adds this to the cactus. His lips are pursed and his face taut. Jeremy tells Raoul that *he* has made a Venus's-flytrap. (The day before, the teacher had shown the children pictures of plants that eat insects.) Raoul leaps up and says, "Let me see." Jeremy points to his painting, and Raoul asks, "Where's the bug?" Jeremy tells him he hasn't put it in yet.

Raoul returns to his seat and carefully twirls his brush in the orange paint. He then paints another figure carefully and says, "This is the butter plant." The teacher asks does he mean butterwort, and he says, "Oh yeah, butterwort." He begins slowly to add more paint to his paper and says as he makes his strokes, "Now I'm gonna make me a bird." He dips his brush in the brown. He slowly outlines a bird on a leaf. He makes a small spot and exclaims, "Look! There's a bug, and the plant's eating it." He invites Jeremy to come and look. Jeremy gets up and comes to Raoul's side. Raoul points to his painting and says, "The plant's eating it. Look at this Venus flytrap. Look at that (pointing to some red color). It's juice from the bug." He points to the bug and says animatedly, "That's the bug," and he begins to paint another one.

Three-year-olds are less aware of themselves as symbol-creators than Raoul. For Julius, the symbol, the action of painting, and the painting itself are one.

Julius is making a low "rrrr" motor-like sound, moving the brush back and forth along a line in a rhythmic way. In a restrained but excited tone he says to the teacher, "Look! They're going skiing. They're going skiing like this." He keeps moving the brush, happily chirping, "Gonna go off a jump!" "Where?" the teacher asks. He points to a rectangular shape on the paper. "Look. This is the thunder. Down the thunder." He swoops down with his brush. "Then up the thunder." He swoops back up the same line. "Down the thunder." Swoop. "Up." Swoop. He continues the same motions, joyfully making "rrrrr" noises.

## Use of Materials and Levels of Symbolic Representation

There is a sequence in a child's use of materials that is related to the child's age and level of development, provided that the material has been available over a span of time. It follows that an older child, coming to the material for the first time, is likely to race through all the earlier stages to reach his own stage fairly quickly. The point at which a child seems to be stabilizing can be considered the current level.

Symbolic representation depends on a technical level of competence and the opportunity to have direct experience with the material so that its properties become familiar. Since the two are tied to each other, an inadequate level of competence may indicate insufficient experience in developing modes of use that support growth in symbolizing capacity. For example, what evidence of growth in symbolization can we observe in children's use of blocks?

***Sequence of Symbolization in Block Building.*** According to Harriet Johnson (cited in Hirsch, 1996), children evolve four basic patterns in block building, *tower, row, bridge,* and *enclosure.* These develop in stages. Complex buildings are adaptations of these four patterns. As generally perceived, the stages of block building are as follows:

1. Making rows, horizontal and vertical
2. Bridging two blocks in a two-step sequence
   » By setting up a vertical block and trying to place a horizontal one on it, then adding a second vertical parallel to the first
   » By setting up two parallel vertical blocks and bridging them with a third

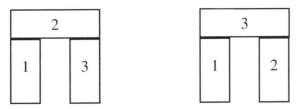

3. Making enclosures with four blocks
4. Decorating unnamed buildings (improvements of shapes)
5. Naming buildings relevant to their function (e.g., house, garage, firehouse)
6. Building reproductions or symbolic renditions of actual structures (e.g., Sears Tower, George Washington Bridge, spaceship, zoo)

Recognizing the basic patterns and stages of block building will inform observations and help in understanding the range of a child's flexibility in a symbolic realm. The following questions are a guide for recording.

- What are the space problems a child is attempting to solve: bridging? enclosure? repetition? decoration?
- Does the 5- to 7-year-old child plan ahead? Are plans carried out? Are there changes in intentions?
- Does the child name the building?
- Can the child predict what will happen with certain placements?
- Can the child reconstruct the building after it has been broken down?
- Is the child's work direct participation (he sits in the building) or symbolic representation (she manipulates the use of the building from outside it)? (For an in-depth examination of these different forms of play, see Cuffaro, 1996.)

**Evidence of Growth in Symbolization in Dramatic Play**

There are developmental changes in children's dramatic play also. Teachers who review records of children's dramatic play taken during a school year, or who have taught children of different ages, will be aware that changes take place; that as children get older, their play becomes more complex, more elaborated.

Here are some examples of changes that a teacher might become aware of:

- The number of symbolic actions that are different from one another, within a play episode, increases; that is, the play becomes more differentiated.
- The child expresses the emotional quality of a role (through actions, language, facial expressions, or body movements) more frequently.
- The play tends to become more coherent, better organized.
- Children tend to play together instead of alone.
- When two or more children play together, they are more likely to play different roles instead of all playing the same one.

These tendencies can be observed, although there usually is a range from simple to more elaborate play in the records of each child.

Changes have been documented in children's use of symbols. As they mature, children "are able to use objects that are increasingly discrepant in form and/or function from the objects" they are symbolizing (Monighan Nourot & Van Hoorn, 1991, p. 41). The younger the child, the more necessary it is to rely on props that resemble what they're supposed to be—a toy plane "flies" as a plane, a doll is the baby. As children mature, such close correspondence is no longer required. A pencil can just as easily "fly," a cardboard box could be a truck or a doll bed.

As children develop, they are also able to increasingly distance themselves from their symbols. The youngest children often put themselves into the doll bed or the block building. As they grow older and their capacity for mental representation matures, they use a doll, a stuffed animal, or a wooden figure instead of themselves. Oddly enough, as children approach 7 or 8 years of age and begin to think more logically, they again become invested in play objects that resemble real objects even as far as scale goes when they are building a miniature world. For example, the chair must resemble a real chair and must not be bigger than the bed.

In observing, it is vital to be aware of the influence of culture and parental values on the nature of children's play (see Haight & Miller, 1993; Monighan Nourot & Van Hoorn, 1991; Singer & Singer, 1990). Some children may not have varied playthings, space, or time to play at home and come to school with play abilities that seem less complex. Others may not engage in complex play inside the classroom but do so outdoors. Teachers should continually evaluate their classroom settings to determine how the environment promotes, extends, and supports play.

## A FRAMEWORK FOR RECORDING DRAMATIC PLAY

When you set out to record play, it may look like a jumble. You may feel overwhelmed: Where to begin? On what or whom to focus? Which details are most important? Try to focus mainly on the child you have chosen to study. Include other children only as they are involved with him or her. If there are four children playing, for example, center your attention on the selected child. The list below will guide your observation of dramatic play and the records that follow provide some examples.

**Details to Observe**

- How does the play get started?
  - » Does the child initiate it? The teacher? Another child?
  - » Does the child join the ongoing play of another child or group of children? What means does the child use?
- Where does the play take place? (block corner, pretend play area, outdoors)
- What is the course of action, or sequence of events?
- What are the child's comments and verbal interactions *about* the play? For example:
  - » What is happening? ("The car is going into the garage.")
  - » What are the roles each child takes and *how* are those roles played? ("I'm the doctor, and I stick you with a needle. You're the baby.")
  - » What are the words the child uses *for* symbolic objects that represent a person? (Jim, speaking for a "child" that is a wooden figure, says in a high, squeaky voice, "I want my fadder!")
- What does the child say in the role (as mother, firefighter, monster), including onomatopoeic sounds uttered ("moo" as a cow, whistle sounds as a train, "grrrr" as a wild animal)?
- What do the other participants in the play say and do?
- What *symbolic* actions are taken by the child in the role? (Justine picks up a very small plastic baby bottle, gets a doll, and sits down. *She puts the bottle to the doll's mouth and holds it there for a moment.* She gets up and puts the doll down and the bottle on the shelf. *She gets a doll bib and puts it on the doll.*)
- What accessories does the child use? (jacket, firefighter's hat, shawl, colored cubes for traffic lights or food)
- What are the child's facial expressions, body movements, tone of voice, that give the role its emotional quality? (She raced frantically around the room, face taut, screaming, "Fire! Fire! Get the hoses!")
- Does the child use any symbolic objects while playing, such as making the object (real or imaginary) perform symbolic actions? (pouring coffee from an empty pot; moving a toy car, or object representing a car, on a road of blocks)
- What does the play reveal about the child's experience within his or her particular culture? "Children's play . . . is an outcome of being a participant within a particular cultural or sub-cultural milieu" (Roopnarine, Johnson, & Hooper, 1994, p. 4).

As you complete the recording, be sure to indicate how the play or game ends. How the child terminates play if playing alone, or leaves a group when playing with others, contributes as much to understanding a child's play behavior as how the child begins play or enters the play of others.

- Does the child leave for some other activity?
- If playing with others, does the other child (or children) leave first?
- Does the teacher interrupt the play? How does the child respond to interruption? (for snack, pickup, story)
- Does the play develop into some other kind of play?
- How long did the child's participation last?
- What or who seems responsible for the ending?
- How do the children disperse?
- What is the feeling tone? (happy, guilty, despairing, belligerent, contented)

## Records of Dramatic Play

In the following record the content comes from real life. It is simple repetitive play with a symbolic object:

Four-year-old Juan takes parts of a construction set and puts them together in the shape of an airplane. Holding the "airplane" in the center, he zooms it through the air making motor noises. He "flies" it to the book corner.

He says to Kevin, who is watching, "I making a airplane." Then he goes over to the teacher, saying, "See, airplane." The teacher admires it, and he leaves her and goes to the book area where he zooms the airplane around.

Kevin, who also has an airplane, joins him, and they both zoom their planes around, making motor noises. Juan lies on the floor and "flies" the plane around over his body, rolling as he does so. He puts the plane on the floor and, with a slowly accelerating noise, has it take off, zoom, and then land. He then goes around the room, zooming his plane and making motor noises. He has the plane touch tabletops as he passes, and go up in the air again, making a louder noise when the plane goes higher in the air.

The teacher says it is time to go out. Juan puts the "plane" in the box and lines up with the other children.

In the following record, two 5-year-old boys engage in Superman play together, using plastic figures.

> Jacob and Alan, each holding a superhero figure, go to the dramatic play area where there is a large empty carton with one side open and a large window cut out of another side. Jacob now gets behind the box and begins to push his figure through the window.
>
> *Alan* (who is in front of the box): Good, Jacob. Okay now, here's a trap. (He then pushes his figure in.)
>
> *Jacob*: That's a good trap. Now we'll pretend that they got out.
>
> *Alan*: Okay, now pretend he got in a truck and got locked up, and then he still got away.
>
> *Jacob*: Now he gets out. He gets away.
>
> *Alan* (talking for his figure): Superman, come and play.
>
> *Jacob* (talking for his figure): I'm coming. I'm out of my trap. (Jacob then pushes his figure into the window and Alan takes it.)
>
> *Jacob* (stands and shouts): Eeeeeek, give it back. (Alan hands it back and Jacob gets right back down on the floor.)
>
> *Alan*: That's fun. Let's do it again.
>
> *Jacob* (Definitively): No. (Both boys leave and go to the book area.)

Since the content of the play and/or the child's role are often ambiguous, all actions and remarks should be recorded whether or not they appear meaningful, at the time, to the recorder, as in the two following short records:

> Eamon (age 3) picks up a figure of a man and lies down on the floor, cradling his own head on one arm. He moves the figure about and says, "Mailman, mailman, boom-da-boom-da-boom."

> At snack time, Mora (age 6) closely examines the breadstick she is holding. She grasps it gently at the base with both hands. In a staccato rhythm she says, "Stop, stop, stop!" as she inches her hands up the breadstick. With the same choppy beat she again says, "Stop, stop, stop!" and repeats the climb of her hands. After a final "Stop!" she takes a bite off the top and begins to nibble the rest.

"Play is an important context or vehicle for cultural learning/transmission" (Schwartzman, 1978, cited in Roopnarine et al., 1994, p. 5), as in the following observation of three 6-year-old girls playing funeral:

One girl is lying perfectly still on the floor covered with a large sheet. Two girls are sitting quietly at her feet, talking in soft tones. Without warning, they put their arms around each other and begin to sob. The teacher goes over quietly and says, "What are you playing?" They look up at her and say, "We're at a funeral," and resume sobbing.

## FOCUSING ON DRAMATIC ROLES

A dramatic role has many facets. Here we will look at the role itself (its content), and the emotional investment in the role.

### The Role Itself, Its Content

Ideas for creating a role may come from many sources in a child's experience. They may come from the tangible world of reality filled with a variety of people children know or have seen such as family members (mother, father, grandparents, baby or grown siblings, uncle, aunt), police officer, storekeeper, firefighter, doctor, or bus driver. The role can be inspired by inanimate objects such as a train, boat, plane, truck, doll, hat, shawl. Ideas for a role may also come from television or from favorite stories.

By reproducing aspects of the real world that they have experienced, or long to experience, children try to fix in their minds the properties, processes, and relationships of what they have encountered. Observations of dramatic play can be used by teachers to assess how well children understand what they are experiencing. Such information furnishes a base for planning opportunities for experiences that can increase and/or clarify children's conceptions of the real world.

Whether the play's content is related to the real world or to stories or television, children use play to work out their feelings as well as their ideas and concepts. Play contributes to children's ability to engage in flexible thinking—to play with ideas and solutions to problems. This is akin to "the way that adults talk through alternatives to problems they face and imagine consequences from varying perspectives" (Monighan Nourot & Van Hoorn, 1991, p. 43). Teachers can learn from play content what is important to children, how they construct and perceive and transform the reality around them, what their misunderstandings are, what they have feelings about, the effects of their social class and their culture, how they form relationships with other children, the quality of their language.

In their make-believe roles, children include that which to their minds and limited experience is the meaningful *quality* and *character* of the person or thing. And how accurately children pinpoint the essence of train, plane, animal, or parent in terms of outstanding action, sound, or feeling value! It takes them longer to see and understand technical details, parts of a whole, ramifications, complexity, variety. We must be careful, however, not to jump to conclusions. Fantasy is a very important part of children's play, and a child may be sitting on what looks like a train and not give us a hint as to whether he is the engineer, the train itself, a passenger, or the cargo.

Records of dramatic play show the level of the child's understanding and comprehension, as well as the content of the role and how the role is played.

Four-year-old Ahmed went straight to the blocks when he came to the classroom. There were only two other children in the center at the time, both at the clay table. Ahmed started to build what looked like a train. He set five blocks in a long row on the floor. At one end he put two blocks on top of each other and sat on them. Danny came in and walked over to Ahmed.

"Is that a bridge?" Danny asked.

"No, it's a train," replied Ahmed.

"Where's it going?" Danny asked.

"To Chicago," answered Ahmed. "I'm the engineer. I build big trains."

"I'm conductor. I drive the train," boasted Danny.

"No, no. I'm the engineer. I made it," responded Ahmed impatiently.

"What can I do?" questioned Danny.

Ahmed replied, "You collect the tickets."

"What tickets?" asked Danny.

"The ones the passengers give you," explained Ahmed. Then he announced in a loud voice, "Who wants a ride on the train? . . . All abo-a-rd . . . All ab-o-oard. Train going. Woo . . . woo . . . It goes so fast."

Francesca came into the room and ran over to the train. "I want to get on." She got another block from the shelf and put it on the middle of the train. She picked up a very small block from the floor and held it to her mouth as she would a telephone and yelled, "Hello, hello. What's wrong with you? We're leaving and we gotta have food. Bring hundreds of boxes . . . right away, you hear?" She slammed the telephone down.

"We got a flat," exclaimed Ahmed. "I'll fix it. Got to fix it now."

With swaggering pretentiousness he removed one of the blocks from the line and turned it upside down and replaced it. Then he got back on the two blocks.

Mitchell came over and got on the train, but Ahmed demanded, "Get off, get off. It's my train. . . . *Go away.*" He gave Mitchell a push to get him off. Mitchell attempted to get on again, and again Ahmed pushed him off. The teacher complimented Ahmed on his train and suggested that he allow other children to share it with him. Ahmed made no response, but did nothing when Mitchell got on again and sat behind him.

Then Ahmed exclaimed, "No gas, no gas. Hey, Mitch, no gas. Ha, Ha! Now no gas. First flat tire, now no gas."

Danny took the block that Francesca had used as a telephone and called on it. "Hey, you. Bring gas. Train needs gas. Ha! Ha! Hurry up, you dope."

Ahmed announced, "All off! It's lunchtime. Let's get some food. Follow me. I'll show you, men."

We can deduce what Ahmed knows about trains from his train play (that they are long, that the engineer sits in the front of the train, that trains have passengers, that the conductor collects tickets). His and the others' confusion of trains with automobiles (the "flat" that must be fixed, the train needs "gas") is also portrayed vividly in his play. In this play lies a clue for the teacher to create opportunities for extending their knowledge at some future time in the form of a discussion and/or storybook about trains and cars, or a ride on or a visit to a train.

In the following record, the source of the content is television. Six-year-old Frankie plays alone for the most part. His occasional contacts with other children are short-lived.

As Frankie gets to the door of the yard, his face broadens into a wide, happy grin, and he races down the steps into the yard. He shouts delightedly, "The monsters!" and begins jumping on one foot and then the other while his arms flap wildly in every direction. He shouts to some nearby children, "Come on!" and begins to race around the playground boundary with his arms waving exuberantly and a wide smile on his face. Two or three of his classmates follow his path and copy his gestures.

Frankie then walks over to a large, circular wooden spool, climbs up effortlessly, and sits down on it cross-legged. He sits for just a few seconds, then stands and leaps off, making flying gestures with his arms. He seems quite excited and delighted with these movements, since there is a broad smile on his face and his joyous shouts ring out.

He runs around the yard again and leaps on the wooden spool. He stays a few seconds and shouts forcefully, "I'm getting outta here," and leaps off again. He turns around and jumps up again. He neither looks at nor talks to the other children on the spool. He seems preoccupied with his own movements at this point.

He stops abruptly and leaps up. He shouts, "I'm Spiderman!" and leaps off the spool and races away. He runs over to the basketball net and begins to climb one of the poles. Using the brick wall in front of him as support for his feet, he extends his arms up the pole, first one hand and then the other, pulling his body up with each reach. He gets to the top and slides down, holding the pole with his hands.

Christa comes over and demands, "Let me try." He turns to her and shouts excitedly, "Try and catch me." He races off with Christa chasing him. He again runs around the perimeter of the yard and back to the basketball pole. He climbs again, making loud, grunting sounds as he pulls himself up. On reaching the top, he yells, "Watch out!" and slides down. He runs over to a group of children and shouts at them, "Bulls." He runs around the yard yelling, "The bulls! The bulls! The bulls!" while putting two fingers on his head to imitate a bull's horns.

Frankie picks out the most obvious aspects of the characters he portrays. He jumps, climbs, and "flies." There is little other developed content because the play tends to be dictated by the script seen on TV. He swiftly changes from one role to another, but the physical activity remains the same.

When children play superhuman/magical roles, they can fulfill certain emotional needs more satisfactorily than in roles with real-life content. These needs, however, are very limited:

- The need or desire to be powerful, more than human—a need that is common to young children because of their powerlessness. (As Superman, they can fly, exhibit superhuman strength.)
- The need or desire to be aggressive. (As Spiderman, they can be aggressive in order to right wrongs, protect the weak.)

Compare Frankie's play above to that of 7-year-old Nolan, who also plays several roles, probably inspired by TV or by watching older students play basketball in the school gym. Notice Nolan's interest in replicating reality in its accurate detail.

Nolan was in the gym shooting baskets and creating a plot—a basketball game between the Boston Celtics and the New York Knicks. The game involved four players, one of whom was Kevin Garnett, somebody named Joe, and two others. Nolan performed the actions of each player. He shot a basket and said, "Good going, Joe," playing two roles at the same time. In addition to portraying the four players, he was also the narrator giving the pretend audience information on the progress of the game. "The score is 5 to 3, the Celtics in the lead." After a basket was shot, he said, "The crowd goes wild." He played for half an hour, an intense expression on his face, eyes open, mouth serious, and complexion flushed from physical exertion. He continually alternated among the five roles. When the teacher asked him who was ahead, or who had scored, he knew right away and seemed to have a clear picture of exactly what was going on. When the game was over and the Knicks had won, he collapsed on the bench, lying on his back, breathing heavily, arms limp and falling off the bench. A smile of satisfaction spread across his face.

In the following record, 6-and-a-half-year-old Brianna has some very definite ideas about the role she has chosen to play:

Brianna moved in a bouncy manner. Smiling and bright-eyed, she removed a chair from under the table and turned it outward. She ran to the doll bed, jerked the sheet from underneath the dolls, and placed the sheet over the back of the chair.

She moved about deliberately, collecting fork, spoon, cup, and plate from the cabinets and placing them on the table. She stared at the items for a moment, then placed the fork and spoon on the plate. She filled the cup with water and set it next to the plate.

Henry stared at Brianna for a moment, then walked over with a curious look on his face. "What are you doing?" he asked. Enthusiastically, she said, "I'm getting my dentist office ready for people to get their teeth fixed. This is the chair that my patients will sit in, and this is a sheet to put around the front of them." Henry began to laugh loudly. "You can't be no dentist because girls are not dentists."

Brianna's lips became tight as she moved closer to Henry with hands on hips. Angrily, she blurted out, "I can too be a dentist because I know what dentists do!" Quickly she turned, and smiling, walked with head high over to Rena. "Would you like to be my first patient?"

## Emotional Investment in the Role

As children play a dramatic part with real-life content—such as doctor, mother, baby, captain—they may give the part an emotional tone that is deeply personal. They may play the role in terms of their feelings and attitudes toward other people. Even though a child is storekeeper, mother, or firefighter, she might choose to be domineering, bossy, timid, conscientious, kind, forceful, subservient, tyrannical, or protective. In dramatic play children may act out feelings not otherwise revealed, for example:

- How they think people feel toward each other (The doctor may be kind, brusque, or scolding; mothers and fathers may be kind, brusque, or scolding.)
- How they wish people would behave toward them (A father is understanding, forceful, positive, kind, a friend; a sibling is a giving, helping person, a pal.)
- How they would express themselves if it were permissible (He plays the baby so he can pretend he is protected and dependent; she becomes a tiger so she can growl with impunity; he plays "boss" so he can dominate; she plays the "bad zoo seal" so she can do naughty things.)

Any of these attitudes could be consistently held in any kind of play. A child would then always be tyrannical or always kind or always meek, whether they be father, mother, captain, police officer, uncle, or aunt. But it is just as likely that attitudes will change with the role as with different play companions. A child could be subservient to a big, strong playmate, but high-handed with a small one, a bossy doctor but a gentle father. We have to observe a child at dramatic play more than once and with many children to see which behavior is characteristic of his relations with others.

What attitudes can be detected in following these 5-and-a-half-year-olds in their roles in the pizza shop? Might their roles be different with other playmates?

Kendra and Solomon are sitting at the play dough table with the teacher. "I'll make you a pizza," Kendra tells the teacher. She begins flattening the play dough with the palm of her hand. Solomon cries out, "Kendra and I are bosses." Kendra acknowledges his statement with her eyes, and, glancing around the table, asks, "Who's in the pizza shop?" She looks back to Solomon and declares, "You're the boss and I'm the assistant boss." In a stern voice, Solomon says, "I'm the real boss, and I'll say who's boss." With his arm outstretched and his finger pointed at Kendra, he says, "You are." Kendra nods her head in agreement and adds, "You and I are the boss of everyone." "Yes," confirms Solomon, "if someone spills water, we have them clean it up." With a complacent smile on her face, Kendra adds, "Yes, and we work in a pizza shop." She cuts a triangular pizza slice out of her round pie and remarks, "This is

our pizza music. It usually plays a song for you. It keeps blowing up."
She then flings it into the air and hands it to the teacher.

"How much are you going to pay us?" she asks the teacher. The
teacher replies, "How much do you want?" "Five dollars plus tax which
is $1. That makes $6," is the answer. The teacher pretends to hand
her money. "I'll keep it," cries Kendra. "No, I keep it," says Solomon in
a commanding voice. After a small verbal battle Kendra says, "Okay,
okay."

Kendra turns to the teacher, "Do you want our new hula drink? It's
$10." "No," Solomon corrects her, "it's $1." With a hint of annoyance
in her voice, Kendra responds, "No. It's $10 off. It was $11, so it's $1."
With a confused look on his face, Solomon yells, "It's free!" Slightly more
irritated, Kendra repeats her prior offer. In a hushed voice, she adds, "I
don't think he's good at math." She turns to the teacher and says, "We'll
deliver it."

The source of the content that inspires children's play seems to
make a difference in the way they are able to adapt the content to
their make-believe. Real-life experiences of actions and processes
they can reproduce seem in general to lead to better-developed, more
sustained, and more productive play than poorly perceived or confusing experiences. The former allow the children and the teacher to
extend the children's knowledge with additional information and/or
clarification.

## SOCIAL ASPECTS OF DRAMATIC PLAY

When two or more children engage in dramatic play together, they
not only express what they know about the world, their fears, wishes,
and aspirations, but they test and modify the effectiveness of their
social attitudes and techniques via the responses of others. Position,
status, and acceptance within a group depend to some extent on an
individual child's actions. But they are affected also by the willing-
ness of other children to see an individual in terms suitable to his
own self-concept, wishes, needs, and wants. The teacher who would
help a child achieve more mature social behavior must know the impact of children on one another in two ways: objectively (this is what
happened), and in the subjective meaning to the youngster involved
(what that child thought happened).

When you observe make-believe play, be aware of how the children interact with one another and what their understanding of that
interaction seems to be. Here are some guiding questions:

- Which children react? To whom?
- What do they do? How do they do it?
- What do they say? How do they say it?
- Do they fit in with others' plans, use others, resist others, follow them under protest?
- Does a child's desire for status, prestige, affection, or attention interfere with the progress of the play situation?
- What is a child's general tone at play—amiable, hostile, creating dissension?

In the following record of a group of 4-year-olds, notice how the shifts in dominance and the conception of gender roles are played out in the social give-and-take.

> Telissa is dressed up in a long skirt. She is moving pots on the stove while Aaron uses a wooden iron on the tablecloth. Aaron says, "Pretend this is an eating table."
>
> Telissa does not reply but keeps on cooking. Aaron ignores the lack of response. He leaves the iron and gets another hat from the dress-up corner. He says, "Look what I brought you, Mother. Does it look nice?" He gives the hat to Telissa and takes the old one. Telissa puts the new hat on her head but says nothing; she continues her cooking.
>
> Aaron gets an apron and puts it on. Telissa turns to him and says reprovingly, "No. That's a girl's suit." Aaron takes it off, and Telissa puts it on over the long skirt.
>
> He gets another apron, a full-sized one with a bib. He asks, looking for approval, "Is this a boy's?" Telissa nods. Aaron persists, "Is this the head?"
>
> Telissa says agreeably, "Yeah." She helps him put it on and fixes it efficiently, adjusting the length so that Aaron doesn't trip. She picks up a flashlight and tries to turn it on. "Turn on the light," she says. The flashlight does not work, and she puts it down after several attempts to turn it on. Aaron and Telissa stand side by side and pretend to cook. They talk quietly about what they are doing as if giving themselves directions.
>
> Sometimes they address each other more directly and seem to expect a reply. For example, "You set the table, right?" Eddie comes up and says, smiling, "Is this a real house?"
>
> Aaron replies, "Would you like to be visitors coming to the house?"
>
> "Okay," Eddie agrees. Donnie joins him and they formally approach, already immersed in the action. They knock at an imaginary door.
>
> Aaron says as he opens the door, "This is a restaurant." Telissa nods her confirmation. Max and Eddie come in and sit at the table.

Eddie calls out imperiously, "Service! Service!"

Telissa comes over and says, "Okay."

Eddie retorts, "I want my dinner. What's for dinner?"

Telissa goes back to the stove and calls over her shoulder crisply, "Hot dogs."

"Okay," Eddie agrees, "hot dogs with mushrooms."

Telissa continues cooking and Aaron joins her, moving pots and pans. Eddie and Max get bored and leave.

Telissa makes coffee in the coffeepot. Aaron takes the kettle and comments, "This is the coffee."

Telissa contradicts him. "No, that's the tea."

Aaron notes, "You'd better hurry up. Here's more customers."

This time the customers are imaginary. They set the table together. Telissa says, "The yellow cups are for coffee, the other ones are for tea."

Eddie returns and seems to want to join the game. Aaron pushes him away roughly. "You're not playing. You can't play." Eddie persists, and Aaron pushes him away again.

Meanwhile, Telissa gets up, goes into the corner, and spins around and around, watching the motion of her long skirt and feeling the motion with her palms.

As soon as Eddie gives up and leaves, both Aaron and Telissa return to the game. They continue playing with a great deal of cooperation.

In this record, Telissa's attitude toward Aaron changes as the play proceeds. At first she ignores him, then disapproves of some of his actions, and finally becomes cooperative and more amiable. Aaron, who obviously is very eager to play with Telissa, accepts her reproofs at first, but persists and comes into his own as an equal partner in the play as Telissa's attitude changes. When Telissa spins around and around, is she deliberately avoiding the confrontation between Eddie and Aaron?

## A Child's Position in Relation to the Others Playing

As the members of a group interact, they tend to find spots for themselves in the group's hierarchy and structure. Some children are leaders, some followers, some peacemakers, and some moralists representing the adult point of view. Some children barely fit into the group as legitimate members at all.

A child's position in the group may be obvious or may be subtly concealed and disguised. A child who seems to be a cooperator may just be passive. Eagerness to be accepted or anxiety about what he has to offer may lead him to a fairly thorough denial of his right to a genuinely cooperative position. The child who is noisiest in a group may seem to be the leader and yet the real direction may be coming from a quiet youngster who controls the play by force of ideas.

Position in the group is one of the important components of interrelating. For one youngster, leadership may be so important that she will resort to any trick she can think up to reach her goal. For another, there may be quiet contentment in not being challenged. Position has two faces—how the adult sees a child's position in the group, and how the child sees and feels about it. Position can appear in many guises—domineering boss, constructive leader, cooperative member, bystander, compromiser, agitator. A child may maintain any of these positions by a variety of means such as bullying, persuading, reasoning, coaxing, bribing, or by the power of ideas. Silence might be another way of asserting position.

In the following record of Peter, age 5, his position in the group, his feelings about maintaining that position, and the reactions of others seem quite clear.

> Several groups of youngsters were scattered through the wooded area of the play yard, some digging, some filling cans, some using a rock for the dinner table in their imaginary home. Peter and cohorts had used cans to collect items for dinner, then to gather maple syrup (sap) from the trees. Peter left his cans by a tree and came swinging past Denise's rock.
>
> Peter announced, "I'm going to get my fishing cast and go out in the boat. Mama (addressing Denise), will you row the boat for me while I'm fishing?" Peter did not wait for an answer but continued on his quest for his fishing rod. From far away he called, "Come on, Mama!"
>
> Denise was adamant. "I need to make the lunch at home on the stove!"
>
> Peter found a long rod-like pole and returning, paused again by Denise. "Come on, Mama. Now you be careful making that lunch." He strode toward his boat rock. "Come on, Mama. Come on, we have to go. You have to row . . . that's the boathouse and you come with me."
>
> Denise kept on with her lunch-making, but called after Peter, "Goodbye!"
>
> Peter was now back on his rock, his fishing rod stowed aboard. He stood there holding on to a tree branch, looking across the woods to Denise and calling. Impatience at being balked was beginning to creep into his tone. "Come on! You have to row me."
>
> Denise says dismissively, "You go on. I can't do it."

Peter, screaming, "Come on! *You have to do it!*" With each word he beat the branch with a short stick for emphasis and to give vent to his feelings, since he couldn't beat Denise but would probably have liked to rush over and do so.

Denise, in a disgruntled, placating voice, "All right. Let me finish the onions. Bring the children. Come on, Jenna." She and her companion moved over to the boat.

Peter now had Henry, Jackson, Robert, Denise, and Jenna on the rock-boat. He was using a stick for an oar. Then he saw Nikki and Julie busy digging. (New fields to conquer!) "Come on, sisters (to Nikki and Julie). Will you row for us, sisters?" They came easily. But soon Julie was in tears. Denise was slapping her hands hard for dumping dirt from her can and getting the boat dirty.

"Stop that, Denise!" Peter commanded. Julie got off the boat, spirits wounded, head bent.

Jenna edged in next to Peter on the rock. "That's where Mama's going to sit. Now get out." He pushed her away so Denise could come.

Then Denise took up Peter's long stick. "Stop! That's my fishing cast," he told her. Denise got off the boat, found herself a long fishing rod, and returned.

Peter asked Jackson, "Brother, will you row?" Jackson refused.

Peter, looking around, "Well, who's going to row?" Spying Denise with her own fishing rod, he says, "Mama, you row. We only want one fishing cast. Look! I caught a big one (a leaf at the end of his stick). *Listen*, who's going to row? Mama, you go over there and fish over there. It's the nicest place on the boat." "Now, man (to Jackson), row with this stick."

Having at last made someone row, he turned to his fishing.

Peter tries to be the boss, but seldom succeeds. He uses several methods to attain his aim—verbal insistence, persistence, and, occasionally, force. His manner provokes considerable resistance from the others.

This anecdote invites the teacher's further inquiry. Is Peter always an unsuccessful "boss" in dramatic play situations, or is he, at other times, comfortable taking orders from other players? In other situations, is he able to lead in a less overbearing style? Information from additional records will guide the teacher in deciding what kind of assistance, if any, Peter may need from her in making and keeping friends.

In the next record, in an after-school program 1st-grader Caitlin demonstrates an entirely different form of leadership:

There are four girls: Caitlin, Hana, Alix, and Marisol. Hana asks, "Who wants to be the dad?" "I don't mind really," answers Caitlin, who plucks a doll from the basket, raises it over her head, and says, "She's 1 year old." Holding the doll tightly, she says authoritatively, "You, mister, have to go to sleep. It's time for bedtime." Then she announces, "I'm setting the dinner table," and puts a plate at each seat. Alix and Marisol approach Caitlin, who gazes seriously at both girls and inquires, "Who's the mom?" Simultaneously, the girls cry out, "I am!" Caitlin points at Alix and says in a commanding voice, "She said it first." To Marisol she says, "You can be the oldest sister."

"Honey," she yells to Alix, "I can't set the table. I must call my boss before I'm fired." Alix approaches Caitlin and gives her a sympathetic smile. Caitlin picks up the phone and says, "Hi, boss. My baby's out of control. Yes, my kid. Yes, I'm having dinner." She hangs up abruptly, then saunters over to a shelf, grabs a container with six small white milk bottles, and addresses Alix, "I'm going to have a couple beers! Do you want a beer?" Alix scrunches up her face with disdain and says, "No, thanks. The phone works, honey. You just have to press zero."

Ignoring this remark, Caitlin plants a man's brown hat firmly on her head, grasps a large black clutch purse, and says to Alix, "I'm going to work." She plops down in a chair and tosses her hat and purse onto a table. After a moment's reprieve she rises and approaches Alix. In a thunderous voice, she declares, "Honey, I'm home."

Hana, who has been playing with blocks, crawls over to Caitlin's feet and says in a baby voice, "Daddy, daddy." Alix says emphatically, "The baby can eat whatever she wants!" Caitlin removes three white milk bottles from the container. With a concerned expression she adds, "She can't have beer, only milk." Caitlin squats down, grabs Hana's shoulders, and says, "Hi, pumpkin." Hana, Alix, and Caitlin walk toward a large chair. Hana blurts out, "It's not a chair, it's a refrigerator." Looking into Caitlin's face, Hana says lovingly, "I'll go to bed early." Caitlin nods with a smile on her face and says to the doll sitting on her lap, "You have to go to sleep as well, mister." She then announces, "You need to wash your hair now." Looking at Alix, she says sweetly, "Honey, I'm giving him a bath now." With concern, Alix says, "Make sure he doesn't splash. We have three babies."

Caitlin becomes the leader of the play by virtue of her good ideas and her ability to include the other members. Is this always her style? Are there instances where her commanding and thunderous voice are used to subjugate rather than to dramatize a role?

## Rules in Play and Games

Alix and Caitlin, in the record above, play according to rules-for-being-parents that they have constructed themselves. One of Alix's rules, for example, is the prevention of splashing. Both Piaget (1965) and Vygotsky (1933/1976) describe the underlying child-established rule-based structure of both play and games. Vygotsky proposes that ". . . there is no such thing as play without rules" (p. 541). There is a difference between the pre-established rules in games and those in play. In play, the rules are dictated by the reality the children have created; for example, the reality of the family as they choose to depict it.

Recording children involved in games with rules provides further insight into the social aspects of play and reveals the collaborative process of rule formation. Young children following the external rules often reconstruct them together. How they turn out depends on the children's age and on their experience. Four-year-olds in the following anecdote gleefully join in a game in which the simple rules of turn-taking and imitation are silently understood by all.

> Saleem, Aimee, and Chana are fighting over who will sit next to whom and who will hold whose hand. Aimee yells, "No! he's holding my hand!" Saleem, suddenly disentangling himself from the other two, directs, "Do this!" He places one hand flat on the table and the other on top of it. Immediately, the others pile their hands on top of his. On completion, the pile instantly flies apart amid shouts of glee. They repeat the game with enthusiasm.

Older children rely on more complex interactions to work out rules of a game. A group of 5- and 6-year-olds, organizing a baseball game, struggle between the external rules and their own internal rules.

> "Let's play ball!" yells Shawn as he runs to get a ball and bat. A large group gathers, all talking at once about rules and bases. Shawn and Darrah lead the discussion. Both argue about who will bat first. "It's not fair. I wanna be first," pouts Shawn. Darrah decides to be second. Shawn continues, "I got the bat so I go first. You be on my team. You go over there, and you be the pitcher, and Angel can be catcher." There's further discussion about rules, positions, and turns. Shawn has held onto the bat and the ball firmly, though other children have made attempts at relieving him of them.

The game begins with Shawn at bat. He bounces the ball on the ground and hits it hard. Everyone runs to get the ball, ignoring Shawn. As the children all throw themselves on top of the ball and one another, laughing, Shawn runs the bases without touching or coming close to them. He circles the field fast. When he touches home plate, he turns to face the others with a big grin on his face. He looks around, picks up the bat, and positions himself to bat again. The game resumes with Shawn batting once more. Again he connects and everyone runs after the ball. Shawn remains standing on home plate.

"Why don't you run?" asks Darrah.

"I don't have to," says Shawn without concern.

"Why?" asks Darrah.

"Because I'll be out," replies Shawn

"That's not how you play baseball," offers Darrah.

Shawn ignores Darrah and swings the bat, warming up. Nick comes over and tells Shawn that it is his turn to bat.

Shawn answers, "No, I go again."

"But you already went," replies Nick.

"So what?" retorts Shawn with authority.

Shawn bats but misses on the first pitch. He connects on the second pitch and runs to first base. He stops there. Nick hits next and Shawn runs to second, third, and on to home base without touching any of them. No one cares, as they are all too busy running after the ball, after Nick, and all over the field.

"Two runs, we're winning," says Shawn with a big smile and reaching for the bat again. "Hey, you don't go again!" someone yells. Shawn gives up reluctantly and wanders away. He goes over to the other side of the field and joins the opposing team. He positions himself, and when the ball is hit he makes a dash for it and catches the fly ball. He runs after the runner, tags him, and yells, "He's out!" When the teams change positions, Shawn becomes the pitcher.

## PATTERNS OF BEHAVIOR

Records of a child involved in dramatic play would not only include evidence about the following aspects of play behavior, but also reflect changes in behavior over a period of time. Records of play in which other children are involved would also shed light on the child's mode of interacting with others and her ability to work out the rules.

1. The extent to which the content of the play concerned real-life or fantasy (superhero, TV, monsters) activities

2. The usual, specific themes of the play (space travel, cooking/eating, being sick, restaurant, death, church)
3. The roles the child usually takes (driver, father, mother, baby, animal, superhero, train)
4. Whether the child tends to play alone or with others
5. When playing with others, whether the child usually takes on a different role from the others (e.g., usually plays the bus driver and the others are passengers)
6. When playing alone, whether a particular content (e.g., playing house, putting out fires) or role (driver of a vehicle or superhero) predominates
7. In assuming a role, the *position* the child takes in relation to others (e.g., when playing such roles as mother, baby, or storekeeper, the *position* could be that of boss, subordinate, leader, cooperator, moralist, scapegoat)
8. The position she takes in relation to specific personalities (i.e., is she always the boss, or only with children who are timid, younger, older, aggressive, boys, or girls?)
9. The way the child's position is maintained (by the enticement of ideas, rationalizing, talking excessively, reasoning, humor, verbal or physical aggression, threats, bribery, voicing protest, acting helpless)

What a rich source of knowledge about children lies in wait for the teacher who can observe unobtrusively and fill a notebook with records of the child involved in make-believe! Observations of children's dramatic play are like a kaleidoscope of their vibrant, zestful life; their thinking, reflective life; their active, social life; their quiet, solitary life. The children tell us many things about themselves through their play when we are present to really listen to them.

# 6

# Recording the Child's Relationships with Adults and in Adult-Directed Activities

Children are born helpless, and for a long time they remain largely dependent on adults. There are individual and cultural variations in the length of time it takes to move toward independence. Yet, to reach mature adulthood, children must somehow make that transition to relative independence. This they accomplish in many steps and stages, sometimes obviously and dramatically, sometimes with quiet ease. The struggle for independence is not waged without qualms and fears. While they are breaking the bonds, children continue to need adults, not only for physical sustenance, affection, and understanding but for moral support in this drive to independence.

From the adults who are most important in the early years—their parents, foster parents, grandparents, other relatives—children learn many things. Their concepts of people and what to expect of them and their concepts of themselves and what they may and may not do are shaped by their daily contacts with these significant adults. Children believe that all adults are like the ones they first knew best until long years of experience beyond early childhood teach them to recognize differences. They assume that what adults tell them about themselves is true, unless other people later teach them otherwise. Consequently, when children enter school or child care for the first time, their behavior with teachers will in large measure reflect their home experience and indicate how far along the road to independence and development of a positive or negative self-concept they have come.

## TEACHERS OBSERVE THEMSELVES

Young children need adults, but they must also gradually loosen the ties. Teachers must be able to observe the relationship in which they are themselves involved with enough dispassionate interest to see the child's dependency needs with objectivity and the denial of dependence with realistic and unbiased appraisal. It is perhaps easier to do this if we ask ourselves about a relationship with a child, "Do I enhance or detract from this child's sense of personal powers?" It is hard to be oneself and the impartial observer at the same time. Our professional selves (objective and educated) must become one with our personal selves (subjective and emotionally involved).

Critical to truly seeing and understanding the children we teach is the courage to reflect on our own behavior. Perhaps the most treacherous aspect of teaching occurs "when teachers face themselves" (Jersild, 1955). Facing biases openly, recognizing the influence of one's own culture and experience, acknowledging values and beliefs, and accepting the influence of emotions on behavior are extraordinary challenges. Ordinarily, teachers are so busy teaching that they are hard pressed to find time for self-reflection. They need to examine how their own backgrounds affect what they believe about children and what children should learn. The accumulated experiences of childhood; the nature of one's family; the character of the larger social, economic, and political community; and the critical experience of oneself as a child in school shape the way teachers look at children. Yet every day teachers make decisions about program content, materials for children, and the arrangement of the physical environment based, perhaps without realizing it, on these beliefs and values.

Reflection on one's own behavior is crucial in articulating one's teaching philosophy and ideas about how children learn. Teachers can learn to think about what they are doing, *while* they are doing it. Donald A. Schön (1983) refers to this capability as "reflection on knowing-in-action" (p. 50). One avenue into such self-awareness is through observing a child's relationship to oneself.

## RECORDING A CHILD'S INTERACTION WITH AN ADULT

Observation of a child's relationship with adults as we see it revealed at school can tell us whether the child feels that adults are to be trusted, or viewed with suspicion; whether they are to be exploited for one's own ends, hated fiercely, or avoided. We can tell, too, whether the child believes it is possible to run the gamut of human feeling from best to worst, break adult taboos of right and wrong, and still remain loved; or whether it is necessary to refrain carefully from doing anything that will offend adult standards and thus bring about a loss of adult love.

The details of the adult-child relationship will, in many instances, be an incidental part of the situations we've dealt with up to now: the child's functioning during routines, with materials, or in relation to children. In addition, however, there are special adult-child contacts, as all teachers know, because they themselves are involved.

There is the time a child grabs one's hand and squeezes it, or catapults out of the doorway and forcefully leaps onto us by way of morning greeting; there is the quiet moment of confidence when a child brings something precious for inspection or holds up a wet nose to be wiped; there is the imperious demand for attention, the teasing, and the shared laughter. Every day brings new relationships with the individual children who make up the group. Every child feels special in the eyes of the teacher and makes individual, "special" contacts with her or him. (If a child does not, it is worthy of note.)

In the following record, the kindergarten teacher responded with emotional honesty to the child and at the same time was able to face her own feelings:

> As Jonathan excitedly climbed on top of the table, the teacher shouted angrily, "Get off the table!" He quickly jumped down, a look of shock on his face. The teacher quickly organized a circle game, which he joined, all the while staring cautiously at her and carefully avoiding her gaze when she looked at him. The children became restless after a few minutes of playing and asked to sing. After the first verse of "You'll sing a song and I'll sing a song," the teacher asked if anyone knew another verse. Jonathan suggested, "How about you bite me, and I'll bite you?" After that verse, he suggested changing "biting" to "hitting." "You're very angry today, aren't you?" the teacher said. Looking directly at her, Jonathan responded, "No, *you're* in the bad mood, not me." The teacher smiled and said warmly, "You know, you're right. How did you know?" "Because you've screamed a lot today," he answered. Then he came over and started to tickle her. Laughing, she said, "You're going to get me out of my bad mood."

Recording adult-child interchanges may provide insights into a child's self-esteem and, as in the following anecdote, challenge the teacher to continue recording as he develops plans for increasing 6-year-old Leslie's comfort with herself in the classroom.

> Leslie is seated at a table alone. Suddenly she grabs the bucket of Unifix cubes and dumps them all over the table and floor. The teacher quietly asks her to pick them up. She sneers at the teacher and screams, "You're

not my father. You think you're my mother? You're not my mother!"
She laughs hysterically. When the teacher repeats, "Leslie, please pick
up the cubes," she roars, "My name's not Leslie. My mother took me
to the place where you change your name. My name is fresh mouth.
Fresh mouth, go ahead, maybe I'll pick them. Call me fresh mouth." She
sticks out her tongue at the teacher. After several repetitions of "Call me
fresh mouth," she begins half-heartedly to gather some of the cubes and
place them in the bucket.

Sometimes children behave one way with a particular adult and
in another manner with someone else. Such situations help us see the
child "in the round," as in the case of a usually independent 7-year-
old who cannot—or will not—remove his own coat when his mother
brings him to school. A child's relation to an adult may be affected by
circumstances occurring outside of school, such as divorce or witness-
ing violence. An example is a garrulous 5-year-old who, during the
time her father is in the hospital, refuses to speak to the teacher.

In the two observations below, 4-and-a-half-year-old Fatima has
such different relationships with the adults in her life that she seems
not to be the same child when she interacts with each of them. In the
first record, perhaps feeling challenged by the teacher's request made
her defensive. In the second, her tentative entry into a familiar situation was due to several days' absence from school. Clearly, one record
alone would skew our picture of Fatima's relations with adults.

Fatima sat in the group directly in front of Mr. Lee, one elbow on her
knee, hand under chin, and a bored expression on her face. Mr. Lee exclaimed, "Fatima, if you had a purple crayon, what would you draw?"
Fatima replied aggressively, "It's none of your business." Mr. Lee countered, "Oh! that's a silly answer. I know someone can give me a better
answer." Taylor, waving her hand high above the others, shouted, "I
know what I would make. A house, that's what I would make." Derrick
interposed, "I would make a face." Tony yelled, "I would make a book."
Fatima intruded hastily, "I would make a monster, stupid!" There was no
response from Mr. Lee. A few minutes passed, and Fatima shouted, "Mr.
Lee, your hair is ugly. You have stupid hair!"

The next observation was made when Fatima returned to school after
an illness:

Fatima entered the room with her father. She stood rigidly in front of
him with a finger in her mouth. Her eyes wandered around the room,

and her lips were taut. Several children were playing at the far end of the room. Fatima's father leaned forward slightly and remonstrated with Fatima, "What's the matter? Go on in." No response. A few minutes passed, then David very pleasantly exclaimed, "Hello, Fatima!" No response. Mr. Lee announced "Look! Fatima's back!" Several children gathered around Fatima, but she did not respond to any of them. She stood rather tense as her father took off her hat, coat, and top sweater. After her belongings were hung up, her father gave her a few gentle pats on the chin before leaving the room. No response. The teacher went directly over to Fatima and placed his arms around her. She then sat in his lap. David came over and said hello again. No response, Fatima just glared at him. Mr. Lee said, "David, Fatima's been out of school for a while, and she must get used to being back in school." As Fatima sat on the teacher's lap, a girl passed by playing with a slinky. Fatima said, smiling, "I have a slinky." The teacher smiled and gave her a big squeeze. She sat quietly swinging her arms and legs, intently observing the other children with a finger in her mouth. She slid off and wandered around the room, joining several children who were watching Gretchen as she fed the guinea pig. Fatima rushed over to the teacher and said excitedly, "Give me some lettuce." The teacher gave her the lettuce. Fatima dropped her lettuce in the cage slowly. Several minutes later when the teacher announced outdoor time, Fatima skipped over to her cubby and took her coat. Carefully, she placed the coat on the floor in the opposite direction of her body. She bent over and placed her right arm into the sleeve of the coat and then the left. Quickly, she flipped the coat over her head, walked directly over to Mr. Lee to do the coat button, then ambled happily toward the door. (Adapted from Cohen, 1971, pp. 40–41)

In the second record of Fatima, we see a familiar early childhood theme played out. The often difficult transition from home to school that occurs at the start of school or group care is often repeated when a child has been away from the group for a period of time. Some aspect of the adult-child relationship is revealed both in the way children say goodbye to parents at the time of separation and in how they respond to the teacher's overtures. In the following records, Ryan is able to make a successful transition while Haley cannot.

Ryan, age 7, has recently entered a new school. The teacher calls for the children to line up for art. Calmly, Ryan asks, "Do I have to go?" "Yes," the teacher answers, "I think you'll enjoy it." Ryan becomes agitated. "But I don't want to go." Sending the group ahead, the teacher remains with Ryan. "Would you like me to come to art with you?" Ryan answers,

"Yes, but if I don't like it, do I have to stay?" She assures him that he doesn't. "Okay," he replies, "I'll try." When they arrive she introduces him to Mr. Cook, the art teacher, who asks, "Have you ever used pipe cleaners?" "Yes!" Ryan says with animation, "Once I made a plane with a little hole in it for the bombs to fall out—BOOM!" "Would you like to make a plane now?" "Yeah!" and he picks out some pipe cleaners with Mr. Cook's help and begins to bend them.

Haley bounces onto the playground where the kindergarten starts the day, with her mother close behind her. When the teacher smiles and says, "Hi, Haley!" Haley walks quickly toward her to show her what she is holding. When her mother calls her back for a kiss, Haley's face becomes serious as she plants a gentle peck on her mother's cheek, and they say goodbye. A few minutes after her mother departs, all the light and cheerfulness leave Haley's face, and she heads directly to the fence from which she routinely waves to her mother. She holds the fence with both hands and stands watching for a long time, then turns to search the playground with her eyes. Her expression is crestfallen, her eyes full of tears. She stands, flamingo-like, on one foot checking the sidewalk outside the fence every 2 seconds. When it is time to go inside, she hangs up her coat, a sad, cold look on her face. She chooses to sit alone at snack time, staring at her cup of juice, nibbling halfheartedly at her cracker.

## Details to Observe

- Where does the episode take place? (the setting)
- Who makes the contact?
  - » If the child makes the contact, is it purposeful? (child asks for help, asks for materials, shows products, asks for comfort when hurt—actual or imagined—seeks help at routines, asks to be played with; bestows affection or asks for it; asks for help in social relationships, expressing ideas) Is it indirectly purposeful? (child seeks attention by excessive talking; by giving a stream of presents; by provocative activity done deliberately—such as screaming, dangerous climbing, breakage, hiding things—with the awareness that it is not acceptable)
  - » If the teacher makes the contact, what is her purpose? (to give assistance with materials or equipment, settle a dispute, enter the play, make suggestions or requests, give directions or orders, give comfort following injury or insult, offer props)

- What attitude and feeling are revealed by the child as evidenced by voice, tempo of speech, facial expression, body positions and movement, body contacts?
- What dialogue occurs? (direct quotes)
- What is the sequence of events?
  - » Include what adult does and says.
  - » Indicate child's responses, both verbal and bodily.
- How does the contact end?
- What does the child do immediately after?

### Records of a Child's Interaction with an Adult

These two children reveal different approaches to a teacher.

Five-year-old Sharon arrives at school with her mother. She walks up the path expressionless, almost dragging her legs. Looking around slowly, she heads toward the teacher. The teacher calls, "Hi, Sharon!" but does not receive a response. She calls again, "Hi, Sharon!" and this time receives a faint smile. Sharon maneuvers toward the swings, where one child is already swinging. She wraps herself around the pole and waits. The other child, paying no attention to Sharon, gets off, and Sharon, still moving slowly, eases herself onto the swing and begins to pump with her legs. Once again she has a slight smile. After a few minutes, she begins to play in the mud, working seriously by herself. Then she slowly stands up, and walks over to the teacher, carrying her mud pie carefully in a dish. Holding the dish, she stands motionless and speechless for several moments. The teacher "tastes" her mud pie and exclaims, "Delicious!" She gives the teacher a slight smile and moves away.

It is picking-up time and 4-year-old Yi-Min comes over to the teacher. "I can count to 10," she offers confidentially. "I'd like to hear you," says the teacher. Hopping on one foot, Yi-Min slowly and accurately counts from 1 to 10, holding her arms out all the time to help her keep balance. She gives the teacher a smile, all front teeth and crinkled eyes, jumps on two feet and runs off.

## GAINING INFORMATION
## ABOUT A CHILD'S LARGER SOCIAL WORLD

When children enter our classrooms, they do not take off and hang up their social environment like a backpack. Their entire world comes in with them: parents, siblings, relatives, friends, child care arrangements, pets, living places, and the cultural, economic, medical, and religious facets of their community. We cannot observe children in isolation from these important sources of socialization, values, and beliefs.

It is through the ongoing contact with children's parents that teachers gain a view of children in their wider, nonschool world. Therefore, supporting parental participation in their children's early education serves a double purpose: It has the potential to empower parents as the natural advocates for their children, and it enables teachers to become familiar with the families' social and cultural context.

The most familiar (but not exclusive) route to forging relationships between home and school is via individual parent-teacher conferences and the more informal day-to-day "kitchen talk" (Powell, 1994). Key to establishing meaningful interchange with parents is teachers' ability to remain *open*, to resist *"telling,"* and to learn from parents by *listening well*. Parents know their children best and, in most instances, are eager to talk about them to a *nonjudgmental listener*. This relationship provides a pathway to enriched knowledge of the child. Parents describe

- Their child's personality and development
- Their expectations and goals for their child from the school experience
- The range of the child's activities at home and in the community
- Their child's playmates
- Situations or persons that frustrate, please, anger, sadden, excite their child
- Out-of-school child care arrangements
- Illness, death, or hospitalization of anyone in, or close to, the family (including pets)
- The child's relations with siblings, relations, friends
- What the child says about school
- Any incident—such as fire, robbery, violence, a move to new living quarters, parents' separation or divorce—that affects the child

Because exchange with parents is a two-way street, teachers can share selected information about their children gleaned from observing and recording. It is important for parents to know that teachers are interested in and understand their children without judging them.

## RECORDING A CHILD IN TEACHER-DIRECTED GROUP ACTIVITIES

The special relationship each child may experience with a teacher exists within a group structure. This means that the one-to-one contacts give way regularly to experiences in which a child must share the teacher with many other children. This sharing takes place in informal situations, as when a child must wait a turn to be helped, and in more formally planned activities, such as music time, a group story, or a trip.

How grown up must a child be to enjoy sharing a common experience with friends? It's one thing to be yourself and get along with others at your own speed. It's another to become an anonymous someone and be moved with a group as an integrated part of it. A child wonders whether to listen for an adult's directions and try to please her, or to listen to the cues the children give and seek to be acceptable to them. For most young children, the group situation offers challenges toward adjustment. The one-to-one relationship is still very meaningful, and individuals vary in the degree to which they can function comfortably outside close and intimate adult-child interaction. Children's responses when the group is directed as a whole may therefore be quite different from their responses when the teacher speaks to each child directly or alone.

For one thing, in teacher-directed group activities, the teacher often speaks to any one child only by inference, because she speaks to all the children at once in a group. (This is often the reason young children do not respond to requests given to the group as a whole for cleanup, dressing, lining up.) For another, the obvious and compelling competition for the teacher's attention may affect a child's feelings about a group activity. If a child is more concerned about the teacher's favor than about the story, for example, he may respond to the most appealing tale by squirming and wriggling, meanwhile pushing and edging toward the beloved adult.

Or, a child's very ability to perform may be affected by the overwhelming presence of nonindulgent peers who all too often compare children with one another, and this is not always easy to tolerate. The group situation established by the teacher (i.e., everybody will do the same thing) may therefore be a challenge to a child that is quite different from the looser group situation in which individual behavior is more closely related to a child's own desires and wants and not as immediately bound by peer involvement. Behavior in a teacher-directed activity may thus have its own meaning to a child, quite unrelated to the intent of the teacher.

Any school activity may be reminiscent to a child of experience outside of school, and this will influence behavior in the group, too. For example, if listening to a story at home is enjoyed as much for snuggling next to an adult as for the story itself, how well can a youngster listen at school, removed from physical contact with the teacher and sharing her with a lot of other youngsters? Or, if a child has been struggling secretly to conquer skipping, or jumping with two feet, or hopping, she may not yet be able to prance unselfconsciously at music time with her better-coordinated peers. And it is easy to understand the panic some children experience as they start across the floor and feel themselves swamped by the stampede of galloping bodies all around them!

## Details to Observe

In observing a child at any teacher-organized activity, we look for the general child-to-group and child-to-adult relationships as well as to the specifics of the activity.

- What is a child's initial reaction to the announcement that the group activity is about to begin?
  - » Acceptance (eager, joyful, ready to discontinue current activity immediately, goes along in a matter-of-fact way)
  - » Resistance (continues with current activity, dawdles, refuses, complains, runs away)
- What is the sequence of events? (the contents of the music period, walking to a trip site, nature and length of the story read, directions given for a project)
- What part is played by the adult? (shows children how to move, keeps children from bumping into one another, plays an instrument, reads aloud)
- How does the child react to sharing the adult with other children or with other adults, as when the teacher is helping other children, talking to another teacher or a parent, directing the entire group in an activity such as a story, game, trip, music, or giving an explanation? (child accepts easily, ignores, interrupts and demands attention, sulks, cries, has tantrums, waits for adult to return, awaits turn patiently but not resignedly)
- What does the child do if he or she participates?
  - » How does the child do it? (responds with body movement, facial expression, speech; is swift, impulsive, interested, involved)

- What does the child do if he or she does not participate? (observes group, disrupts, clings to teacher, turns back on group, does something else, runs out of room)
- How does the child respond to adult directions? (blankly, agreeably, happily, reluctantly, petulantly, tearfully, angrily)

## Records of a Child in Group Activities

Since a child's participation in a teacher-directed activity may also reveal a child's level of interest and functioning in the activity itself, recording the details of the child's involvement gives us additional data by which to measure the effect of the relationship with the teacher and the other children. A child who can cope with feelings about adults, children, and an activity in a reasonably balanced way is clearly one who has integrated the several areas of relating. Many children are still working at achieving this balance. Four-year-old Juanita, in the next record, is clearly one such child:

> It is 9:30 A.M. and the teacher is singing with the class. Juanita sits near the teacher. The children have been singing a song about animals and are discussing what kind of sound a turkey makes. Juanita looks around at the children, and her face lights up in a bright, full smile. Her body is in motion, switching rapidly from one position to another. She makes hand motions. Focusing on the teacher now, her eyes are darting around the circle of children, her mouth working, and her brow slightly knit.
>
> The teacher is now telling a story. Juanita looks around at the other children, then looks pertly at the teacher and seems to be listening carefully. She fingers her dress, turns to watch another child who is making a scratching sound, and turns her attention back to the teacher.
>
> Her face is alive, interested; sometimes she seems to slip off into her own world, then comes back. She is extremely attentive to the other children. She watches carefully as they respond, although she says nothing in response to the teacher's questions directed to the group.
>
> The children are taking parts to act out the story. Hassan is a frog. Juanita says, "I wanna be a frog, too." She becomes very involved in being a frog, joyfully jumping around. She continues being a frog after the time for the frog part is finished. Then her concentration breaks, and she makes contact with Natasha.

## PATTERNS OF BEHAVIOR

The pattern of a child's relationships with adults can be drawn from many areas of school living, such as casual adult-child contacts throughout the day (what the child says and does); the relationship at routines and while using materials and equipment; through the roles (and the meaning given to them) adopted during dramatic play; and the child's behavior during teacher-directed activities.

### Summary of a Child's Relationships with Adults

This summary may be all of a piece or as many-faceted as a millipede has legs. So much depends on how much you are able to record and on how constant or changeable the child is in exchanges with adults. Be aware of the following:

1. How frequently are contacts made with the adult and in what situations? (routines; coming for approval, for help in conflicts, with materials, with ideas; to give or get affection, be comforted; to express hostility; to involve adult in play, seek attention—directly or indirectly; group activities)
   » Is there a special quality in contacts with adults? (whining, demanding, trusting, coy, timid, belligerent, clinging, openly hostile, matter-of-fact, warmhearted, reserved)
   » What are the child's special mechanisms for gaining attention? (excessive talking; tattling; showing clothes, toys, products, bruises; bringing presents; telling about family; sidling up and touching, hanging on)
2. How does the child react when the teacher behaves in a giving manner?
   » When the teacher offers affection, does the child return it, look uncomfortable, squirm, seem startled, stiffen up, become effusive and gushy, reject the offering?
   » When she offers help, does the child accept it as a right, become clingy and helpless, brush it away, become angry, discuss it, become interested in procedures?
   » When she offers suggestions, does the child follow through reluctantly, eagerly; ignore her, appear grateful; follow through mechanically; reject, discuss questions?

The summary of a child's total response to the teacher as a giving person would indicate:

» Dependence on this adult (and possibly all adults)
» Rejection of this adult (and possibly all adults)
» Ability to meet adults on equal terms, to accept or reject the adults' overtures as appropriate

3. How does the child react when the teacher acts in a controlling, inhibiting way, curtailing child's actions and feelings?

» When limits are set, such as group rules and/or personal denial, child defies openly; resists passively by lingering, slowing up, remaining at another task; accepts with overt seriousness; accepts with no emotional investment; accepts with a verbalization of the reason; accepts and repeats instructions with parrot-like insistence.
» When criticism is given, child cries, pouts, accepts cheerfully, shows interest, becomes belligerent, sulks.

The summary of a child's total responses to the adult as an authority figure would show the child to be someone who:

» Typically does as told, to whom following adult direction seems more important than his own ideas, who has a consistent pattern of subordination to adult wishes—who is compliant
» Resists authority by any one of a number of patterns: by defiance, questioning, or indifference
» Finds a balance between carrying out her own independent ideas and wishes and accepting reasonable restrictions

4. What evidence is there of growing independence from adults, as seen in routines, use of materials, relationships with other children, identification with other children rather than with adults (perhaps is even against adults)?
5. How does the child manage direct verbal expressions?
6. Does the child exhibit overdependence; excessive insistence on independence; fear of new adults; persistent hostility to adults; excessive displays toward adults, including strangers?

## Records of Children's Behavior with Adults

The following summaries of two 4-year-olds show José's expanding relationships with adults in contrast to Amanda's more insistent method of securing contacts:

The first 2 months José was at school he seemed to need a lot of reassurance from the teacher that he was doing the right thing. He seldom talked, but would raise his eyes questioningly as if to say, "Is this all right?" With a nod and a smile from her, he would take paper and crayons, or some other material, and proceed to work. But again and again he would seek the teacher out with his eyes. After finishing any work, he would always walk slowly and proudly to the teacher and say, "See, it's for my mommy!" Since he often wandered out into the hall leading into the kitchen, the teacher asked him one day if he would like to accompany her to get the juice. He nodded enthusiastically and walked faster than usual down the hall and into the kitchen. There he struck up the beginning of his friendship with the cook. He remarked to her after a few minutes of observation, "I like it here. What are we going to eat?" After that, José accompanied the teacher into the kitchen every morning, and he talked to the cook as the juice was being prepared.

José seems drawn to any visiting adults and will always edge his way slowly and cautiously to their side, usually displaying something he has made for approval and appreciation. For a long time he just smiled and dropped his head if spoken to. But by now he has gained enough courage to tell his name and age if asked. He is very happy if they praise his work and lingers nearby until they leave.

At the beginning of the year it was evident that Amanda was embarrassed by any attention shown to her by adults, except in the routines of help with clothing or toilet. She showed this by her posture, gestures, voice, facial expression, and jerky movement of her body. Next came her bid for attention by loud and excessive talking, laughing, antics, climbing performances, and pretended inability to dress herself (this last was in spite of the fact that in the beginning she never needed help with dressing, with the exception of placing a garment into proper position). At present, she is still behaving in this attention-demanding way, but not as frequently as before. She comes to show us her dresses (she usually wears slacks), asks to pass out items when the need arises. She also seeks help in toileting. Help is not actually needed, but she apparently wants the presence of the teacher in the bathroom.

# 7

# Clues to Cognitive Functioning: Developmental Approach

How do we recognize that a child is a learning child who is able to make sense of the world and his or her experiences? As in the preceding chapters' focus on other areas of functioning, we concern ourselves here with the *how* and the *what*: how a child goes about the business of learning; what a child knows.

Studies by Piaget (1962a, 1962b, 1965), Vygotsky (1934/1962, 1933/1976, 1930/1978), and Gardner (1999), among others, make us realize that children work hard and steadily at finding meaning in everything they encounter and that "intelligence" is actually a multifaceted set of abilities not confined solely to the more traditional view of verbal competence and math facility. Young children continuously shape a reality that makes sense to them out of their interactions with the people, places, and things in their everyday lives. Naturally, their understanding is limited by an egocentric interpretation of things they encounter; yet unless adults restrict them to learn only what adults want them to learn, they tend to explore freely and happily in a variety of directions. Children need to learn from adults, of course, but do not feel constrained to focus only on adult-directed paths unless parents and teachers misunderstand the motivating force of childhood curiosity and insist on repressing it.

Thus, the capacity to learn feeds, and blooms, on curiosity, a human birthright that goes into action the day a child is born. Read the following description from 1900 of a baby less than 1 month old and see how early curiosity appears:

> This was on the 25th day, toward evening, when the baby was lying on her mother's knee by the fire in a condition of high well-being and content,

gazing at her grandmother's face with an expression of attention. I came and sat down close by, leaning over the baby, so that my face must have come within the direct range of her vision. At that she turned her eyes and gazed at it with the same appearance of attention, and even of some effort, shown by a slight tension of brows and lips, then turned her eyes back to her grandmother's face, and again to mine, and so several times. The last time she seemed to catch sight of my shoulder on which a high light struck from the lamp, and not only moved her eyes, but threw her head far back to see it better, and gazed for some time with a new expression on her face—"a sort of dim and rudimentary eagerness," says my note. She no longer stared, but really looked. (Shinn, 1900/1985, pp. 65–66)

The same intense curiosity in exploring the environment normally continues all through childhood. Here is how it looked in a rural kindergarten classroom:

When the class gerbil died, the teacher led the children to a corner of the yard where they buried the pet, marking the grave with a small sign. The next day, several children who wondered when the gerbil would go to heaven asked if they could check by digging up the remains. The teacher agreed. After a few days, their curiosity satisfied, they discontinued this activity.

Here it is again in a self-directed activity of two 1st-graders at school. Notice how Ariella directs her own attention to the snake's characteristics through using "private speech"—a clue to her ability to think (Berk, 1985, 1994; this item is discussed later in this chapter).

It's early in the morning, and 6-year-old Ariella is the first child in the room. After wandering around for a few minutes, she asks if she may hold the male garter snake, Stinker. She gets permission and takes the snake out of the tank with the teacher's help. Suddenly Ariella looks up and asks curiously, "What's that on his tail?" Holding the snake with one hand, she gently strokes his tail with the other. The snake coils itself into a complicated knot on her hand. She remarks, half to herself, "Look at his shape," and continues to stroke and watch the snake. Then she begins to shift her weight back and forth excitedly as she watches the snake's gymnastics. She looks down at the snake and softly croons its name, drawing out the syllables, "Stin–ker." She does this several times. Mary Ann comes over holding the female snake, Diamonds. She says to Ariella, "Under here she's really cold." Mary Ann lifts up the snake and peers at its underside. Ariella glances over at Diamonds quickly, and Mary Ann walks away to play with the snake on the rug.

## DEVELOPMENTAL APPROACH
## TO THINKING IN EARLY CHILDHOOD

Curiosity about the environment, the desire to explore new situations and places, the need to manipulate and experiment with new objects and materials—these are the natural ways of childhood. They are the key elements in learning and as important as the ability to remember what one has learned. So basic to humanity are these characteristics that they do not have to be taught to children anywhere, unless development has been compromised by delay or environmental assault.

As a result of this biological need to find out, all peoples everywhere seem to have tackled certain common aspects of physical and social reality and given them form and meaning, though perhaps in different ways as a function of culture. Among these are the phenomena of matter, number, space, weight, time, perspective, volume, distance, morality, social interaction, and justice.

Piaget's studies of children (1962a, 1962b, 1965, Piaget & Inhelder, 1969) reveal that in every society every child pursues the search for physical and social meaning over and over again as a way of understanding the world. It is not possible to know how much understanding of such phenomena a given child has developed by using standardized tests even though the extensive use of tests is currently pervasive. The conceptualization that marks true mental growth is not solely *quantitative*—the sheer accumulation of facts—for equally important is the *qualitative*—the growth in capacity to understand. This growth creates a basic change in a child's way of perceiving and knowing. Such change, being qualitative, is not measurable by quantitative means. It is therefore necessary for teachers to know what are the important processes of mental growth in early childhood so as to document them and consider the implications for curriculum planning. This means looking for, and finding, the evidence that a child is thinking and therefore developing intellectually. *What* a child knows (i.e., information) can also be documented by good observation (see Chapter 8).

### Two Important Ideas: Assimilation and Accomodation

As observers of young children, we rely on Piaget's concepts to give meaning to their thinking. All human beings are constantly involved in making sense of the information coming in all around them. According to Piaget, two *lifelong* processes, assimilation and accommodation, drive cognitive development.

1. *Assimilation* is the process of making sense of experience and fitting it into current cognitive concepts.
2. *Accommodation* is the complementary process of adapting concepts about the world to fit reality.

These are *lifelong processes* because "when one cognitive scheme becomes inadequate for making sense of the world it is replaced by another" (Goswami, 1998, p. 260). Here is an example of assimilation/accommodation at work in a young child:

> Two 4-year-olds examine a large black pet rabbit that has recently inhabited their classroom. They call it a "dog" (their current cognitive concept). They had never before seen a rabbit. After a few days' experience holding and watching the rabbit—it hops, it has long ears and whiskers, it doesn't bark—the children experience some cognitive discomfort. They begin to assimilate these un-dog-like features and over time accommodate their concept to include "rabbit," discarding "dog."

### Sequential Development of Thinking in Early Childhood

In Piaget's stage theory (1962a, 1962b, 1965; Piaget & Inhelder, 1969), a young child's approach to learning about the physical world is initially *sensorimotor,* seen as children taking in information about the world through their senses and their own physical activity. For example, an 8-month-old chewing on the corner of a soft block is learning about texture, weight, and shape. As children mature, they have new experiences and their ways of thinking change. Sometime between ages 2 and 3, their approach to thinking becomes *pre-operational* and later, around 7, it becomes *concrete-operational.* The terms *sensori-motor, pre-operational,* and *concrete operational* refer to specific ways of thinking.

*Pre-Operational Thinking.* Children at this stage believe mainly what appears to be obvious to their senses. They are literal; they think in concrete terms. They are perception-bound. "Pennies can't make a dime," says the pre-operational child. "A dime is smaller." Pre-operational children, according to Piaget, regard the physical world from a primarily "egocentric" point of view, meaning that young children are unable to see things from another person's perspective. Comprehending that one person might have more than one role can be problematic for young children, for example, that a firefighter is also a father or a doctor a mother.

The pre-operational 4-year-old in the following anecdote doesn't understand that teaching 4-year-olds and "working in the square" are both *work*.

> Zach asked his teacher if she went to work. (His own mother worked as a salesperson in a large store in the main square of the town.)
> "Yes, I do go to work," said the teacher.
> Zach responded, "Where do you work? In the square?"

Other examples of pre-operational thinking reveal that because children often have difficulty understanding the difference between animate and inanimate, they frequently project life onto that which is inanimate. They may perceive the moving shadows of leaves or swiftly traveling clouds as alive. It may be even harder to understand that difference when death is actually involved. Listen to these 3-year-olds.

> Katya and Antonio find the class fish bloated and floating in the tank. They call to the teacher. "Hey, something's happened to our fish." The teacher tells them that the fish is dead. She takes it out with a small net and places it on a piece of paper.
> "Look, it isn't moving," says Antonio. "It isn't moving because it's dead," explains the teacher. "What do you think we should do with it?"
> "Put it back in the water so it can swim," replies Katya.

However, intimate, personal experiences of children, such as the death of a family member or a pet, may well affect their understanding of the world and their larger understanding of death.

*A Transition Period.* Between the pre-operational stage and the subsequent concrete-operational stage, there is a transition period, according to Piaget and Inhelder (1969), during which the pre-operational child starts to shake loose from earlier forms of thinking. Children who are just approaching this level of understanding do not rely solely on their perceptions. They begin to be able to "conserve." For example, they no longer believe that breaking a cookie into several pieces gives them more to eat. They can "conserve" the original whole quantity in their mind despite the perceptual change.

The ability to conserve does not develop all at once, evenly, in every arena. A 6-year-old who may be confident with the abstract idea of quantity (that the whole cookie equals the sum of the parts) may be unsure about the concept of number (that 10 pennies is the same as a dime).

*Concrete-Operational Thinking.* Once children have made the transition, or, in Piaget's term, have achieved conservation, they speak with certainty about what they know to be true despite what their eyes see and *they can explain why.* They are no longer perception-bound. An understanding of abstract characteristics such as volume or mass allows a child to realize, for example, that a chunk of clay transformed first into a long, slithery snake, then into a series of small balls, then into one large ball, and finally into a snowman is still the same quantity of clay throughout.

After children have grasped the notion that objects and events may have characteristics that are not necessarily apparent to the senses of sight, hearing, touch, smell, or taste but that nevertheless do exist, they become less dependent on their senses as the primary source of meaning and therefore less *egocentric*; they can deal with some nonconcrete reality. For example, having learned by experience that many things that look very different from one another can all be warm, they can now grasp the existence of an abstraction, the concept of warmth; knowing that light and dark are not always related to their own waking up and going to bed, they can grasp the concept that light and darkness have objective existence; knowing that the same numerical symbol, for instance, 4, can be used to measure age (4 years old), time (4 o'clock), place (4th floor), weight (4 pounds), quantity (4 wheels on a car), and so on, children can now grasp the concept of number as an abstraction that has a meaning of its own. Number is no longer perceived as an integral part of a child, a building, a car, or a television set; it has an existence of its own. Once children grasp this, they can understand and develop relations with numbers, play around with parts of the whole, and reverse relationships within the whole. They grow ready to deal with a wide variety of abstract concepts—provided these are perceivable in connection with some concrete base of action. For example, while using a scale to balance various items of different size and weight (a hammer, six pencils, a bag of corks, a small stapler, a large cardboard box), children are now able to recognize that size and weight do not have a necessary relationship to each other. According to Piaget (1962a, 1962b; Piaget & Inhelder, 1969), they could not understand this concept if it were taught to them by words alone, and it is not possible to grasp at the pre-operational level at all. Children who conserve, however, can understand many relationships of an abstract nature if they discover them through concrete experience and their discovery is labeled and validated by the teacher, by themselves, or by a peer. Their thinking has transformed so they can usually rely on mental processes, no longer tied solely to perceptions.

## HOW CAN WE KNOW A CHILD'S APPROACH TO THINKING?

Children's approach to thinking is affected by two influences. One of these develops sequentially, while the other does not. The sequential development in the approach to thinking is related to the growth that occurs as a result of both maturation *and* experience in a social and cultural milieu. The nonsequential element is the personal, idiosyncratic way in which an individual functions all through life, although possibly with modifications caused by self-learning and/or the guidance of others (see Chapter 8). Although we can look separately at each of these influences on the approach to thinking, in reality they function together (along with feelings), because children always act as whole beings.

Children's approach to thinking can be observed while they are using play materials, involved in drawing pictures, writing or dictating stories, doing specific academic activities, experimenting, and talking with one another.

### Language and Learning in Early Childhood

Most children love to talk, and as soon as they begin to master language, they use it steadily, increasing in skill all the time. Through listening to what children say to one another and to adults, teachers can learn not only what they know or misunderstand, but what their thinking is like. During the early years, children's involvement in the *process of thinking* is of greater, more far-reaching effect than whether they know many right answers to adult questions. According to Carew, Chan, and Halfar's (1976) extensive observational records of intellectual growth in toddlers, "Wrong answers after a struggle are indicative of intellectual development; clumsy execution is as acceptable as smooth" (p. 11). The *process* by which children arrive at conclusions is thus more significant at this age than the answers, valuable as these are.

In addition to observing children's language use with one another and with adults, it is fruitful to attend to their talk-to-themselves— their private speech. Piaget refers to this as egocentric speech, an "indication of the young child's cognitive immaturity" (cited in Berk, 1985, p. 47). In contrast, Vygotsky (1962) regards private speech as originating in the social context of infant and parent communication and as a pathway to problem solving and internal verbal thought. Research (Berk, 1985, 1994; Berk & Winsler, 1995) reveals that children accomplish much when they use self-directed private speech. "Private speech is an important way in which children organize, understand, and gain control over their environment" (Berk, 1985, p. 50). Children derive a host of benefits from talking to themselves such as expressing affect, playing with language, describing their own activity, regulating motor activity, focusing their own attention, emotionally integrating thoughts and experiences, engaging in self-directed fantasy play, and solving problems (Berk, 1985).

> Research indicates that private speech is a problem-solving tool universally available to children who grow up in rich, socially interactive environments. Several interdependent factors—the demands of a task, its social context and individual characteristics of a child—govern the extent and ease with which any one child uses self-directed speech to guide behavior. (Berk, 1994, p. 83)

Some young children who come from a bilingual environment may not initially produce as much language as monolingual children (Tabors, 1997). However, "experience with two language systems can enhance mental flexibility, concept formation, and metalinguistic abilities" (National Research Council, 1998, cited in Meece, 2002, p. 263).

Children's language, while important, is not the only clue to their thinking processes and understanding. For some children it is not even the major clue. So much of young children's thinking is done with their bodies that it is often possible to deduce the thinking process directly from their behavior. One can easily see curiosity in their eyes and faces; exploration and experimentation in their active hands; concentration and attention in their postures and expressions; persistence and involvement in the continuity with which they pursue their tasks; creativity and imagination in their pretend and fantasy play. By the same token, one might also see behavior that appears distracted, characterized by seemingly random, empty gestures that lead nowhere. Learning is an active process in early childhood, and it is through a child's activity that one can infer the presence or absence of investment, struggle, purposefulness, imagination, and organization, all elements of thinking. Observe this 3-and-a-half-year-old child.

> Eneida walks to the table where the teacher has set down two cartons of milk, four paper cups in a stack, and a serving dish with graham crackers. Without a word, Eneida takes a milk carton and opens it with deliberation. "Look," she says, smiling with pride. (She was shown how to open a milk carton without touching the part that becomes the spout, and she has done it well.) Eneida separates the paper cups. Silently she

counts the four cups with her eyes, not pointing, and then with her eyes
counts the three children at the table. She gets up and puts one of the
cups back on the cart. Cheryl sits down next to Eneida, and, smiling,
Eneida says, "Wait," and goes to the cart to get a cup for her.

Is there any question that this child is thinking and reasoning? In a
quite different situation, 4-year-old Rosalie is also intently absorbed in
what she is doing. Is she learning anything? How is she going about
the process of learning? How does her talking to herself reveal her
thinking?

At the water table, Rosalie poured water through a funnel into a tall
bottle. She did this very contentedly—slowly, with rhythm. She noticed
water trickling from a small hole in the bottle; she said, "Peepee," and
continued pouring water into the bottle. She stopped and just watched
the water stream out. She then took a water wheel and poured water
into it very quickly with a scoop, picked up another bottle, filled it, and
poured the whole contents onto the wheel. This made the wheel turn
very quickly for a long time. Smiling, she said, to no one in particular,
"Whee . . . whee . . ." She then became interested in the sponge, putting
it under water, slowly squeezing it downward, then releasing it again and
again, with her whole body going up and down as she did this.

This child is methodical and systematic in her efforts. From an
intellectual point of view, she is gaining something. In exploring the
properties of water, she has made a connection between the stream
of water and the more familiar, personal stream that flows from her
body. She has learned how to act quickly and apply pressure to keep a
water wheel turning. She has also gained knowledge about the properties of a sponge. Throughout, she was strengthening a bodily sense
of rhythm that pervaded all her observation, exploration, and experimentation.

In the following record we see a 2-year-old doing "math" without
any words.

Zaida, sitting in the sandbox, picked up four items: a small shovel the
size of a tablespoon, a medium-sized shovel the size of a half-cup, a
large shovel of about two cups, and a very large bucket. He placed
the bucket between his legs. He filled the smallest shovel with sand.
Then poured that into the medium-sized shovel. He dropped the small
shovel and picked up the largest shovel. He then dumped the sand from
the medium-sized shovel into the largest shovel, which he ultimately

dumped into the bucket. He dropped the largest shovel, picked up the smallest shovel, and began to repeat the process. He continued his process until the bucket was full. He turned the bucket over and dumped out the sand. He stood up, stomped on the pile of sand, and walked away. (Brown-Murray, 2006)

Following is a record of some 3-year-olds who are struggling with a different kind of intellectual task, that of perceiving the relationship of parts to a whole. They are putting a puzzle together. Here, too, while the major evidence of their thinking is in their activity, their private speech reveals how they direct and label their own solutions to the puzzle. The help provided by Darcy is clearly a learning situation for Abigail:

Abigail sat by herself working intently on a puzzle. After quickly placing the most obvious pieces, she began to struggle with the rest. She tried one, then another, a slight grimace passing across her face after each failure. The teacher suggested that Darcy could help because she knew that puzzle well. Darcy sat on one side of the puzzle, Abigail on the other. Neither said a word. Darcy picked up a piece, trying it in several places before she found a fit. "Goes there," she said softly, more to herself than to Abigail. Abigail sat back watching carefully, with a puzzle piece in each hand. She watched with interest as Darcy placed another piece.

Then Abigail leaned forward and tried to put a piece in. "It goes there," she stated with authority to Darcy. "No-o-o!" Darcy argued as she grabbed the piece out of the spot and fitted in another piece. Abigail sat back looking a little surprised but seemed resigned to letting Darcy have her way. They finished the puzzle together, taking turns placing pieces. The only verbal communication was an occasional "There," or "It goes here."

As they finished, Abigail patted the puzzle, grinned, and proudly called out, "It's done, Miss Behan." She then turned the puzzle upside down and started doing it again, working intently and silently.

Socially mediated language plays a significant role in children's learning, according to Vygotsky (1930/1978). In the following anecdote, the teacher discovers the nature of Helen's approach to thinking:

Seven-year-old Bettina takes apart a triple-layered, three-dimensional puzzle but does not know how to begin putting it together. She is sitting at a table with two other children and Ms. Weiss, the student teacher. Ms. Olivo, the teacher, points out that the outside edges of the puzzle are smooth while the inside edges are curvy. Together they find the outside, smooth pieces. By holding two pieces next to each other, Ms. Olivo points out that each succeeding layer of the puzzle is thicker. Bettina begins to put the pieces together with Ms. Olivo's guidance. On the third and top layer Bettina says, "Let me do this one by myself." She proceeds to do the puzzle twice more. Each time less assistance from Ms. Olivo is necessary. Finally, Bettina takes the puzzle to Ms. Weiss, the student teacher, and, using Ms. Olivo's words and techniques, teaches Ms. Weiss how to do it.

Ms. Olivo's supportive behavior can be defined as "scaffolding" (Berk & Winsler, 1995), the way the adult guides the child's learning via focused questions and positive interactions. Ms. Olivo's guided participation enabled Bettina to do a task that at first she was unable to do alone and that later, with practice, was able to do by herself as well as to teach it to someone else. Vygotsky refers to this increasing independent ability as occurring within the child's "zone of proximal development" (1930/1978, p. 86). Ms. Olivo helped Helen move to a higher level of competence and in the process became familiar with Bettina's ability to think, her style of learning, and her persistence.

According to Vygotsky (1930/1978), the role of social interaction and informal teaching is paramount in a child's learning. This view of children's thinking and learning has implications for the teacher's role. Rather than waiting for a child's readiness, it encourages contingent teaching, which involves pacing the amount of help children are given on the basis of their moment-to-moment understanding. Teachers are engaged in structuring the task and the surrounding environment so that the demands on the child at any given time are at an appropriately challenging level, and in "providing assistance when children need help and reducing the amount of assistance as children's competence increases" (Berk & Winsler, 1995, p. 29).

### Listening to What Children Say

The most direct and obvious way to find out what children know is to listen closely to what they say. In the following records the children are all under 6:

Mariam comments during a class discussion, "After 14 is my favorite number; it's 15. That's the floor I live on."

Noah arrives at school and heads straight for Farhad. One fist is tightly closed, but when Noah gets to Farhad, he opens his hand and shows him its contents. "What is it?" Farhad asks.

"It's not an 'it,'" answers Noah. "It's a seed. If you plant it, you get more."

A teacher threading needles for children staves off pressure for help by asking, "Why can't I do more than one at a time?"

Says Charles, "Because you only have one pair of hands."

Esther, suddenly animated, bursts out, "A squid could do anything."

"Why could a squid?" the teacher asks.

"Because he has eight legs," Esther replies.

Nicole says at meeting time, "I'm flying to Worcester tonight. It's a very short flight."

To which Owen adds, "Well, I've flown to Boston, and Boston is near Worcester."

Such different things children get to think about, know, and understand without being formally taught. Listening to them closely, one also finds out what a child misunderstands or misinterprets or "knows" differently from adults. In the example below, Liam "knows" his age, and he may also "know" how to count to 5, by rote or with objects, but he doesn't yet understand numbers. Here he is focused on the most personally salient aspect of the count.

As the teacher counts heads in the 3-year-old group, she chants, "One, two, three, four, five." She is interrupted by Liam, who says seriously as she taps his head on the five, "No, I'm 3."

Observing and recording what children say provides insights into their acquisition of relevant information and their manner of solving problems. These preschoolers know something about "money" and something about numbers but perhaps not a total concept of either. What they don't understand are quantity words.

At the collage table, Josy and Meryl, both 4, are cutting and gluing. Josy looks up and says, "Me and my brother has the most money in the whole wide world. We have a hundred."

Tara, almost 5, pipes up, "We have a hundred million. That's less than a thousand, you know."

Josy states firmly, "And we get allowances. I get a dime, and my brother gets a quarter. *So there*," she adds firmly.

Tara responds, "I get allowance of a penny a week . . . when I take the baby downstairs."

While the boys in the next anecdote understand that wars take place between differing groups, they are unclear about the meaning of the names they use as identification.

Three 5- and 6-year-old boys building helicopters, machine guns, and motorcycles out of blocks have the following conversation while playing:
*Dwayne*: The war is between the bad guys and the Americans.
*Harley*: The war is between Darth Vader and the Americans.
*Noel*: South America is against America.

The 5-year-olds in the following example are engaged in a conversation that reflects the process of their thinking and problem solving within a social framework. There are implications here for the teacher to "provide sensitive and contingent assistance, facilitating children's representational and strategic thinking" (Berk & Winsler, 1995, p. 32) that will enable the children to wrestle further with the inconsistency of Zoe's solution that the next baby may be Black.

Zoe (White) is washing a Black baby doll. Will (African American) is watching.
*Zoe*: You can watch but don't touch the baby. My aunt is having a baby today.
*Will*: How do you know it's today?
*Zoe*: My mother told me.
*Will*: Oh yeah? What's it going to be?
*Zoe*: How do I know?
*Will*: Well, if you know it's today, why don't you know what it's going to be?
*Zoe* (in a disgusted tone): 'Cause I don't, that's why!
*Will*: Well, will it be Black or White?
*Zoe* (looking down at the doll): Maybe Black.
*Will*: What color is your aunt?
*Zoe*: She's White.
*Will*: Oh.
*Zoe*: Anyway, I'll know when I get home.
The next day Will and Zoe are sitting together at lunch.
*Will*: So did your aunt have the baby?
*Zoe*: Yes, and it was a girl. I'm glad.

*Will*: Was it Black or White?
*Zoe*: This one was White. Maybe the next one will be Black.

## Details to Observe as Shown in Records of a Child's Approach to Thinking

Observant teachers will look for the following kinds of evidence of children's approaches to thinking. The records after some questions provide examples.

- Does the child make generalizations from examining and using specific materials? (e.g., "The clay gets too mushy from too much water." "If you press too hard on the crayon, it breaks.")
- Does the child rely totally or partially on the use of concrete objects or experiences to understand ideas and to learn? (e.g., One child counts five children waiting to paint, gathers five paintbrushes and hands one to each. Another child gives out one brush at a time until each has one.)
- How accurate is the child's understanding when concrete materials are absent? Is the child confused? Does the child "catch on" after a while?
- Can the child understand an event from another's perspective? (In the following example, one child can take another's perspective while the other can't: Two 5-year-olds are looking at a classmate's hair. Salma says, "She got a haircut, and now Ms. Parchment won't recognize her." Diego replies, "Yes she will—by the face.")
- Can the child be logical?

The following two records of 4-year-olds reveal logic in their problem solving.

Zofia and Valerie had built a "two-room house" of large hollow blocks connected to Benjamin and Raymond's house. Benjamin was wearing a hard hat and was attempting to carry one of the small chairs into his house.

"How can I get in there?" he puzzled. The opening for a door was not wide enough, although the blocks were only up to his waist.

Zofia glanced over and suggested, "Take your hat off. Hold it [the chair] over your head."

Benjamin shook his head, but Raymond picked up the chair for Benjamin, held it high over his head, and carried it into the building.

A passage from Paley (1984) of kindergarten children discussing "the best way to choose a daily leader" (p. 17) reveals a certain kind of logic:

*Jonathan*: Why can't we have a boys' line and a girls' line like that other class?

*Teacher*: They were going to the bathroom—and older boys and girls go to separate bathrooms. We have our own toilets.

*Jonathan*: Can't we go to theirs?

*Teacher*: No, but you will in 1st grade.

*Charlotte*: That reminds me. I want leaders to be from cubbies and not from the list on the wall because then it'll be quicker to be your turn again.

*Teacher*: Why is it quicker to go cubby by cubby instead of name by name from the list?

*Charlotte*: Because when you go down the list and the last person they would have to wait a little longer than the cubby way.

*Paul*: She's right. Because there are not so many cubbies. There are more names.

*Teacher*: Doesn't each name have a cubby?

*Clarice*: He means the names are littler than the cubbies.

*Charlotte*: So you could look better at the cubbies.

*Andrew*: No, it's the same thing. Everyone has a cubby.

*Charlotte*: Yeah, but the list is longer.

*Teacher*: Let's do this. I'll call every name on the list. When I call your name, stand in front of your cubby. (There is an attitude of suspense as the children fill up the spaces in front of each cubby.) Now, let's count the list names. (We count to 24.) Okay, count cubbies (We count again to 24).

*Paul*: It takes longer to call the names.

*Teacher*: Charlotte, we counted 24 names and 24 cubbies. Do you still think you'll get your turn faster if we go by cubbies?

*Charlotte*: I do a little bit.

*Mary Ann*: No it won't, Charlotte. It'll be the same.

*Jeremy*: It *will* be shorter.

*Andrew*: It has to be the same.

*Jeremy*: It can't be, because they're both different. You can even see the cubbies faster.

*Mary Ann*: No. See, it's really like the same thing except for being in a different place.

> *Charlotte*: It really is shorter by cubbies. Just *look*. Can't you see your cubby quicker?
>
> *Teacher*: How many agree with Charlotte, that you'll have your turn to be leader sooner if we go cubby by cubby? (Every hand but two goes up.) How many want to make the change? (Every hand goes up.)

The following is a letter written by a 6-year-old that indicates her ability to think back in time and her understanding of the sequential nature of human life and relationships:

Dear Mom,

   Happy Mother's Day. I love you because you invented me. If your mom was not invented by her mom you wood [sic] not be there to invent me.

Love from Migdalia

- Does the child see part-to-whole relationships? In what contexts? Which are missed? Does the child think that breaking up a cracker, a piece of clay, or a crayon gives him more?

  When young children understand the relation of part to whole, they are able to demonstrate that knowledge in various ways. See how Marcy, almost 3 years old, revealed what she knew:

  Marcy, helping the teacher clear the table, gathered pieces of a puzzle together and put them in their places. When all the pieces were in, she stuck her finger in the one empty space left and announced gravely, "We missed a piece there. There's one piece missing there." The teacher found the missing piece mixed in with another puzzle and gave it to Marcy, who pushed the last piece in and shrieked, "I did it!," jumping up and down in her seat.

- Does the child see sequence? In what situations, content, or experiences? Which are missed?
- Does the child understand causal relationships? Which ones? Which are confusing?
- What criterion does the child use as the basis for grouping objects? Is it interest? Function? Theme? Color? Any other? (e.g., loading same-shape blocks before putting away; putting paintbrushes, crayons, or pegs into their appropriate containers; categorizing children as older and younger)
- Does the child use more than one criterion for grouping or categorizing? For example, does she know her teacher as a

teacher *and* a father? (See also earlier example of the child who thinks his teacher works in the square.) As a child categorizes materials and play objects, do the categories change along the way or remain stable?

A small group of 5-year-olds create their own categories in a sorting activity with an array of buttons in a tray with six containers. One child takes the lead in creating the categories as he begins to sort, ". . . ones with two holes, ones with four holes, yellow ones, blue ones, brown ones . . ." Then he picks up a couple of buttons, one in the shape of a hand and one in the shape of an elephant. He puts these in the sixth container and says, "Interesting buttons."

- Play, artwork, writing, movement, are all symbols for experience. In what way does the child use symbols? conventionally? freely? uniquely? often? seldom? For example, does the child adapt materials for props in dramatic play? Does the child use letters to make up or figure out words?

Hai-yen, a 1st-grader with a command of letter-sound associations, uses invented spelling to write a story. In a story about eating lobster with her family, she writes, "I took off a *pice* and *tryed* it with some *buter*. I told my sister to *tast* it but she did not *here* me, so I said "Pay *attenshion!* Im telling you something *importent*."

- Can the child sometimes "play" with abstract ideas? Which ones?
- Does the child form and express concepts? What sorts? How? Verbally? Via movement? In play?

During lunchtime in a 2nd-grade classroom, Lily, an English Language Learner, is seated at the table, eating her lunch. She picks up her water bottle and holds it up directly in front of her face, examining it. She comments, "The water not melt," and then makes eye contact with the teacher and repeats what she just said.

- Does the child have a sense of humor? What does he find funny?

As a group of young 4s are making their way to the school gym, a teacher says, "Henry, stay with your partner." His partner says, "Henry spells prenry" and begins to laugh. Henry laughs along with him.

- Does the child have a variety of responses to questions? Does she search for answers?

- Does the child enjoy and play with words?

  A 3-year-old is jumping along a long line of large outdoor blocks, half singing aloud to herself: "A horsey, of coursey, horsey, horsey, horsey."

- Is the child an adventurous learner? Does he take chances intellectually? Does he exhibit competence?
- Is the child persistent in working on a task or exploring a problem?
- What is the child's emotional tone in academic situations like reading or math?
- What is the child's approach to problem solving? timid? impulsive? thoughtful?

  Joaquin, a 3-year-old, puts two long blocks on top of each other to create a road. He puts an arch over the road and tries to run a small fire truck under the arch, but it doesn't fit because the road is too high and too close to the arch. He says, "Small tunnel!" He looks at the blocks and then removes one of the long blocks. Now the fire truck fits as he runs it under the arch. He announces, "Big tunnel."

- How does the child respond to adult or peer support in problem solving?

  Six-year-old Mia has built a low square structure. A long flat block rests on the "roof" and extends to the shelf holding other blocks. Cindy, the student teacher, asks, "What are you building?" "A super-market," Mia replies.
  *Cindy*: So what is this long block for leading to the roof?
  *Mia*: That's where the trucks come in with food. They unload on the roof.
  *Cindy*: How do they get it into the store?
  *Mia*: They throw it down.
  *Cindy*: Oh. Suppose it's eggs?
  *Mia* (staring at Cindy): Would you please help someone else?

# 8

# Clues to Cognitive Functioning: Individual Approach

Quite separate from the influence of children's development, yet embedded within it, is the unique individual approach to cognitive functioning that emerges because children have differing temperaments, personalities, cultures, and languages. The inborn differences in temperament show up at birth, and interwoven with them thereafter are the diverging experiences with their families and their communities. All affect a child's cognitive approach.

## IDIOSYNCRATIC APPROACH TO THINKING

A child's unique individual approach to thinking reflects temperament and culture. One aspect of inborn temperament has to do with the pace of development. Some children seem not to be progressing, and then growth emerges dramatically; others grow steadily, with regularity and evenness. Other aspects of temperament, as defined in the seminal work of Thomas and Chess (1977), are such qualities as *adaptability, quality of mood, intensity of response, distractibility, attention span*, and *persistence*. Adaptability means that some children make easy adjustments to new experiences; others are more cautious. Temperament shows up in cognitive style as impulsive or reflective reactions to stimuli; as dependence on external stimuli or being tuned in more to inner stimuli; as persistence or impatience; in degrees of being playful and imaginative; or in the strength of enduring in the face of difficulty. Attention span, persistence, concentration, and distractibility can be inferred from almost any activity in which a child engages.

> During quiet time, 5-year-old Yael works with rubber bands and a geoboard studded with small nails. She stares at the board as she makes a series of three squares with rubber bands. She works confidently and

quickly but at a methodical pace. She seems to have a preconceived pattern in her head, as she doesn't hesitate when placing the rubber bands on the board.

Her mouth is slightly opened as she stretches the rubber bands when they are too tight to reach the nails. Each time she selects a rubber band, she looks into the box and carefully chooses one. When the bands are too large, she makes them go around four nails instead of two. Occasionally she is distracted by noises in the room and looks over her shoulder to see what is happening and then returns to her board.

As she works, she stares at the board. When a rubber band doesn't fit, she makes a sound, "ts," with her lips as if she were annoyed. She makes another small square. The next band drops to the floor, and she bends down and picks it up with ease.

"I'm all finished," she says with a smile when the pattern looks complete, and she pushes her hair behind her ear. She carefully removes the rubber bands but has some problems getting them around the nails, and she pulls at them. She smiles at the board, and then at the teacher when she is quite finished.

It is important for the teacher to be aware of the degree to which a child is able to persist despite difficulties and frustrations and to ignore distracting environmental stimuli. It is important to observe these in relation to many activities and at different times. For example, on one day a child may spend half an hour on a swing but only 5 minutes on writing a story. On other days the time spans may be quite different or even reversed. For records of all activities in which a child engages, if the time at which the activity begins and ends is noted, the assessment will be easier and more objective.

Keep in mind the following questions when observing intellectual involvement:

- Does the child have a variety of responses to questions or does she tend to stick to one answer?
- Is the child relaxed or anxious in academic situations?
- Does the child work steadily? withdraw? whine? bite nails? attack problems cheerfully? share information with others?
- How does the child respond to academic challenge? Eagerly? Indifferently? Seriously? Fearfully?

*Life experience* seems to influence such aspects of learning as feelings about failing (is it a spur or a dampener to a child?) and standards for self (are they too high, too low, or realistic?). Either temperament or experience or a combination of both is responsible for a child's ability to cope with ambiguity and uncertainty, to control impulses, to take chances, and to view clues as relevant or irrelevant.

Two children in the same family, examining the same statue in the park, have very different approaches, related, perhaps, to their particular type of intelligence—the first more personal, the second more musical or linguistic:

> A mother, 6-year-old Cora, and 2-year-old Becky are walking in the park and come upon a statue.
>> *Cora*: Who's that? Why does he have a statue?
>> *Mother*: That's Garibaldi (and provides a little background information).
>> *Cora*: How old was he? What's a hero? What's independence? How old is his horse? Where's Italy?
> Several years later when the younger child, Becky, is 6, they come to the statue again.
>> *Becky*: Who's that?
>> *Mother*: Garibaldi.
>> *Becky* (in a dreamy voice): Garibaldi . . .Garibaldi . . . Garibaldi (long pause). What a beautiful name!

Yet age is a factor in all these things, too. How then can one ever be sure about what causes one child to think in a linear fashion, another to think in an associative manner, and yet another to think analytically? It is perhaps wise for teachers to concern themselves with recognizing where each child is in the development of intellectual processes so as to be able to support growth in each child without worrying excessively about why individual children are not all growing in the same way.

Individual differences in approach to thinking are clearly shaped by the range and character of children's life experiences and the expectations and values of their families and their cultures. These approaches, however, may differ substantially from the approaches valued by teachers and may not be recognized as *differences* in approach. Instead, they may be mistakenly viewed as less able approaches, which is a kind of cultural conflict. Philips's comparison of Native American and Anglo children (cited in Lubeck, 1994) attending four different classrooms serves as an illustration of such conflict. In the first two classrooms the teacher called on individual children as she worked with either the whole class or a small group. In the third classroom, students worked alone, approaching the teacher for help as needed. In the fourth, where students worked independently in small groups, the Anglo children were less comfortable than in the first three classrooms. They argued more and tended to defer to an appointed leader. In contrast, the Native American children became deeply involved and worked closely with one another, but were reluctant to participate in the first two types of classrooms because they perceived being called on as learning through public mistakes. Might a teacher interpret the Native American children's reluctance to speak out when called on (in classrooms one and two) as a deficiency in their ability to think?

Teachers are challenged to gain an understanding of the cultural heritage of the children in their classrooms by tuning in to the "contexts of children's lives, informed by genuine and ongoing conversations with parents, [thereby] making classrooms compatible to children of various cultural groups" (New, 1994, p. 77).

In addition to being affected by their particular environment, cultural values, and beliefs, children's approach to thinking may be shaped by what Gardner (1999) posits as "multiple intelligences." Gardner proposes multiple intelligences such as linguistic, musical, logical-mathematical, spatial, bodily-kinesthetic, and personal, which cut across cultural variations.

> If we define intelligence as Howard Gardner does, as "the ability to solve a problem or fashion a product that is valued in at least one culture or community," we might dare to imagine that a dancer, athlete, or musician is the most intellectually advanced member of a culture. (Bowman & Stott, 1994, p. 124)

We must consider that a child's individual approach to thinking may be influenced by a proclivity to one or more of these intelligences.

### Details to Observe

How do we know a child is thinking and learning? Teachers should look for evidence from the following questions:

- Is the child physically involved in learning? Is the child verbally reflective? How would you describe the children in these records?

  Brian, 3-and-a-half, spent an hour experimenting with Scotch tape and masking tape. He put it on his head; put it on a piece of paper and colored the paper (discovering that there was nothing on that part of the paper when he pulled the tape off); cut the paper with a pair of scissors and taped the two pieces together; put the tape on his finger as a bandage; felt the stickiness; tasted it; taped his mouth; covered his eyes.

Six-year-old Ayesha held a thin twig on which she had placed a caterpillar. She began to move the twig vertically to watch as the caterpillar moved along. She commented to herself, "He's walking back and forth." She picked a leaf from a bush, held the leaf close to the caterpillar and said to herself, "He likes the stick better than the leaf." She continued poking the leaf at the caterpillar and then asked, "Are you going to change into a butterfly?"

- Does the child show curiosity? About what?
  - » How often does he show it? In what way?
  - » How does the child go about satisfying her curiosity?
  - » Does the child experiment? Is the search persistent?
- Does the child ask questions? What kinds?
  - » Does the questioning seem to come out of a desire to find answers or to develop relationships?
  - » Do the questions make sense immediately to the teacher, or do they require explanations from the child?
  - » Do the answers lead to action? To reflection?
- During a story, does a child ask questions about what is in the pictures or why a character does something?
  - » Or on a class trip, about the things she sees or hears, or about the people?
  - » Or about what is happening around him—in the classroom or outside—for example, what a truck is delivering or a worker repairing?
- What kinds of risks does the child take in learning?
  - » During reading, does he sound out an initial letter? Does he get a clue from the picture?
  - » Does he, must he, do things the "right" way? For example, when painting, does the child always use the same kind of stroke, or try new ones? (e.g., swirling lines, dotting with hard and soft motions)
  - » Does she enjoy mixing colors and creating new ones?
  - » During music and movement, story, or group discussions are his contributions unique and idiosyncratic, conventional, flamboyant, or perceptive?
- By what means does the child make an effort to understand what is going on? To master a skill? To solve a problem?

- Is the child easily sidetracked?
  - » Is she easily distracted by other children? By noises? By arrivals and departures?
- Does the child go through a series of steps in developing a product or an idea?
  - » Does he act hastily? Reflectively? Timidly?
- Does the child show persistence in exploring? in manipulating? in trial-and-error approaches?
  - » Does she jump from one thing to another, trying varied approaches?
- How does the child start an attack on a problem?
  - » By saying "I can't" or "I don't understand it"?
  - » By examining the situation and arriving at a thought-out action?
  - » By eliminating extraneous factors?
  - » By picking a solution out of the air?
  - » By impulsively jumping in?
  - » By testing each possibility in turn in some kind of order?
  - » By selecting the important cues?
  - » By referring to the teacher? or another child?
  - » Does the child have difficulty knowing what to do first?
- Are there indications of persistence in working on a task?
  - » Does the child concentrate on finding an answer and learning facts?
  - » Are the facts important to the child to know?
  - » Or is the process of finding out itself exciting enough? Or both?
- Which details, and how much, can the child remember of a story that has been read many times over or of an experience in or out of school?
- When games are played in which each child has a turn to guess what object or objects of a number of objects displayed have been taken away, does the child remember the missing items?
  - » Is the child aware of who is absent? Who came back to school?
- What is the child interested in?
  - » What gives him satisfaction?
- What is frustrating?
- To what is the child typically indifferent?
- Does the child seem to feel competent as a learner?
- What is important for the child to learn?
  - » What does the child's family believe is important to learn?

- Is there congruence between what the teacher wants the child to learn and what the child wants to learn?

Most of the questions in the cognitive realm will be answered in observational records that show a child in the typical actions of the day. It is not necessary to ask young children how they think or to set up special tasks for them. Thinking skills are used and strengthened by the children—and best observed by teachers—in the everyday situations of life that demand them and in the use of materials, dramatic play, and interactions with peers and adults. And that is just about everywhere.

## Records of Children Learning

In the following records of two 5-year-olds, the first child, Malik, though very controlled in his use of the paints, turned his painting into something useful and logical—an interesting game. In the second record, the children experiment with mixing paint, which becomes the focus of their activity. Is there risk-taking here?

> Malik took his smock off a nearby hook. The teacher helped him put it on, and he quickly buttoned up the front. He stepped up to the easel and looked behind it, where he found a pencil hanging by a string. Holding the pencil lightly, he leaned forward. His right arm hardly moved as, with his left hand, he meticulously wrote the letters of his name in the upper-left corner. He wrote slowly with his eyes steadfastly fixed on his task. When he finished writing his name, he carefully picked up a brush loaded with blue paint. Gradually he proceeded to move the brush across the middle of the page. He continued with this punctilious method, using only one other color, red. After carefully adding a few more horizontal and vertical lines, he stood back and made a forceful announcement: "I'm finished." He continued to study the painting. In a pleasant voice he said, "How do you like it? It's a game." He then picked up a crayon and began to draw inside the rectangles of the grid that he had painted. Slowly he drew small circles, carefully writing numbers inside of each.
> "This is a 10," he said casually, never taking his eyes off the work. He drew several more circles and put a number in each one. He stepped back and studied for a moment. "This is where you stop," he said decisively. Turning to the teacher, his eyes full of accomplishment, he asked, "How is it?"

Dean was painting one color at a time, but when he noticed two children mixing their colors, he was inspired to try to do the same.

Watching Martiza and Marcus, Dean said, "I don't like to mix my paints."

Marcus responded, "We do, because we make different colors, and you don't."

Dean then slid his painting toward the center of the table, saying, "Sometimes I mix mine, like now I'm gonna mix my red with my blue." As he said this, he carefully picked up a paint dish with his thumb and index finger. He tipped it slightly to pour a tiny bit into another paint dish. He grabbed a brush and with big swishes stirred the two colors, splashing some out of the dish. He began to rock from side to side and chant, "Stir, stir, stir," as he stirred with strokes much too big for the dish. Martiza spoke to him excitedly.

"Now it's purple! I think it's gonna make pink," she squealed.

Dean slowly and emphatically said, "It's not that purple." He stopped stirring and rocking, dropped the brush on the tray, and began to pour the red into the yellow. He was precise in his movements.

Dean, pouring, announced, "Now we're gonna make . . ." (His voice trailed off as he poured.) "Then see what we get." He grabbed the nearest brush and began to stir in short, fast strokes. He exclaimed, "I'm getting orange!"

Martiza, across the table, said smugly, "So we already got orange."

Dean didn't focus on Martiza but began to mix two more colors. His movements were quick and jerky, his eyes were wide open and gleaming, and he had a big grin on his face.

Sometimes a child may start an activity with a plan and lose it along the way. What happened to Chad in this next episode?

The children's outdoor playtime is over. The 1st-grade teacher has called for the leader and door-holders to line up. Chad, who is playing near the door, transforms himself into a locomotive. Holding his tight fists in front of his body, he pushes one hand forward sharply and along with the motion whispers "Choo." Drawing the other hand back and thrusting the first hand forward, he continues, "Choo-choo-choo-choo." His steps are short, and he skids along the ground. Suddenly, with a twirl and a flourish, he waves his arm and announces, "Batman!" The children have gathered, and he then begins stomping with one boot on a rock. As he stomps, he says loudly to the onlookers, "I'm

Superman. I'm getting more superpowers . . . Watch!" He jumps and stomps on the rock. Turning to Jessica and retaining his composure, he says authoritatively, "We're lining up now, Okay?"

Jessica makes a dash for a last turn on the slide. Then Chad makes a dash for the slide as he explains to a bewildered crowd of onlookers, "I'm locking it up now." He stops suddenly, turns sharply, and, swinging his mittens, marches to the end of the line.

Learning and thinking are both affective and cognitive. Here are several children involved in academic work. See how differently they respond emotionally and socially as well as cognitively.

The assignment was to copy groups of different shapes from the board and color them the designated colors. Tiffany was coloring quietly and seemed to be concentrating quite hard, as her eyes were fixed on her paper and she was curling her bottom lip over her teeth with her mouth open slightly. She finished coloring a group of circles and then looked up at the board, giving it a long, hard look. Then she looked at her paper. She nodded her head in surprise with her eyes and mouth wide open. She carefully erased something on her paper, then counted the circles on her paper, whispering aloud and touching each one as she counted it. But she seemed still to be unsure, for she stood up and looked carefully at Samora's paper. She erased something on Samora's paper and then something on her own. Still standing and with a serious expression on her face, she touched one area of Samora's paper and commented, "This side—more better." She helped Samora by erasing and writing on her paper, then turned and scurried to the blackboard with a quizzical look on her face. She counted the shapes, touching each one. Her knitted brow suggested intense concentration. She scurried back to her seat and counted the shapes on her own paper, on Samora's, and on those of other children at her table. After counting the shapes on the paper of the girl across from her, she sat down slowly, turned to Samora, and said, "She got 10, and I got 10."

The student teacher came to the table and complimented Samora on her work. Tiffany stared at them. Billy came over and announced, "I always get mine right." Tiffany boasted haughtily, "I always get mine right too—and it's not crooked like yours."

Ms. Chu reminds Bryant that he needs to work on his math. Slowly he drags himself to the shelves, bypassing the math folders, and pulls out a basket of Unifix cubes. He hauls the basket to an unoccupied table as if it weighed a thousand pounds. Barely lifting the basket, he slides it to the middle of the table, then drops into an empty seat and stares at the cubes.

Bryant turns to watch someone walk by, then returns to staring at the cubes. He drops one hand limply into the basket and sifts through the cubes. Finally, he pulls out three red cubes and places them on the table. He picks out a few more red cubes and a few blue ones. He starts stacking them neatly on top of one another. Then, scooting closer to the edge of the chair and using both hands, he begins to arrange the stacks vertically and horizontally to form a geometric structure. Thoughtfully, he begins to test and balance the stacks in a purposeful effort to arrange them to his satisfaction. Now his tongue appears, pointing toward his nose. Slowly it begins to move from one corner of his mouth to the other as he concentrates on placing the red cubes diagonally across the blues.

Luke bounces over and wiggles into the chair next to Bryant. He starts talking a mile a minute as he begins stacking some cubes. They talk about forts and canons. Luke demonstrates a canon's blast with a loud "Pooooouush!"

Bryant brings his attention back to his own structure and becomes intently involved in his project once again. He looks only at his creation and does not become involved with Luke. He says something to himself about the stacks, and then, for no apparent reason, one of the stacks topples over. His eyes and mouth open wide in shock. "Oh-h-h-h," he whines sadly as he bends over to pick up the fallen cubes from the floor. As he returns to an upright position, he clenches his fists and thrusts them downward to show his frustration.

Ava walks by and accidentally bumps into the table. "Oops, sorry," she says as half of Bryant's creation crumbles and falls. A long drawn-out "Oooooo" pierces the air as Bryant's shoulders go up and his hands make an ineffective attempt to catch the pieces. His face is red with anger but slowly turns to pink as he begins once more to rebuild. Eventually his face regains its natural color and composure.

Now the structure is complete, and Bryant looks proudly at it. When anyone gets too close or even breathes on it, he puts his hands up as if to catch it.

The teacher informs everyone that it is time to come to a short meeting and that all the children must clean up their work materials. Bryant is reluctant to disassemble his creation, but he finally does, very slowly and painfully.

## HOW MUCH DOES A CHILD KNOW?

There are certain kinds of information about the world and the self that most children with average opportunities seem to learn on their own, and it is reasonable to expect a young child to have the beginnings of information in many of the areas indicated below. Naturally, age makes a difference in the accumulation of knowledge and what children make of that information; so does opportunity (including the role of helpful adults), and so do individual interests and readiness for certain kinds of information. To some extent, however, knowledge gathered by children is an indicator of curiosity as well as of memory. But misconceptions abound in childhood, even in the most knowledgeable children, so teachers need to be sensitive to how accurate—or how confused—children's information is within the limitations imposed by their level of development. Be careful not to be misled by an easy flow of words that children could be repeating without understanding.

### Details to Observe

The suggested questions that follow should not be used as a list of what every child *should* know. Your records will be a source from which you may extrapolate evidence of the child's arena of knowledge.

- What does the child know about the body?
  - » Can she name the body parts? Which parts?
  - » Does he know what different body parts do?
  - » Does the child refer to him or herself as a boy or a girl?
- What does a child know about his family?
  - » Does the child know who is in her immediate family? Extended family? Her relation to them?
  - » Does the child understand the meaning of words such as *daughter, son, sister, brother, grandmother, uncle, aunt,* and their relationship to *self, mother, father*?
- What does the child know about family structures other than his own?
  - » Does she recognize that differences exist among families?
  - » Can he generalize a definition of "family"?
- What does the child know about work roles?
  - » Does she know what members of her family work at?
  - » Does he know what storekeepers, police officers, garbage collectors, coin booth agents, garage mechanics actually do?

» Does the child have a sense of what a community is and why people work?

A glimmer of the difference between the reality of adult work and the preparatory nature of child's play appears in this 4-year-old's astute comment:

> Watching his parents painting the kitchen, Tyrone asked several times if he could paint too and they said no. Finally, he said pensively, "Grown-ups have lots of things, and kids have just one thing, right?"
> "What do you mean, one thing?" his mother asked.
> "Grownups have lots of things," he said, "and kids just have toys."

> Four-year-old Farah, who had visited her father's law office, described his work as follows: "He just sits there and gives out pencils and paper clips when the people need them." In the same vein, when Mark brought some tapes to school, he explained to the teacher, "My uncle gave them to me when he opened his store. He sells tapes, money, and children."

Lawyers and selling are difficult concepts for 4-year-olds.

- Does the child have knowledge of observable, concrete, mechanical processes?
  » Does the child know what makes a car go? Is it the adult? Gas? The steering wheel? The engine?
  » Does she know what makes electric lights go on and off? Is it the switch? Wires in the wall?
  » Does he know what makes water flow in a sink? Is it turning on the faucet? Is it the pipes below?
- Does she have knowledge of natural processes of birth, growth, death, the sources of food?
  » Does he know where babies come from?
  » Does she know what a flower, a fish, or a child need in order to grow? For example, when Shari, age 4, says, "The plant needs water to grow and then it will open by magic," what is she clear about, and what does she mean by magic?
  » Does the child have an idea of what happens when a flower or a person dies? Where eggs come from? Oranges? Milk? Cheese? Tuna fish? Bacon?
- Does he have knowledge of animals—domestic, wild, prehistoric, imaginary? At first children generalize from the one animal they know, and all four-legged creatures could be

dogs, cows, or whatever. In time they differentiate one animal from another.

» Does she know the names of common domestic animals?
» Does he know anything about the life-styles and habits of common domestic animals?
» Is she able to recognize pictures or models of wild or prehistoric animals?
» Does he know which animals are alive now and which lived long ago?
» Does she recognize the difference between imaginary and real animals?
» Does he make up imaginary animals?
• Does he have knowledge from specialized experience?

Children from a range of economic and cultural backgrounds may have particular information stemming from their experiences. They may know about varied kinds of food; about techniques of gathering fruit from trees; about what happens in churches, hospital emergency rooms, public assistance offices, or shelters; about country homes or jet trips; about nannies and play dates; about how to go alone to the supermarket and back along the safest route; or even about what happens at racetracks. This knowledge is a valid indicator that a child is learning and requires acceptance and understanding by the teacher.

### How Do Teachers Find Out What Children Know?

Children's knowledge about themselves in relation to their families, about what they like and what they feel, is likely to be verbalized mainly in intimate situations—alone with the teacher, in conversations with other children, or in discussions focused on family life and relationships. It is tempting to ask young children personal questions, but this is not fair and to an extent is an invasion of privacy.

When children trust adults, they will speak of what is important to them. Evidence of the child's knowledge of the world and self will probably come mostly from remarks made by the child; from questions the child asks during class trips and subsequent group discussions; from responses to stories read by the teacher or to a book a child is looking at alone; from questions or remarks during cooking or science experiments or while building with blocks. Records of these activities are likely to be a more valid indicator of what a child knows than what he does during dramatic play, although information is revealed there too.

During dramatic play the child's feelings and needs often dominate what is said and done. Fantasy mingles with reality as children work away at resolving issues related to their wishes, fears, aggressions, and ambitions in self-created, imaginary situations. During dramatic play children may drive a car up the side of a building, or put cows in the bedroom with the baby, although they may recognize, if asked, that such things do not really happen. For this reason, teachers need to be wary of hastening to correct inaccuracies revealed during dramatic play, and while the play may offer rich material for interpretation, such interpretation should be done cautiously.

Books and pictures and play materials must contain images with which young children can identify. Books must show children and adults of color, of varied cultural groups, with disabilities; and families that include single parents (either mother or father), grandparents, and families with two mothers or two fathers, with one child or several. We must bring the wide world of children and adults into our classrooms so that no child feels excluded by the available representation.

As has been indicated, actual information is as much the result of opportunity to experience as of readiness to learn. All too often, the information a child has is unfamiliar to a teacher who does not know the context in which it is valid, and it is therefore underestimated. However, every child, within any context, can and does reveal the capacity for thought in a number of processes that reveal a mind at work. For example, a 5-year-old child worked away at a fairly intricate puzzle showing a steam shovel at work while men were setting dynamite. The child worked through trial and error, and then his perception improved visibly as he sought matching shapes. He completed the puzzle in good time, but when asked about the picture, he shrugged his shoulders and said, "I dunno." The capacity to do a puzzle showed a good mind. The lack of knowledge showed a different world of exposure. The two must not be confused, and certainly one realm of knowledge is not more or less valuable than another.

It is not in the children's best interest to consider the rote accumulation of information as the goal of intellectual development. Knowledge of facts is by no means the only or even the best indication of a mind at work, although it is one. Especially among children whose lives were begun in one kind of environment and for whom school represents a very different one, it is important, as the children's teacher, to place greater emphasis on trying to understand *how* these children approach learning than on *what*, at their very young ages, they already know. But this truth is valid for all children; a good attitude toward learning will carry them through life much more effectively than specific information learned earlier rather than later.

# 9

# Observing Children
# Develop the Power to Think

In Chapters 7 and 8 we focused on both the developmental aspects and the individual characteristics of children's approach to thinking. These approaches are embedded in *thought processes* that characterize children's burgeoning intellectual power during the early childhood years. By observing children closely in many kinds of situations, such as their involvement in dramatic play, their use of materials, and their relationships to adults and other children, we can see what we assume to be indications of these thought processes developing. This chapter focuses on behaviors that have become associated with those internal, impossible-to-observe-directly processes we call "cognition." The following described processes are meant to serve as a *guide to better understanding of children*—not as a standard for measuring children's intellectual abilities. This may seem to be a subtle difference, but the key word here is *understanding*, not *measuring*.

## FORMING GENERALIZATIONS

Out of their play, experimentation, exploration, and varied experiences with their families, friends, cultures, and communities, children form generalizations, which are for them true discoveries because they are based on their own observations. This process begins early in infancy and never really ceases.

> For several days after a heavy snowfall, 2-year-old Mike spent a good part of the outdoor playtime gleefully throwing snowballs against a wall of the school building. Finally, he went to the teacher and said, "Snow breaks into little pieces."

Uncovering principles is a major occupation of children who are learning. It is most effective when children come to conclusions on their own or with the guidance of an adult or another child (Rogoff, 1990). Teaching them to repeat a principle verbally, by rote, does not have the same effect.

> Six-year-old Kara is working on a building in the block area. She goes to the shelf and counts out the number of unit blocks as she removes them. "One, two, three, four, five, six." She lifts the stack of blocks into her hands and rests her chin on top to hold the stack in place.
>
> She looks at the teacher, who comments, "You have a lot of blocks there."
>
> "I needed an even number so I picked six," she says.
>
> "Why an even number?" the teacher inquired.
>
> "Because," she explains, "I need to stack them in two, and I would have one left over, and then I'd have to go back."

## ABILITY TO DIFFERENTIATE

Children's generalizations enable them in time to make comparisons among objects, people, or events. Using all their senses, they learn to differentiate:

- Between themselves and others
  - » Does a child speak of himself in the third person or as I, me, mine?
- Between family members and friends
  - » Does the child know which are friends?
  - » Which are family? (a distinction that can be both cultural and family-specific, e.g., "Aunt" Ettie may be a close family friend)
  - » Which are older? Which are younger?

> Daniel and his friend Tanisha (both 5) are visiting Daniel's grandmother. They are drawing. Suddenly Daniel asks his grandmother, "Are you Tanisha'a grandma?"
>
> Tanisha intercepts, "No—she's not my grandma."
>
> "Why not?" asks his grandmother.
>
> "Because Daniel's my *friend*," says Tanisha.

- Between animate and inanimate
  - » Does a child know whether a stone, a bug, a tree is alive?
- Between fantasy and reality
  - » Does the child know whether Superman is real?

&raquo; When do children begin to understand that fairy tales or television programs are make-believe?

- Between male and female.

  Carmella, age 3, observes a female student teacher with facial hair and asks, "Are you a boy or a girl?" The student teacher replies, "I'm a girl." The child then says, "But you have a mustache."

- Among people of different skin colors

  Mattie (age 6) comes up to the teacher, stretches her arms, rotates them, and says, "My arm is darker on the outside than the inside because my father is dark and my mother is light."

  Cody's father, who is White, brings Cody, who is African American, to kindergarten every day. One day, Brenda, curious, asks "Is *that* Cody's father?"

  Natan (White, 11 months) has a caregiver named Charlotte who has dark skin. He calls her "Da-da." When he is on the street with his mother, he points to each woman with dark skin and says "da da."

### ABILITY TO PERCEIVE SIMILARITIES AND DIFFERENCES

Children's ability to see that similarities and differences exist in objects as well as people prevents them from coming to mistaken conclusions. Comparisons enrich children's perception of the reality around them, add to their vocabulary, and help them distinguish the salient properties of materials and objects. Such comparisons are critical in reading, for example, to know that "was" and "saw" or "feel" and "feet," while similar, are different.

> Two 4-year-olds are fingering their short ponytails.
> *Sophie*: Mine is longer.
> *Karena*: No, the same.
> (They come closer and touch each other's hair.)
> *Sophie*: My ponytail has more hair.

### ABILITY TO DRAW ANALOGIES

Drawing analogies, or creating metaphors, is another form of symbolization. Instead of using their bodies in the play-mode to understand parts of their experience, children use words to link together two unlike actions or objects in order to more clearly comprehend them.

Franklin, who has had a fracture, remarks knowingly at lunchtime, "Peeling a banana is like taking a cast off."

Avram, examining carrot tops set in a dish of water that have just started to sprout, says, "These look like my daddy's little whiskers."

Shi-jen, gazing at a huge crane with two arms atop the steel skeleton of a skyscraper, says, "It looks like a giant bird."

## ABILITY TO PERCEIVE CAUSE AND EFFECT

It is easier for children to understand causality in physical phenomena than to understand it in social relations, where their feelings are involved. It is important to listen for the causes children attribute to specific events and phenomena as a way of assessing what they do and do not understand and what they are confused about. Even their errors reveal their struggle to understand, as in these records, where they are groping for an explanation of cause. The first record is from 2-year-olds; the second, from 4-year-olds; the last, from 6-year-olds.

Ellen hits Joe, and Joe cries. Ellen asks her teacher, "Why Joe crying?"

*Joel*: I'm the sunshine. I'm going up in the sky and stay there.
*Steve*: Won't you ever come down?
*Joel*: The sun doesn't shine all the time. When it gets dark, I'll come down.
*Teacher*: What makes it get dark?
*Joel*: The moon makes it get dark.
*Vincent*: Oh, no. God makes it get dark.

"Why did you stick your tongue out at me on the playground?" asks Nicholas.
Seth, still a little angry, replies, "Just because Mr. Carr said I knocked Gabe's building down, and he made me sit alone."
They both walk over to their lunch boxes, and Nicholas says in a very serious tone, "I still don't like that, Seth."

Some of this understanding, or lack of it, is a matter of age. But a good deal is due to experience (or lack of experience) with the specific phenomenon or event. A 4- to 6-year-old may say that the food she eats stays in her stomach, and after she has eaten a lot of food, her stomach will get fat and there will be a baby in her stomach. At this stage of development, a child is aware that there is a cause for the presence of the baby, but she attributes the wrong cause for the effect, selecting as the cause a personally experienced happening. Older children are able to solve problems even with more abstract or less directly experienced actions.

## TIME ORIENTATION

Children learn to use the words *when, soon, later, remember, last, next week, next year* before they can fully conceptualize the meaning of time. They incorporate the words in their play as well as in their communication with others, using them correctly in context on the whole but missing out on the more remote, abstract concept of what time is. Simultaneously, however, in their use of language in play and conversation, children may be engaging in a process of learning more precisely what the conceptual meanings of words are.

> "And every day I go to work, all right?" says Angelo in the housekeeping corner.

> "In two weeks is Christmas," says Cynthia, although it is actually a month away.

When a child says that he visited his grandma in Florida yesterday (but you saw him in school), does he know that he really didn't? Or does he categorize all past events as occurring "yesterday?" And a 4-year-old, who was told the birds were migrating because the seasons were changing, agreed heartily. "Yes," he said. "The birds will fly north in the summer and south in the winter, and time will fly."

How well do children understand time? *Now* is more convincing than *tomorrow* and far more concrete than *yesterday.*

> Alfredo, age 4, arrived in school after an absence and burst into the room exuberantly, shouting, "I'm here!"
> "Were you sick?" the teacher asked.
> "No," Alfredo answered, "in Puerto Rico."
> "Did you get back yesterday?" asked the teacher.
> "No," answered Alfredo, "tomorrow, in 3 weeks."

Time is an elusive concept, and even as late as 5, children can show both their beginning grasp of it and their resistance to accepting its structure over their egocentric wishes, or their ability to use the language of time in a precise manner, as the following record of two 5-year-olds shows:

> *Abdulla*: You're always hitting me. I'm not playing with you anymore.
> *Ronnie*: Are you sorry when you hit me?
> *Abdulla*: Yes, but I'm not playing space creatures with you.
> *Ronnie*: But you said yesterday you'd play space creatures with me, and that's today.
> *Abdulla*: I didn't mean today. This isn't the tomorrow I meant. I meant another tomorrow.

A sense of time begins with a sense of order and sequence:

- Does the child know the usual daily schedules? For example, does she know she goes outdoors to play first, that a snack is before a story?
- Does he know on which days of the week he stays home and on which days he goes to school?
- Does she know the order of the days of the week? The order of the seasons?

## ABILITY TO CLASSIFY

Children reveal their ability to classify and seriate in informal as well as formal situations. Often they combine the two, as 5-year-old Jasper did with classroom material deliberately designed to encourage classification. The record also reveals his ability to symbolize—the circles stand for hamburgers and, when rearranged, a snowman.

> Jasper has just walked over to the shelf and taken down a box divided into three compartments, each containing circles, squares, and triangles of varying size. He quietly places the box on his table, takes off the lid, using both hands, and places it under the box.
> He removes the circles first, looks up, and says, "Hamburgers." He looks around for Bobby, spots him at a nearby table, and says playfully, "Bobby, want some hamburgers?" He then arranges the circles in a sequential order from largest to smallest across the table. He then looks up, makes eye contact with the teacher, points, and says "Largest, smallest." His voice is loud and animated. He seems pleased with himself and his work. A huge smile appears on his face.

He rearranges the circles and says, "A snowman." He is aware of other activities in the room, since he leaves his work and walks over to Bobby to see what he is making.

When Jasper returns to his table, he pauses for a few seconds and then announces, "I want to make a car. I've got to try and do a car." As he slowly removes the squares, he looks over at Tiernan, who has the same materials. They begin chatting excitedly about monsters, and when the conversation ends, Jasper hums contentedly as he arranges the squares in various patterns. First he arranges them in a sequence from largest to smallest, proceeding from left to right. Then he takes the triangles out and places them above the squares, again in sequential order of size. He observes that two are missing and looks over at Tiernan's table. He sees that Tiernan's set is complete and asks the teacher where the missing triangles are. She tells him she doesn't know, and he comments ruefully, "Probably lost." He has difficulty picking the pieces up and experiments with many gestures of his fingers. Finally, he slides the pieces off the edge of the table one at a time and places them in the box, again from largest to smallest.

The ability to classify is likely to develop from recognition of concrete qualities that are observable through the senses to recognition of abstract ones that must be conceptualized. Color, shape, and size can be seen and are easier to learn about and to categorize than something nonconcrete like direction or theme. All classification, however, depends on the perception of similarities and differences. When there has been a good deal of concrete experience in perceiving similarity and difference, with and without adult guidance, children will often attempt to classify at a simple level of abstraction. Thus, a child who tried to place a newcomer to the classroom into a recently grasped understanding of group membership asked, "What are you? Christmas, Chanukah, or Vegetarian?" The facts may have been distorted, but the thinking process was on target. (Note: It is easier to correct facts than to change processes.)

## PERCEIVING PATTERNS

The ability to perceive patterns (visually, tactually, or aurally) is a basic underpinning for learning to read. The patterns of the written language vary from one culture to another. The descriptions that follow are focused on languages that are encoded from left to right. In Western societies, children must learn the pattern of moving their eyes from left to right across the page and down to the left for the beginning of the next line. They must recognize the pattern of left to right in the letters of each word and the pattern of words and spaces across a page. They must learn not only the pattern of marks made up of letters for each word but that patterns of words vary in sizes—from little patterns ("it") to big patterns ("there")—and that some patterns are alike ("the," "the") and others are not alike ("dog," "mouse"). (For an excellent discussion of this, see Clay, 1991.)

See how differently two 5-year-old children respond to the opportunity to form patterns out of colored pegs. Jessie proceeds smoothly, while Anya does not seem to notice:

> Anya and Jessie are sitting next to each other, each with her own peg board but sharing a basket of wooden pegs. There are cardboard pattern cards in a box in the middle of the table, created by the teacher to help children work on directionality. The cards are the same size as the peg board and have differently colored dots in patterns. Jessie selects a pattern card with an alternating pattern of red, yellow, and blue dots going around the perimeter. She places the card to the left of the board so that the card and the board are adjacent to each other. She begins to replicate the pattern from the card onto the board, going from left to right across the bottom. Meanwhile, Anya, who did not select a pattern card, haphazardly places pegs in the board without producing any apparent pattern. She says to Jessie, "Look what I made." Jessie looks up, regards Anya's board, and shrugs.

The differences in their responses offers clues to the teacher. Does Anya choose to ignore the opportunity to create a pattern, or does she fail to notice it?

## UNDERSTANDING SPATIAL RELATIONSHIPS

A child's sensitivity to pattern and awareness of space is readily observed during music and movement and when using puzzles, building with blocks, and playing outdoors. The following list of details to observe will enable you to expand your appreciation of the child's comfort or discomfort in space.

- Does the child respond with bodily movements or instruments to the rhythm of the music being played, the drumbeat, or the teacher's clapping?

- Does the child maintain an individual rhythm at variance with or in accordance with the rhythm being played?
- How does the child use space? (sweeps the room, stays in one spot, likes to jump)
- Does the child move with, or against, others? Does he seem confused as to which way to go?
- During group games does the child follow patterns and directions?

When a child doing a jigsaw puzzle tries every piece in order to find out which fits, it is clear that she is working by trial and error and is not yet able to perceive either visually or tactually the relationship between a space and the corresponding shape of the piece of the puzzle. By the same token, the child who holds a piece while her eyes roam over the puzzle and then places the piece accurately shows a grasp of spatial relationships that marks a different level of development. Many of the materials and equipment that children use will demand awareness of spatial relationships, and teachers can be thinking of a number of questions as they observe children at play with puzzles or blocks.

- Does the child recognize that a space between two block buildings is large enough for the truck to get through? That a double-unit block will just bridge the space between two upright blocks?
- Does the child know how to get from the classroom to the kitchen? How to get to school from home?
- In solving spatial, construction, and other physical problems, does the child manipulate the objects involved? For example, in order to determine how to place a "Stop" sign in the road Luis has built so that it could be seen from the road, he first placed it on one side, apparently realized that it was not visible there, and then placed it on the other side of the road, where it was visible.
- Does the child recognize that a box is too large for the available space on the shelf?
- Are children aware of space relationships in drawing?

Shannon and Keisha, both 7, are carefully sketching a face on the class pumpkin preparatory to carving it. Shannon decides she will do the eyes and nose and Keisha can do the mouth. They agree. Shannon begins to design her part, carefully sketching the eyes first and then the nose. She checks the placement and appropriate size of the nose. As she finishes, she says to Keisha, "Make a mouth that goes with what I do." After a few minutes of laughing and giggling, Keisha suggests they cut out the parts they have drawn. Shannon notices Keisha's mouth drawing and says, "You should have made it a little smaller, but my nose is too fat too."

Young children work very hard and seriously in their attempt to understand the world of people, events, and objects. Observations done with respect for the child's thought processes, awareness of the content and extent of his knowledge, and understanding of the effects of culture, family, community, and school will yield information to help teachers choose appropriate materials and plan relevant curriculum.

# 10

# Recording Children's Developing Language and Emerging Literacy

All children in every community who are in contact with more mature speakers learn to speak unless they have a specific impairment. In learning language children simultaneously learn the values and shared meanings of their culture. By means of language they construct the reality in which they live and form a way of being related to others.

They acquire this astonishing linguistic ability, which seems nothing short of a miracle, in the context of their interaction with intimately related people during "shared activities" (Rogoff, 1990, p. 209). Children learn right off in babyhood that language is for communication and for sharing meanings about experience (Stern, 1985) in which they, as well as adults and older children, play a central role. They pick up the sounds, meaning, and syntax of the language they hear and use it creatively to say what they need to say. Through language, children begin to create "a narrative of [their] own life" (p. 162).

## LANGUAGE AND CULTURE

The amount and style of children's language use differs depending on what's important in the particular social and cultural environment in which they are reared.

> The *sequence* of language development (i.e., cooing, babbling, first-word production, etc.) in young children is biologically determined and follows a fairly consistent pattern, regardless of one's cultural context. What we do see vary from culture to culture is how parents think about children as communication partners, which in turn influences language development. . . . Anderson and Battle (1993) have identified the following aspects of communicative competence that vary from culture to culture:
> - The child's main communication partners
> - The interaction styles that are encouraged or discouraged between the child and her communication partners

- The topics of conversation that are allowed or forbidden
- How highly participants value talk
- What the caretakers believe about teaching language and how consciously structured the language teaching is. (Mann, Steward, Eggbeer, & Norton, 2007, p. 10)

The language and social interaction aspects of a child's community influence that child's ability to adapt to the school's literacy expectations. Some families are more likely than others to socialize their children into the authority of books and the question/answer sequences in story reading that is so often used in classrooms. Some children are not reared in settings where they learn school discourse. While it may be important in certain communities for young children to

> learn to attend to the nuances of differences between small, two-dimensional shapes, . . . such a focus may not matter in other communities, where it may be more important for young children to learn to attend to the nuances of weather patterns or of social cues, to use words cleverly to joust, or to understand the relations between human and supernatural events. (Rogoff, Mistry, Goncu, & Mosier, 1993, pp. 9–10)

Awareness of these variations is critical for teachers in order to understand that what appears to be a deficit in language or in literacy may be a cultural difference. According to Hurley and Tinajero (2001), "speakers of languages other than English use discourse styles and patterns that vary greatly from English." They specify Spanish and Native American languages as nonlinear. Spanish-speaking students writing in English

> often use discourse patterns of their native language. . . . [T]herefore, a writing rubric that is based on the linear logic of English may have as a standard that good stories have a beginning, middle, and end. Students writing in Spanish may not use this linear logic when writing and, thus, be judged as noncompetent writers. (p. 46)

Observing and recording children's language introduces teachers to children's understanding of their world, to what is meaningful to them and their families, and to each child's unique approach to solving problems. In order to truly learn about children from their language, *teachers must try to avoid assigning the goals of their own language to those of the child.* For example, although a teacher may value verbal give-and-take with children, other adults with whom a child is affiliated may not. Understanding that a child's language is a reflection of deeply held beliefs challenges teachers to examine their own language as an indication of their own cherished values.

Teachers also need to think about ways to foster children's primary language in school. Observing and recording children's language involves accepting and respecting the broad diversity with which children speak. Although teachers may be tempted to correct children's use of nonstandard linguistic forms, Delpit (1995) states that this has no effect on altering children's manner of speaking and may, as stated in the seminal work of Cazden, John, and Hymes (1972), produce negative effects such as resistance to learning standard forms. Delpit (2002) urges teachers of children who speak nonstandard forms to recognize the meaning conveyed and to provide opportunities to "become involved with standard forms through various kinds of role play. . . . Young students can create puppet shows or role play cartoon characters" (pp. 125–126). This provides young children with practice using the standard form. When children present puppet shows featuring well-known characters who speak standard forms, the *characters* are held to the standard, eliminating any intimation that the *child's* language is inadequate.

As in all growth that is developmental, the interaction of environmental support, individual differences, and culture may bring children of the same age to different levels and styles of language facility. Awareness of those elements of language that give children the full power they need to express anything will facilitate teachers' observation of what use the children make of the language they do use. Teachers are reminded that

> It is not that a child does not know a word, but that he pronounces it in one social dialect, rather than another. Not that a child cannot express himself or that a thought cannot be required of him, but that he expresses it in one style of expression rather than another. Not that a child cannot answer questions, but that questions and answers are defined for him in terms of one set of community norms rather than another, as to what count as questions and answers and as to what it means to be asked or to answer. (Cazden, John, & Hymes, 1972, p. xxx)

Language, according to the seminal work of Bram (1955), "initiates the child to the esprit de corps of his speech community . . . and provides the feeling of belonging" (p. 19).

## RECORDING CHILDREN'S USE OF LANGUAGE

What discoveries await you when you begin recording children's language! Something of children's social interchanges, their humor, and their comprehension will be there in your records. You will also be able to reflect on children's differing narrative styles, especially through capturing storytellers-in-action. The range and use of vocabulary will yield clues about a child's facility with words.

## Social Purposes

Most children experience language in a social context even before uttering their own first murmurs and coos. Through the verbal (and nonverbal) intimacy of their earliest relationships, children experience turn-taking—the basis of all conversation.

- What is the range of the child's use of language for social purposes? To express wants and needs? To share pleasures? To complain? To demand, plead, beseech, cajole, or control? To give, share, or gain information?
- Is the child's language directed to adults or to children, or is it equally distributed?
- In what manner does the child communicate as she goes through the normal activities of the day? With facility? With assertion? With restraint? With affection? With hostility?

The following 3-year-olds are struggling to develop relationships, and it is quite a feat to put their needs into verbal terms. A year earlier they could not have done it.

Kristen and Jill are sitting in a small barrel very close to each other, their bodies touching. Their knees are bent, and they are crouching in the small space. They nuzzle up closer together and casually touch heads. They stay in this position for a while without saying a word. Kristen pulls her head away, moves closer to Jill, and gently kisses her on the cheek. Jill lowers her head slightly, and Kristen lifts her arm and puts it gently around Jill's shoulder. Their heads touch. Suddenly a loud voice comes from the barrel. "Are you my friend? Are you my friend?" It is Kristen. She continues to ask the question in a moderately loud and clear voice. She raises herself up onto her knees and brings her head close to Jill's face. Jill sits with one arm resting on the side of the barrel and looks away from Kristen.

Kristen urgently asks again, "Are you my friend?" Jill turns her head further away. Kristen puckers her lips and, looking at the teacher, says, "I want Jill to be my friend, but she won't listen to me."

"That's a problem," the teacher says sympathetically. Kristen continues to look at the teacher and puckers her mouth. The teacher approaches the girls and tries to make eye contact with Jill, but Jill continues to look away. The teacher says to Jill, "Jill, Kristen is asking you a question, and you need to answer her." Jill continues to look away. The teacher looks at Kristen and suggests she ask Jill again.

"Jill, are you my friend?" Without looking at her, Jill replies in a whining voice, "No, I don't want to." She seems to be forcefully pushing the words out of her mouth.

It is in a social context that language learning and understanding relationships take place, first in the family and increasingly within the child care and school environment. Because Jill and Kristen's language and their social experience are still developing, their means of resolving their relationship is limited. A teacher, working with 3-year-olds, perceived that

> of all the relationships children explore in the classroom setting, making friends is arguably the most important to them . . . . As I continued to observe the transitory nature of their friendships, I realized that the youngsters used these phrases *in order to find out what they mean*. This realization cast the issue in a different light. I slowly came to understand that, similar to the resistance to routines, moments of conflict provided opportunities for the children to explore and experience the skills of seeking and maintaining friendships. (Gibson, 1989, pp. 40–41; emphasis in original)

The next episode is a typical social situation among 4-year-olds who are using language instead of hands and feet to try to resolve a difference in views:

> Joey walks determinedly up to Anthony and Juan Carlos after cleanup time, angrily pokes his finger repeatedly at the two boys, and cries bossily, "What's the big idea! I was sitting here."
>
> Anthony and Juan Carlos ignore him by looking the other way and talking to the other children around them. Joey, however, insists. "I was sitting here! I was sitting here! I was sitting here!"
>
> Anthony impishly raises his eyebrows, looks Joey right in the eye, points his finger at Juan Carlos, and says in self-defense, "He took your seat."
>
> Juan Carlos starts to defend himself, "Well, I—" Joey haughtily cuts him off declaring, "I'm not going to give you this," and takes a shiny turquoise-blue butterfly pin from his pocket and handles it admiringly.

As the 1st-grade boy and girl in the following anecdote explore social conventions, they make some discoveries about contrasting family experiences:

> Lucy and Julian are holding hands. Lucy says, "I want you to be my boyfriend. You are very pretty." She stretches her face toward him, puckers her lips, and closes her eyes, waiting for him to kiss her. He looks at her with amazement. In an annoyed tone she asks, "Why don't you want to kiss me? You never kissed a girl before?"
>
> Julian says, "Yes, my sister."
>
> Lucy replies, "Well, you are dumb. I have lots of boyfriends, and they kiss me on the lips. Like this." With that, she plants a sloppy kiss on his face. Shocked and annoyed, he wipes off the moisture from his face.
>
> Lucy asks, "Did you like that, Julian?"
>
> He wrinkles his brow and exclaims, "What! That sloppy thing you did on my face? I hated it! Don't do it again or else I will punch you in the nose!"
>
> Lucy moans, "You are really dumb if you call it sloppy. My mommy and daddy do it."
>
> Julian grunts, "My daddy wouldn't do something like that. He is real big and strong, and if my mommy does kiss him like that, he would slap her."
>
> Lucy's eyes open wide. "Your daddy slap your mommy?"
>
> "All the time," Julian replies. "And my mommy cries and my baby sister cries, but I don't cry. I just close my room door."
>
> Lucy opens her mouth as if to speak, but no words come out. She shakes her head and whispers, "My daddy never hits my mommy, only kisses her."

Since the revelation of such intimate information is not unusual for some young children, hearing it, teachers may experience a conflict with their own cultural values. There are implications for the teacher's role in recording this conversation. Surely this role is to help Julian and Lucy in a nonjudgmental, supportive manner to understand that families differ without exposing either of them to criticism or ridicule. The observation is also a signal for the teacher to consult with another professional on how to assess this information about a possibly abusive situation and what steps are appropriate.

As you record children talking to one another, or to an adult, you will find instances of using language to express thinking, to exchange information, to conceptualize, to reason, and to describe. Children in a social context ask questions and wonder. Listen to two 2nd-graders thinking together about some basic questions.

> Ernest says to Gustav, "Let's go see the gerbil's grave."
>
> Gustav objects, "She's in heaven."

> Ernest confidently explains, "Not to heaven yet. Once I buried a
> bird, and it took a long time for it to go to heaven."

How much of young children's social language is without words!
Who has not heard a child use "noises" to communicate opinions or
feelings—"yuk," or vomit, belch, or flatulence sounds? In the following
record, a 3- and a 4-year-old's social exchange is mainly nonverbal.

> Shau Lee is a 3-year-old, Chinese-speaking child. Enrico, age 4, speaks
> only Spanish. They are playing at the foot of the slide, pushing one little
> car at a time up the ramp to another child at the top, who then sends it
> back down. When Shau Lee sends her car up the third time, the child at
> the top walks away with it. So Shau Lee grabs Enrico's car. He hangs on
> to it and yells, "*Mio!*" Shau Lee cries out, "Teach!" but the teacher is out
> of earshot. Enrico joins in with "Teach! Teach!" All the while both chil-
> dren are hanging on to and pulling on the car. Shau Lee raises her hand
> and touches Enrico's hair as if to pull it. He does the same, but neither
> actually pulls hair. They push one another. Suddenly the child returns
> with Shau Lee's car and slides it down. Shau Lee lets go, grabs her own
> car, and smiles. Enrico smiles at her and says, "*Te lo dije este era mio* (I
> told you that was mine)." They continue on the slide as if nothing had
> happened.

**Humor**

Humor comes from the recognition of incongruities. Young children laugh heartily when they experience the unexpected, such as a
sudden bump at the end of a slide, or when they fool the teacher by
asking for help, then help themselves. Their newly achieved physical
control makes noncontrol incongruous and therefore very funny. But
it takes a certain level of maturity in comprehending both words and
concepts to see incongruity in verbal terms. You have to know what is
incongruous before you can find it funny. In the following episodes,
the references were concrete and comprehensible to the 4-year-old
children:

> Elliot, his eyes sparkling, says, "You don't eat lunch boxes!"
> Keith responds, "You eat Cheerios." And both giggle at their joke.

> Nils spies Candy, who has just come in out of the rain. He asks, quite
> seriously, "Candy, do you have a haircut today?" Candy laughs delight-
> edly and tells him she washed her hair in the rain.

To these 5-year-olds, the incongruity is in areas a bit more abstract:

> Yoni tells the children in an authoritative voice, "My coat is not to go in the rain." Someone asks why. Yoni's face lights up and he says, delightedly, "It melts!"

> Scott says to Leni, the cook, who has entered the classroom, "You cook good, Leni."
> Leni replies gushingly, "Oh, thank you sweetie."
> Scott giggles with Pablo, as they both repeat, "Sweetie?" Later Leni reenters, and Scott says, "Hello sweetie, hello sweetie," with a mischievous giggle.
> Pablo imitates him, saying to Leni, "Hello darling."
> Scott tells Leni, "He called you darling."
> Leni says, "That's okay. He's my boyfriend."
> Scott and Pablo look at each other with a jerk of the head, pursed lips, and feigned surprise and shock, and then erupt into gales of laughter.

Does a child understand and use puns? Here's a dialogue showing how 5-and-a-half-year-old Francesco does.

> *Francesco*: Knock knock.
> *Teacher*: Who's there?
> *Francesco*: Banana. Knock knock.
> *Teacher*: Who's there?
> *Francesco*: Banana. Knock knock.
> *Teacher*: Who's there?
> *Francesco*: Orange.
> *Teacher*: Orange who?
> *Francesco*: Orange you glad I didn't say banana?
> He folds over in laughter.

Does a child make up chants? Three-year-old Kai is in the bathroom enjoying a soapy sponge and chanting:

> Aren't you glad I cleaned the mirror?
> Aren't you glad I cleaned the wall?
> Aren't you glad I cleaned the floor?

Nikki, age 6, is playing checkers and chanting:

> Ha Ha! Two against one.
> I let you jump me

Only because I show you-u-u
That one . . . goes . . . there.

When the class hamster died, this 7-year-old chanted:

I'm sad that Tabby died.
We buried her with no flowers.
So we're going to get a new hamster.

## Comprehension

Teachers will find evidence that children understand what adults are saying, what is required of them, what choices are available to them, and what they are to do through:

Their facial expressions: agreement, irritation, anger, fear, delight
Their actions: positive or negative in response to adult speech
Their nonverbal expressions of feeling: laughter, tears, hand-clapping, foot-stamping, hooting, lowering of eyes
Their verbal responses: "Okay!" "No, I won't." "Don't talk to me."

Here are some questions to guide you in recording evidence of children's comprehension.

- Does a child listen, remember, and follow instructions? For example, when the teacher says, "After you have put away your puzzle, you may wash your hands and come to lunch," what does a child do?
- What are the children's responses to stories read by the teacher?
  » Do they understand the concepts and meaning?
  » Do they connect the story to personal experience?
  » Do they understand all the words? Which words are unfamiliar? Of these, which are everyday words? Literary words? Culturally specific words? Regional words?
- Does a child appropriately require visual aids to comprehend a story?
- Does a child grasp nonverbal clues to meaning, such as the reader's facial expression, actions, pitch and volume of voice, as a story is read? (Some children, particularly bilingual children, can understand what is being said even though

they may have difficulty expressing themselves adequately in English.)

- Does a child shut his eyes in order to listen better? Or cover the ears to watch better? (These may indicate problems of perceptual processing.)
- Does a child pick up and use phrases, chants, and words from stories or conversations?

Young children often understand only the literal meaning of words and respond in kind. Sometimes children misinterpret adult language and insert their own private meanings.

> Five-year-old Jorge, at the water table, became soaking wet. He complained to the teacher, who said, "Don't worry, I'll change you."
> "Change me? Into . . . ?" sobbed Jorge.
> "I mean," the teacher explained when she understood his fear, "I'll change *your clothes*." (Harriet Cuffaro, personal communication, 1995)

## Vocabulary

The characteristics of children's vocabulary are very much influenced by their family and their community. Some children hail from families in which talk is a prominent aspect of their lives, while others live in families where talk is less important. As we saw above, the same words can have varied meanings. What does the child's use of vocabulary tell us about the child's thinking? The following list is a guide for observation, for "getting the picture," not for judging.

- Is the child's vocabulary adequate to make her needs known?
- How does the child's vocabulary compare with that of other children the same age and of similar background?
- Is the child an English language learner? Does he or she code-switch between the first language and English?
- Does the child's vocabulary reflect a regional variation?

> What *sack* and *pop* are to the Midwestern American are *bag* and *soda* to the Middle Atlantic speaker. The Italian sandwich changes to *submarine, torpedo, hero, wedge, hoagie,* and *po'boy* as it moves about the United States. Within each region there is no confusion. Order a milkshake in Massachusetts and that's what you get—flavored milk that's been shaken. If you want ice cream in it, you need to ask for a *frappe*. (Owens, 2001, p. 413)

Understanding and expressing ideas about time and place is shaped (though not determined) by a child's culture and experience. For example, some families follow a regular schedule, while others are very flexible about dinner time and bedtime.

- Has the child developed the ability to use words to denote place? For example, "I'm putting the wooden people on top of the chair and the animals under the chair."
- Does a child's language contain unexpected words for a child of that age? These words might cover a spectrum that includes those with specialized meaning ("cooperation") and those that are scatological or indicate a child's exposure to or witness of adult behavior or events.

Two almost 4-year-old boys were arguing loudly over a sawhorse. The teacher asked them to share it. Mariah walked over to see what was going on and said with authority, "They need to have cop-er-a-shun."
"What does that mean?" asked the teacher.
Mariah replied assuredly, "It's when each one has a turn."

- Has the child developed an awareness of more than one meaning for words that sound alike, such as *pair, pear; dear, deer; see, sea*?
- Does the child like to play with words? In what way? Is the play with words within the context of dramatic play or more concerned with the relationships of sounds?

Ron, age 4, climbs up onto the structure he has made and begins calling, "Avocados, avocados, get your fresh avocados." The other children do not respond, but Ron continues his game, calling persistently, "A-vo-ca-dos, a-vo-ca-dos, fresh avocados."
Micky, standing within her own climbing structure, calls out defiantly, "Those are not fresh avocados. They're poison."
Albert, mischievous and laughing, but not mean, mimics, "Get your nasty avocados."
Micky, disparagingly, "Get your fool avocados." Micky and Albert are both inside the climbing apparatus and laughing together.
Ron (continuing unabashed) calls out, "Get . . . your . . . fresh . . . avo-ca-dos."

- Can the child make rhymes?

A 3-year-old sings "Butterfly, butterfly, flyeeee, flyee. Butterfly flies, bird flies, bird, bird, butterfly flies, flies, flies."

A 2-year-old chants as she plays, "Let's go sleepy in a deepy."

## Narrative Style

Young children may relate incidents and tell stories in a style that is highly personal. Observe to see whether the sequence is linear with one event following another—"topic-centered"—or whether several incidents are linked together in an "associated" thematic manner.

Michaels (1981) has described these two differing narrative styles in a group of Black and White children from different backgrounds. In her report, the White children tended to use a topic-centered style characterized by information that moved forward in a linear fashion, much like the White teacher's own style. The Black children tended to use a topic-associated style, characterized by a series of personal anecdotes that were connected by implication. The teacher assumed that the Black children were rambling or unfocused and attempted to make them more topic-centered. The children perceived these efforts negatively as interruption and interference.

This study helps us realize how challenging it is for teachers to understand and accept children's differing narrative styles. In the above example, Michaels (1981) herself was

> unable, on the spot, to follow this kind of discourse thematically and ask appropriately focused questions, . . . [while] a black instructional aide . . . was better able to pick up on the narrative intentions of the topic associating children, ask them thematically appropriate questions, and help them round out and organize their narrative accounts. (p. 440)

Recording, without interruption, a child's narrative may help teachers gain insight into, and appreciate, the child's particular style. Narratives also open the teacher's eyes to the child's experiences.

What might the teacher think about 5-year-old Sean's dictated narrative?

> This was a castle. One day there was a problem. There were soldiers from different countries. The countries were England and Chicago and New York City and Africa. And Africa was on New York City's side. They started fighting. Hooray! Hooray! New York City won. They had a baby. Every other day it was nice. New York City was happy that they won. They almost lived happily ever after. They were good guys.

The following story by a 4-year-old seems to be topic-centered.

Once there was a girl who wished she had a dog. One night she had a dream that she had so many dogs. It made her think that the next morning she would have a dog. And it turned out that she did have a dog. (Hayes, 1993, p. 63)

The following story dictated by a child almost 4 years old appears to be a mixture of styles and reveals bits and pieces of her attempt to understand complex relationships and events:

Once upon a time there was a little girl and she was very poor. Because she didn't have a mother. Then out popped a baby from her bottom. Then her mother grew and grew and out popped a boy baby from her mother's bottom. Then the baby grew and grew and grew tall to be the father. Then they were not poor. Then the mommy and the girl and the daddy went out shopping to the store, and they found a real turkey that goes "gobble gobble." Then they came back and caught some fish. Then they went out to dinner and had a movie about Superman and Superlady. And then they saw Lois Lane, and then they went to sleep, and they woke up and went on a subway train. And then they went back home and went to sleep. And at the morning went to school. The end.

Through language and stories, children bring their social and cultural selves into the classroom. Sometimes a child will narrate a story to accompany a drawing. Then style may not be the issue, but content is. Are teachers able to accept some of the frightening aspects of children's lives as well as the conventional aspects? A 2nd-grader told the teacher the following story about his drawing, which she wrote down:

This is the sun wearing sunglasses, and the sun is trying not to see the drugs. These are all beer cans and drugs and dead birds dying, and the grass is dying and the trees are dying and the leaves are falling down and dying. (Project Healthy Choices, n.d., p. 13)

## OBSERVING SPEECH PATTERNS

Most children by age 4 use the basic form and structure of their language correctly. However, the English language has many irregularities, which are usually learned between 4 and 8, and there are also words and forms for which a child's mental structures must develop before they can be used; for example, mixed tenses ("I used to live in the country, but after our dog died, we went to live in the city, and that's where we live now").

## Sentence Structure

Observe whether the child talks in words, phrases, or sentences (simple or complex, correct or incorrect for the language being used).

- Does the child's speech fall into a pattern consistent with the spoken language—for instance, in English, the word order of subject, verb, object, as in "I want milk"?
- Does the child show understanding of the regularities of the language, such as *walk, walked; girl, girls*?
- Does the child show knowledge of the irregularities, as in *sing, sang; buy, bought; mouse, mice*? (This is evidence of more advanced awareness of language and can be as much a result of hearing appropriate models as of stage of development.)
- How does the child use tense—for example, present tense only? ("I go home." "I buy candy." "I'm playing with blocks.") Or overgeneralization ("I goed home." "I buyed candy.")? Or does he use present, past, and future? Correctly or incorrectly? ("Where were you when I looked for you?" "I will come to your house on Saturday.")
- Does the child use pronouns appropriately, or confuse them?

In the following record we see not only the children's competent use of English speech patterns but their interest in language itself. They attempt to understand the implications of the deep connection of language to family and culture.

Justen is sitting at a table with Pedro looking at a book. Justen softly asks Pedro, "How do you say 'love' in Spanish?"

Pedro is startled, "Love? You wanna learn Spanish?"

"Yeah!"

"Why do you wanna learn Spanish?"

"So I can say, 'Everybody loves everybody!'"

Pedro then asks, angrily, "Are you American?"

Justen replies, "Yep."

Pedro retorts, "Then you can't learn Spanish!"

Justen sticks his chin out, squints his eyes, and demands, "Are you Spanish? Then you shouldn't be in New York!"

Pedro explains, "I could be in New York if I'm Spanish. Everybody in Brooklyn is Puerto Rican and Black and Brown like me."

Having recorded this conversation, the teacher now has an incomparable opportunity for cultural mediation, not only for Justen and Pedro but for other children who may be listening. A discussion about who "owns" language and whether a language is limited to a particular place will afford these 6- and 7-year-olds a chance to understand what language means to them and thus to know one another better.

If the child's dominant language is other than English, try to discover whether the child demonstrates competent use of that language. In order to make such an assessment, a teacher who is not fluent in the child's language would need the opinion of a professional who is proficient in that language. (For more information about English language learners, see Tabors, 1997.)

In the following conversation, Fernando and Tania (both 4-and-a-half) demonstrate a command of Spanish plus an ability to switch to English when addressing Nathania.

> Fernando, Tania, and Nathania are playing with plastic boats, but Fernando wants the larger boat that Tania has and takes it. Tania complains to Fernando, "*¿Por que tu me molesta?*" (Why are you bothering me?) Fernando replies "*Eso no es tuyo.*" (This is not yours.) "*Tania, es lo mismo.*" (They are the same.) Tania insists, "*Yo quiero ese.*" (I want this one.) But Fernando presses his case, "*Pero es lo mismo.*" (But they are the same.) Frustrated, Tania yells, "*¡Ai, ai, ai! Yo quiero ese.*" (I want this one.) Not easily swayed, Fernando repeats "*Pero es lo mismo.*" In desperation, Tania tries another tack, "*Si me lo das, mañana te traigo candy.*" (If you give it to me, tomorrow I will bring you candy.) She begins to cry. Fernando finally gives back the big boat. Tania turns to Nathania and says, "Come on, Nathania!" They make racing noises. "Vrr . . . vrr . . . beep . . . beep . . . beep." Fernando declares, "I win!" Nathania counters with a loud "NO!" Suddenly Brett approaches and tries to get the big boat from Tania saying, "Gimme it!" Tania whines, "*¡No me mate! ¡No me mate!*" (Don't kill me). Brett leaves.
>
> Later on Fernando and Tania are punching one another, and Fernando pushes Tania away, saying, "No fighting! No fighting!" Tania continues, "Pow! Pow!" Fernando in a loud voice says, "I said no fighting!"

Is the child whose dominant language is not English able to "switch codes" (as Fernando does in the above example)? Code-switching indicates that a child can apply rules to both languages. Although this is sometimes regarded as a lack of command of both languages, in reality, it is quite the contrary. Code-switching is a complex skill that demonstrates the speaker's flexibility in each language (Perez & Torres-Guzman, 1992).

## Dialects

Dialects of English have their own forms of regularity. If you have questions about a child's usage, find out whether she is following a different cultural pattern before you decide the child is confused.

In the following anecdote, the use of the adjective *bad* meant "great!" to the speakers but not to the child.

> Three-year-old Lucas heard one woman joking with another saying, "Oh, Lynette, you one b-a-a-a-d *girl!*" Lucas, who had a special close relationship with Lynette, rose up in her defense. "She is *not* a bad girl!" "Oh, Lucas, we were just joking." No amount of explanation helped. He puffed out his lips, folded his arms, and remained indignant.

Trying to correct children's dialect by directing them to imitate you is more likely to give them the message that their communications are unworthy. The child in the following example, however, assumed that something was wrong with the teacher. She had been drilling her 3- and 4-year-olds to respond to her morning greeting, "How are you?" with "I'm fine, thank you."

> *Teacher:* Good morning, Tony, how are you?
> *Tony:* I be's fine.
> *Teacher:* Tony, I said, How *are* you?
> *Tony* (with raised voice): I be's *fine.*
> *Teacher:* No, Tony, I said, *how are you?*
> *Tony* (angrily): I done told you *I be's fine* and I ain't telling you no more! (Delpit, 1995, p. 51)

## Pronunciation and Enunciation

Records of children at play, of the stories a child makes up, of the retelling of a known story; records of conversations, of participation in discussion, of anything a child says at any time, all provide evidence of a child's language use.

- Does a child have difficulty pronouncing certain words? Certain letters?
- Is there change over time in the clarity and precision of pronunciation and enunciation?
- Are some letters not sounded out in words? Can you tell which ones?

- Is the child's inability to pronounce certain words and sounds due to the fact that English is not her first language?

For example, because the *r* sound is absent in Chinese, the tongue is not trained to make that movement. Likewise, English speakers are unable to make certain sounds in other languages. In the following anecdote it is the *child* who detects an incorrect pronunciation of her language by an English-speaking adult and attempts to correct her.

> A bilingual (Portuguese/English) 3-and-a-half-year-old was anticipating her aunt's arrival from Brazil. Her teacher said, "I hear that your Aunt Melina is coming to your house today." The child, correcting her, says, "*MAH*-lina." The teacher says cheerfully, "Right. Melina." The child, emphasizing the first syllable, repeats, "No. *MAH*-lina." The teacher finally realizes that she has missed a message and asks, "What?" The child, slowly, with some degree of impatience, repeats, "*MAH*-lina." Teacher, imitating slowly, says, "*MAH*-lina?" Child, relieved, sighs, "Yes."

In Spanish, the sound *st* is always preceded by *e* so that a child may say "estreet" for "street" in keeping with the rules of Spanish. Other pronunciation conflicts may arise, such as "shoes" for "choose" or "seen" for "sing." Such a conflict is well illustrated in the following anecdote where Carlos, unable to pronounce the "st" sound, uses the word "sump" for "stump."

> The 1st-grade teacher is distributing corrected worksheets. She is seated on a low chair in front of the children, who are squatting or sitting on the floor. She calls the children one by one and comments on their work.
>
> Carlos is seated directly in front of her, practically at her feet. He is eagerly looking up at her, awaiting his turn. The teacher comes to his paper. "Carlos . . . Beautiful work!" She beams with approval. "Everybody wrote just one example. But Carlos wrote *bat, cat, rat, hat* for *sat*; and *they, hay, may* for *play*; and *bump, hump, sump* for *lump* . . . Only I'm not sure what that word is—*sump*?
>
> Carlos appears bewildered at first. Then, looking up at the teacher directly, he lifts his shoulders and says in a clear, confident tone, "That is *sump* (emphasizing the word), like in a tree!"

Another example points to the realization that what appears to be a grammatical error might better be understood as a difference in pronunciation. In the process of learning English, 6-year-old Lily, whose first language is Korean, seems unable to pronounce the final consonant.

> The teacher tells Mia that the Korean word for *friend* is *chingu*. Mia asks Lily, "Are you my *chingu*?" Lily takes both Mia's hands, breaks into a big smile, and says, "How do you know that word?" Lily announces proudly that she can write her own name in "Korea." Mia corrects her, "You mean in Korean." Lily repeats, "Yes, I write my name in Korea." Mia says, emphasizing the *n* in "Korean." Mia asks, "Can you write my name in Korean?" Lily says, "No, I just learning."

Language is learned from models and through use. When opportunities for both are available to children, language develops, broadens, and deepens. Records over time will show the developmental changes that occur.

Children have their own ideas about how language develops. The following excerpt from a teacher's log reveals some deep thinking by a group of 8-year-olds in response to her question, "Why do you think people speak different languages?"

> "Well," said Eddie thoughtfully, "it depends on what language is in your vocal cords." . . . "You see," said Brandy, glibly picking the story up, "everybody has three languages inside his body, but the vocal cords are only attached to one of them, and that's the language you speak.". . . Ramon continued, "Actually, you speak a language because your mother speaks that language. You see, when the baby is in the mother's stomach, there's an English tube from the mother's vocal cords to the baby, and when the mother talks, some of the English goes out of her mouth and some of it goes down the tube to the baby, and that's how the baby learns how to talk English." "Uh-uh," said Myriam, "that can't be because I have a friend who's Filipino and her mother speaks Filipino, but she only speaks English." After only a few seconds, Ramon had a ready answer. Patiently he explained, "You see, the language tubes that are connected to the baby from the mother are different shapes. Now the English tube is round and it works really good, but the Filipino language tube is sort of funny-shaped like a triangle and it doesn't work so good."

Encouraging children to express their ideas about language (and about anything else) may bring out countless tales. Never lack a pencil and pad lest these escape you!

## OBSERVING EMERGENT LITERACY

In many parts of the world, language, writing, and reading are understood to spring from children's passionate thrust to join the human community. Just as language emerges before, but is necessary for, writing, so writing emerges before and is a "necessary complement" to reading (Clay, 1975, p. 2). Writing and reading, woven upon the warp and woof of language, create the fabric of literacy. Children's progress from scribbling to writing is nourished and supported when teachers supply both the materials (paper, crayons, pencils, notebooks, space) and the models (announce as they write, take dictation from children, use experience charts, create signs) of literacy (Hayes, 1990).

Observations of children's emerging literacy can be drawn from their development as writers as well as from their language use. It is important for teachers to attend to not only the content of their language use but also "how" children function in such situations as the following. (For greater detail about observing the development of writing, see Clay, 2002.)

- Does the child make the connection between "talk" and written words? The following anecdote illustrates that "the representation of things not present is of key significance in learning how to deal with the world of print" (Gibson, 1989, p. 16).

   Three-year-old Max sits in front of paper and crayons and says to the teacher, "I want bubble gum." She asks what he means, since there is no gum in school. "I mean you spell it—and I'll spell it (he points to the paper). I mean you spell it and I'll draw it. 'Cause I want it." As the teacher says each letter slowly, he writes each letter. His lips are pursed and it looks as if he is sounding out a *b* sound as he writes the letter *b*. Sometimes he blows out some air in a soft sputtering sound. He is wholly involved in his task. He writes with his right hand, his left hand tensing and gripping the paper. After writing each letter, he says the name of the letter in a sing-song tone, an exaggeration of the teacher's tone, and holds up the paper for the teacher to see. As she says the third *b*, he looks up, his lips and eyebrows screwed up in a frown. "I did that already!" he says with annoyance. When the teacher explains that there are three *b*'s in bubble, he goes back to writing. When she gets to *l*, he stops, eyebrows furrowed, "Show me *l*." The teacher makes a lowercase *l*. When Eve, who is looking on, says, "Another line," Max seems to have a quick realization. "I know how to make a real one," and makes an uppercase *L*. "Eeeeee," he says as he writes *e*. Max and the teacher go through this process of spelling and writing *bubble* twice more. Then he rolls up his paper carefully, asks for tape, and asks the teacher to write "Mommy and Daddy" on it. At the end of the day, Max's mother comes to pick him up. Max hands her his rolled-up paper, saying, "I want bubble gum."

- Is the child stymied by the writing task? Or interested and eager?
- Is there evidence over time (in the child's notebook or folder or in his drawings) of scribbles becoming letters, letter strings, words, names, word groups, and eventually sentences?
- Does the child trace and/or copy the teacher's written words, or signs, or her own writing? Does the child "read" her own scribbles?
- Does the child demonstrate an understanding that writing moves from left to right?
- Does the child "read" books to himself? To others? Is the book properly oriented? Does he turn the pages sequentially? Does he like to be read to?
- If English is the child's second language, or if the child speaks a dialect of English, how is this reflected in the child's writing? (Writing can be used to learn standard form.)
- Does the child display flexibility and/or experimentation in writing?
- What indication does the child's invented spelling give about her intuition concerning the alphabet and how it works?

A figure with a large smile, drawn by a 4-year-old, has a slim body, stick arms and legs. Under it the child has written "PRSN" (person). (Hayes, 1993, p. 67)

- Does the child use writing for social purposes? Notes to friends or family? To convey ideas and experiences?

A drawing by a 4-year-old of three fish contains writing at the top of the picture—"Are FISH SIM ALAt." and includes the period. (Our fish swim a lot.) (Hayes, 1993, p. 35)

- Has the child progressed in writing over time?
- Do the child's errors make sense?

Literacy begins at birth, develops through language, and flowers into writing and reading. Children display great variation as they tackle these skills. Observation and recording illuminate the many paths children take as they become increasingly literate.

# 11

# Observing and Recording the Behavior of Infants and Toddlers

Observing infants and toddlers in group care or family child care above all requires a keen eye and patient perseverance. The observer's pen appears to fly across the page, for the movements of children under 3 seem to be calibrated in milliseconds. One action follows another, often with such disjointed quality that we are roused to wonder how so small a person can think of so many things to do, so many ways to move, in so short a span of time. At the table, under the table, beside the table, on top of the table, all activities take place within a few moments, leaving the recorder, but hardly the baby, nearly breathless.

The recorder, thus poised for action, may suddenly face another condition—that of no identifiable activity at all. The child is momentarily still, or staring into space, or repeatedly fingering or mouthing a tuft of fringe. Recorders may find themselves "tuning out," restless or possibly bored. How very unlike observing and recording 3- to 6-year-olds is this endeavor with the under-3s!

## MAKING SENSE OF WHAT YOU SEE

To make sense out of all this random movement, it is wise to consider each action from the infant's or toddler's point of view—as a completed event. When seen in this way, through the eyes of the child, these seemingly disconnected events begin to take on a new meaning. For that reason, records can be taken in 3- to 5-minute periods and should include as much detail as possible.

Perhaps some activity may seem too insignificant, too trivial, or too fleeting to record. It should be written down anyway, for it is in the accumulation of these bits of lively evidence that the wider picture of this elusive baby will emerge. Every scrap of observed behavior becomes important when it is finally collated into a pattern.

For example, in this record of 19-month-old Danielle, no startling action occurs. Yet it is a completed behavior. It has a beginning, a middle, and an end.

> Danielle walks steadily over to a crib where 7-month-old Claudia has just awakened. Putting her two hands on the crib bars, she regards the sleepy baby with a long look. She laughs gently and then walks away.

We do not know the meaning of this action to the toddler, but as more data are collected on Danielle, other evidence of her interest in, her pleasure in, and/or her stresses with other children will begin to surface in an emerging pattern of her relations with children.

Therefore, in order to capture the mercurial lives of these under-3s, it will be necessary to record as frequently as possible, without a preselection of events. In that way, some anecdotes, as that of Danielle, will be brief, and others will be more lengthy, as is the following record of 15-month-old Jared, who is eating lunch, making connections with the caregiver, and receiving loving attention from another toddler.

> Jared is eating cottage cheese for lunch. He holds a spoonful and examines the cheese as he bounces the spoon up and down in front of him. He sets it back in the bowl. Then he takes a spoonful again, but this time the cheese drops to the table as he becomes involved in watching Aram, who sits across the table. "Eating your cheese?" comments Lois, the caregiver, who did not notice that it had dropped off the spoon. He looks at her impishly out of the corner of his eye, puts the spoon to his mouth, and licks off what is left on the spoon.
>
> He moves his body forward in the small chair, perhaps to be closer to the table, or perhaps to reorganize his body in the chair's space. In doing this, he loses his balance, falls forward, strikes his head on the edge of the table, and cries. Lois takes him on her lap and he molds to her body. Aram, 32 months, looks at Jared with wide eyes. "He's crying," he says, and leans over to plant a kiss on Jared's wet cheek. Jared slides off Lois's lap and walks steadily over to touch a toy telephone that is lying on the couch.

## THE VALUE OF RECORDING

The value of these records lies in their almost microscopic focus on the details of toddler and infant life that often slide by in the hurly-burly of day-to-day caregiving. The preponderant load of physical care necessary for infants and toddlers, plus their rapid developmental changes, means that caregivers must make many shifts in their own behavior in order to accommodate to these factors, often without conscious thought. Taking this sort of recording "time out" during a busy day can be viewed as putting "time in," since it provides teachers and caregivers with a deep view into the lives of the children as well as the program.

In such a yeasty situation, it is imperative that caregivers grasp as much time as possible to record these tumultuous developmental changes as they occur. Such recorded data are a unique source of enrichment and growth for the infant/toddler program itself. Records, for example, lend themselves to sharing among a staff, forming the basis for regular, ongoing, content-laden meetings. The function of such record-sharing is twofold. First, one or more staff members may be recording the same child over a period of time and these shared anecdotes help the staff understand not only the child in focus, but some developmental characteristics of that specific age as well. Second, the very process of recording adds to staff development by serving as a basis for adult reflection about the refinements of caregiving practice as well as connecting staff members to their own individual differences in observing.

Written anecdotes provide concrete illustrations of the continually unfolding saga of development. Against this hard recorded evidence, the teacher's knowledge will be honed, for it is the teacher who must decide whether the observed characteristics fit with the age of the child, and appreciate, at the same time, the great variations produced by individual differences.

## TIME

Recording at different times of the day becomes especially significant in observing children under 3. The influence of the hour on the mood and the state of the very young child is often pronounced. Babies who are bubbly at 9:30 in the morning may be limp and whimpering at noon or outraged at 4:00 P.M. A record taken before lunch may be at serious odds with one taken after the meal. It might not even appear to be the same child. Time of day has an influence on the tempo of the child's entire environment. For instance, caregivers themselves flag and revive at different times during the day. In a child care setting, as a further example, time dictates which staff members will be present and which absent. Obviously, different people set different tones in a classroom. Similarly, the presence and absence of some children, often dictated by the time of day, makes an impact on the environment. This, in turn, affects other children as well as the caregivers.

## WHAT TO OBSERVE

An infant or toddler's day in group care is unlikely to fall into a distinct pattern of planned activity as it might in a preschool setting. Therefore, it will frequently be necessary to record at random. However, taking records in the following situations will provide a comprehensive view of the child's life in the group:

- Arrival and departure
- Caregiving routines
    » Diapering/toileting
    » Eating/feeding
    » Napping
    » Outings
- Playing and exploring
- Interaction with adults and children
- Language

An in-depth examination of each of these situations, one by one, will illustrate the range of information that can be mined through recording.

### Arrival and Departure

During the first few years of life, children form deep attachments to the person who provides them with primary care, usually a parent, grandparent, or other relative. (The designation "parent" may refer to a relative, a foster parent, or the person who is the primary caregiver at home.) This attachment provides the base from which children begin to separate themselves in their efforts to become individuals with a distinct sense of self. In both the arrival at group care and the departure from it, the infant or toddler is, in most instances, accompanied by the primary caregiving person.

Records taken at these times provide the professional staff with an opportunity to understand the unique quality in each parent-child pair's negotiation of the separation as well as the reunion. Records will also help the staff focus more deliberately on the influence the child's age and developmental characteristics have on the nature of these events. A baby of 5 months, for example, would be unlikely to react to these events with the verve and display of feelings of a 21-month-old toddler. On the other hand, certain idiosyncratic characteristics may appear as a continual thread over time. Recorded evidence will help place these developmental differences in proper perspective.

The following questions are designed to sharpen the caregiver's awareness of arrivals and departures and to act as a guide in the recording process. Thinking about these items will involve an understanding that some behaviors observed at one age may not be observed at another. Thus, these and other questions are intended as guides and assume the teacher's familiarity with broad age-connected developmental differences (for more information, see Cole & Cole, 2005).

*Arrival of Infant/Toddler—Departure of Parent.* Children under 3 and their parents have many ambivalent feelings about leaving one another, and later rejoining, in a group care situation. Even though parents and children are assured that the child care, preschool, or play group offers good, loving care, it is not always easy for them to leave one another. These feelings are expressed in a multitude of ways.

- Does the infant/toddler make eye contact with the parent?
- Does she follow the parent to the door with a gaze, or by crawling or walking?
- Does the baby make any spoken sound or protest? Of what sort?
- Does the child verbally or motorically signal "goodbye"?
- Does the infant/toddler ignore the parent or behave as though the parent weren't there?
- How does the baby react to the receiving caregiver?
- If the child is distressed, is he able to find a means of self-comfort, such as thumb-sucking, becoming involved with a plaything, or accepting the caregiver's attention?

Here is 18-month-old Skye, whose father has just brought him to the child care center:

Skye's dad starts to leave, and Skye bolts out the door after him, without a sound. He is caught up by Kim, the caregiver, hugged, and taken over to the table for snack. He sits quietly, somewhat subdued, face blank, next to Kim. He munches on a slice of apple.

Bart, at 14 months, is younger, and has another style of parting with his parent:

> Bart's mother brings him into the room and sits down, holding him on her lap. As Sylvie, the caregiver, approaches, Bart jumps down off his mother's lap and runs to her. Sylvie swoops him up in her arms and sets him on a chair at the table where other children are eating breakfast. He gazes blankly at the recorder, a stranger. His mother says cheerfully, "Bye honey," and smiles at him. He looks at her with a blank expression, sucking on his pacifier. Mother exchanges glances with caregiver and leaves.

Younger infants may display their feelings in more subtle ways through gaze or cries of distress.

*Arrival of Parent—Departure of Infant/Toddler with Parent.* Leaving group care at the end of the day to go home presents another adjustment for the baby-and-parent pair. It involves a reunion that might or might not be totally joyous. Perhaps feelings associated with leaving one another in the morning well up when the pair is reunited. The sad, angry, and ambivalent feelings aroused by separating are usually diluted by the day's activity, but by the end of the day there is little activity to stand between those feelings and their expression, as in this incident with 26-month-old Maya, usually a sweet-tempered child, when her father picked her up to go home:

> As Maya's father enters the room to take her home, she picks up a book and a lunch box that is used for play. "I want the book inside the box. I want to take it home," she insisted. "You can't take the lunch box, but you can put the book inside your bag. Here," her father says in a calm tone. He holds out a small canvas bag to her. She holds on tightly to the lunch box, pouts, stands resolutely, stares into space, and screams, "No! I wanna put it inside. I want it. No!" She clutches the lunch box. "I wanna *borrow.*" (The teacher has made the rule that the children may borrow one thing.) Father, becoming edgy, says, "Look, if you make a fuss, you can't even take the book. Do you want the book?" At this moment, Josepha, the teacher, steps in. "Look, Maya, I'll put the book into your bag," and begins to do this. "No!" screams Maya, holding more tightly to the lunch box. "You can't have the box and the book," her father states flatly. "I am going to," she insists loudly. "Are we going to have a fight?" her exasperated father groans. "I want it!" she shrieks. "I've got an idea," her father says brightly, "how

about leaving the book and taking the lunch box?" She drops the book on the chair, takes her father's hand, and bounces on her toes as they go out the door.

Another child, Sally, 21 months, handles her ambivalent feelings about the reunion with her mother in her characteristically low-key manner:

Sally's mother comes quietly into the room. "Mommy!" Sally says aloud in a rising tone of pleasure as she spies her mother. She stops in her tracks and looks at her mother with a blank expression for several seconds. Mother crouches down and opens her arms expectantly, saying, "Sally! Sally!" Sally continues to stare blankly for a few seconds, then finally runs to her mother's open arms. Her mother lifts her up. Sally maintains a blank expression and then suddenly breaks into a wreath of smiles as she hugs her mother.

Watching and recording arrival and departure situations over time provides insights into how parent-child pairs negotiate these events, what the child's particular coping style is, and how it evolves as the child grows older. Some periods of time and some stages of development may be more trying for the child and parent than others. Collecting samples of such arrival and departure events over a period of several months will reveal trends in this delicate relationship that are often the bellwether for describing parent-child attachment. (For full details on how to evolve patterns, see Chapter 13.)

### Caregiving Routines

A considerable portion of an infant/toddler's day is defined through the routines of daily living. The performance of these routines is often dismissed as solely physical care. Not so! The social, emotional, and intellectual capacities of children are deeply engaged in these caretaking exchanges. Observation of routine caregiving situations, while they occur as well as before and after, may reveal the degree of children's ability to inhibit impulse and desire, to distract or comfort themselves, and to trust adults. These records may also indicate the infant/toddler's thrust toward autonomy, as sense of self expands with increasing age and experience. The observer may spot the baby's autonomous grab for the spoon during feeding, or the toddler's assertion of self in pushing another toddler out of the way. Such observations will contain clues to the following:

- Does the child seem to feel competent about her own effectiveness and skills?
- How does the time of day and/or the style of the caregiver's interactions affect the child's behavior?
- Is the child's behavior from one routine to another predictable and consistent, or is it different with each routine?
- What is the salient characteristic of the child's behavior? (compliance, restlessness, rebellion, teasing)
- Has the child's behavior changed significantly over time in relation to any particular routine(s)? In what ways?

Examining more closely the routines of diapering/toileting, eating/feeding, napping, and outings will also shed light on the relationship between the caregiving person and the baby or toddler. Such records can be treasures in the hands of a staff that seeks opportunities to develop itself.

*Diapering/Toileting.* Here is 30-month-old Raphael, who wants to control his diaper change. His preference cannot be accommodated at the moment, so the caregiver handles the situation by acknowledging his desire, but not giving in to it. A "natural phenomenon" saves the day.

Anna, the caregiver, leads Raphael by the hand into the bathroom for a diaper change. He breaks loose from her grasp by pulling away and wresting his hand from hers. He runs pell-mell out of the bathroom toward Lena, another caregiver, who is playing with two children on the floor. "Mmm. I want Lena!" he bellows, pointing at her. Anna, who has followed him, picks him up gently. He screams a piercing, loud cry, *"Lena!"* *"You* want Lena, but she's busy," Anna tells him. "I think I am going to do it. Quick. Then you and Lena can read a book together. Quick, I'll do it." She smiles at him. He continues to cry and she says several times, reassuringly, "I'll do it." Suddenly a fly buzzes by him and he points at it. They both watch the fly for a moment. He stops crying and stands quietly, helping to secure the diaper.

Sometimes the diapering situation is an opportunity for a special private time with a child and it becomes a social occasion. Here is 2-year-old Jonas, involved in a delightful give-and-take with his caregiver:

Gloria (the teacher), who is in the bathroom, calls, "Jonas, come into the bathroom so I can change your diaper." Jonas pushes his head forward, says an emphatic no, and pouts, jutting out his lower lip. When the teacher repeats her request, Jonas starts to cry, grabs his blanket, hugging it very closely to his chest, and says, "Put in cubby." He runs out of the room, presumably to his cubby, and then runs back in. He pauses, looks at Gloria, and then with a stern look on his face, trots into the bathroom.

Gloria greets Jonas as he walks over to the low table, stretches his upper body across it, and hoists himself up. Jonas stands up on the table and moves very close to Gloria. She compliments him on the way he remembered exactly what to do when he is in the bathroom. As she takes down Jonas's overalls, she continues to talk to him in a conversational way. Jonas leans very close to her. He is playing with the buttons on her shirt, and he is laughing. He stands motionless as she moves away to get a clean diaper. When he begins to scratch a slight rash on his thigh, she tells him that is not a good idea. He points to the supply cabinet, saying, "Eh, eh, eh, powder." Gloria gets the powder and he holds out his hand for some. She pours it into his hand and he pats a little on his penis. He begins to manipulate his penis, bending his legs and looking down with curiosity. When Gloria puts him down on the table to put on the diaper, she leans close to his face and talks to him. Jonas smiles, reaches up, grabs her hair, and pushes it in front of her eyes. The two of them laugh. Jonas then starts to play with Gloria's face, saying nonsense words in a singsong way. After Jonas is fully dressed, he looks up at Gloria and says, "Kiss," puckering his lips. The teacher bends her head and he gives her a quick kiss on the cheek. She lifts him off the table and he shuffles into the other room, saying, "Choo, choo," pretending he is a train.

Records of diapering and toileting help to focus on children's feelings about their bodily processes as well as about those who care for them. As you record, ask yourself:

- How aware is the baby/toddler of what the diapering activity means?
- Does the child cooperate with or struggle against the person who is diapering?
- Does the child behave in the same way with all caregivers who diaper him?
- Is there any opportunity for the child to take an active role in the process, or is the diapering mostly peremptory?
- What is the quality of the adult-child interaction? Is there eye contact? Is there conversation?

In the following record, the caregiver deliberately involves the baby in her own care:

> Rachel, 17 months, stands in front of the caregiver. They smile at each other. "Are you wet, Rachel?" the caregiver asks, stretching out her arms. When Rachel stretches out her arms, the caregiver picks her up. "Yes, indeed, you've got to be changed," she says to Rachel as she carries her to the changing table. She sets Rachel, standing, on the table. Rachel begins to pull on her pants. "You are really good at taking off your pants, Rachel," the caregiver grins as she gently pulls Rachel's pants down, carefully avoiding interference with the baby's own action. "There, you've done it, they're down. Now let's get your feet out." And as Rachel pulls on her feet, the caregiver removes them from the pants. Now Rachel tugs at her diaper. The caregiver loosens the tabs; Rachel tugs again, and then hands the wet diaper to the caregiver. "Wet," says Rachel. "It is wet," says the caregiver, "and here's a dry one." She hands the dry one to Rachel and waits while Rachel tries to put it between her legs, then carefully arranges it so that Rachel can be involved in pressing the tabs together. After putting on her pants halfway, she waits, as Rachel begins to tug at them, then pulls them up. "What a great diaper changer you are, Rachel!" says the caregiver as she hugs Rachel before setting her down on the floor.

Since diapering and toileting occur with such frequency in an infant/toddler program, they carry a powerful message to children and offer one way through which children learn how adults take care of them, and how adults feel about the products of their bodies. In this record of a 23-month-old, the teacher is in the bathroom with three children. One has just used the potty and another, the toilet. The third, Laurie, has other ideas.

> "It's your turn to use the potty, Laurie," the teacher tells her matter-of-factly. "Let me help you take off your diaper." Laurie pouts, turns up her head, swerves her body swiftly out of the teacher's reach, and stands resolutely, looking her in the eye. "Are you sure you don't want to use the potty?" the teacher asks again. Looking at the frozen figure of Laurie, she adds, "Okay, but let me know if you want help," and she moves toward the entry to the bathroom, discreetly looking in the other direction from which Laurie is standing. Laurie checks out the caregiver's gaze and when she is sure that it is not on her, she moves toward the potty. She turns her body in line with the potty, takes a step backward and sits on it, fully clothed, for a few moments, then gets up and walks

with a confident stride out of the bathroom. She is smiling the smallest of smiles.

The tone of these episodes is revealed through the words chosen to describe the baby's facial expressions, body movements, and verbalizations. Gentleness is communicated through the description of the teacher's movements, the expression on her face. Tension, disgust, or annoyance would be revealed in the same way, through words that describe a baby's irritable crying and a caregiver's flatness or impatience of tone, choice of words, or efficient coldness.

An obvious pattern of tension or unhappiness seen over a period of time in records of diapering/toileting demands the attention of the staff. What do these repeated records say regarding the baby's feelings about diaper changes or trips to the potty? What do they tell the staff about the handling of the child at these times? Teachers can be mutually helpful if records are considered tools for their own development and learning.

*Eating/Feeding.* Since eating and feeding take place with repeated regularity in an infant/toddler program, it is not difficult to take such records. Someone, it seems, is almost always eating or being fed. The range of eating situations is wide: from a baby of a few months being held for a bottle to a 2-and-a-half-year-old independently enjoying a snack or munching lunch.

Feeding and eating are situations through which the observer is able to become acquainted with the baby's style of satisfaction, level of enjoyment, and thrusts toward autonomy. Some babies are lusty lovers of the bottle and enjoy it to the last drop, often falling into a contented sleep when it is done. Others are more cautious, taking in small amounts and pausing for burps or rest between sucking. Some children experience discomfort in feeding, which may produce irritable crying or restlessness. The point is that not all babies take a bottle or solid food in the same way.

Close observation of several feeding situations with a baby will throw light on the baby's approach to the bottle. Is it eager or hesitant, lustful or languorous? Whether the baby is in or out of step with the caregiver will be detected through such details as these: Does the baby mold to the caregiver's body? Flail around uncomfortably? Struggle to get up? Does the caregiver respond to the baby's signals and make appropriate adjustments?

Through feeding and eating, infants and toddlers form an opinion of the world. Is the world a friendly place where needs are met? Is food proffered by loving people and consumed in an atmosphere of patience and pleasure? In the following record the caregiver and the 7-month-old baby are very much in tune with each other and the level of the baby's pleasure is obviously high.

> Deirdre, who is being held in Josephine's lap, says, "Mmmmmmm," looks around at the children who are playing nearby, moves her legs up and down, and chomps slowly on the fruit and cereal that Josephine is carefully feeding to her. Deirdre's legs circle in the air as her body reclines against Josephine's breast. "You like that? My goodness-mmmm," purrs Josephine. Deirdre begins to struggle, reaching with her arms, arching her back. Josephine shifts her own body and adjusts her position so that the baby is now sitting higher, her back straighter. She is able now to look around. She relaxes and resumes the meal, opening her mouth for the next spoonful.

Bottle feeding is often a source of comfort, relaxation, and enjoyment for both the caregiver and the baby.

> Four-month-old Andre is lying on the floor underneath a hanging toy. He begins to fuss. "Oh, you're getting hungry," says Hal as he picks up Andre. As Hal gets a bottle from the refrigerator, Andre wiggles excitedly in his arms. Hal sits on the couch holding Andre and offers the bottle. Andre opens his mouth and puts one hand on the side of the bottle as he begins to suck, clenching his other hand into a fist. While Andre drinks, Hal rubs his small foot.

Toddlers and 2-year-olds, in large part, like to be in charge of feeding and eating. Sometimes it means waiting for the caregiver to bring the food or, as in the following case, the juice. We see Hester, 17 months, who uses several skills to help herself wait.

> Hester is sitting on a small chair at a round table with other toddlers who have been eating pancakes for breakfast. "Ah. Du," she says to the caregiver, Ruth. "You want juice," Ruth confirms. "I'll get your juice for you." Ruth washes Hester's sticky hands with a cloth. She willingly allows Ruth to do this and makes a squeaking sound. "Okay. I'll have to get your juice." Hester looks around at the other children. Her body is composed, her gaze relaxed. "Ruth, Ruth," she calls as the caregiver walks away from the table to take a child to the bathroom. Hester sits still and begins to suck her thumb. She screams gently, making guttural sounds and waving her hand to the caregiver, who has come back to the table

without the juice. "You sound like a little tiger," Ruth says and laughs. Hester laughs, too. Then she pounds her hands on the table saying, "Ah. Ah." Two other toddlers at the table begin to pound their hands on the table. Meanwhile, Ruth, who had gone during the pounding, arrives with a small cup of juice and hands it to Hester who, with great serious-ness, holds it firmly in her two hands and drinks it with gusto.

Other toddlers are not so patient or so able to distract themselves as Hester, and sometimes they cannot tolerate the ministrations of adults who attempt to feed them when they do not want to be fed.

Sarah, 19 months, is seated next to the caregiver at a small table. The caregiver, seated between Sarah and Eli, alternately offers a spoonful of food to each child. In this position she makes eye contact with neither child, nor can she see their facial expressions. Eli willingly opens his mouth with each proferred spoonful of peas. Sarah, however, clamps her mouth shut, turns her whole body sideways in the chair, and clenches her fists on the table top. Suddenly, she emits a piercing scream, reaches over to the plate of peas, and, rummaging her hands about in them, scatters the peas across the table and onto the floor.

"Well, Sarah," says the amazed caregiver, "what's gotten into you?" Another caregiver, Marian, enters the room at this moment and says, "Do you think she wants to eat the peas from the plate herself?" Marian sets the plate of peas in front of Sarah, who deftly begins to pick up one at a time with her thumb and forefinger, daintily placing them in her mouth.

While not all toddlers are such neat eaters, most of them are intent on doing it themselves. At 11 months, Nadia had a second breakfast, quite unknown to the caregivers. She was quiet and out of sight until she popped into their view.

Nadia is crawling on the floor. When she nears the high chair in which Denise sits, she pulls herself to stand, says, "Da!" and laughs. She drops deftly to the floor, crawls to a small chair, pulls herself to stand, cruises to the table next to the chair, drops to the floor, and proceeds to visu-ally examine the floor around her. Looking ahead of her, she crawls un-der the table and continues slowly until she reaches the center. Seeing a paper napkin on the floor near her, she grasps it, sits up, and waves the napkin in the air. She reaches out and grabs the legs of Teddy, 18 months, who is sitting at the table for breakfast. She notices on the floor within her reach a piece of waffle that had been dropped by one of the breakfast eaters. She stuffs it into her mouth with the palm of her hand and sits, for a few seconds, chewing contentedly. Turning herself around, she crawls out from under the table. Pulling herself to stand on a nearby chair, she shifts to the table edge and cruises over to Teddy, who is busy eating his waffle. She reaches over to Teddy's plate and takes a big chunk of his waffle, stuffing it all into her mouth. "Don't take his food," the caregiver says gently. Nadia gives the caregiver a big grin.

What can be said of Nadia? Toddlers' persistent curiosity about the surrounding environment is very powerful, and their reality testing takes place primarily through the senses. Perhaps Nadia had asked herself, "What is this stuff? It looks familiar. It really tastes good." Perhaps the heady feeling of discovering it herself and of controlling it herself fueled her continuing investigation. Had she been seen while she was under the table, would her behavior have been understood in the same way she experienced it?

Sometimes eating episodes reveal glimpses of how the toddler thinks and how the toddler's visual-motor coordination functions. Kira, 12 months, is not only involved in the joy of eating, but she is practicing the coordinated use of her hands and eyes, as well as the skill of following the path of a falling object. Both are necessary for the development of object permanence.

Kira, at her mother's side, walks through the classroom door with a bumpy gait and goes right to the caregiver, who picks her up and puts her in a high chair near the table where other children are sitting on small chairs. "Ee—ee," she says. "Say bye-bye," the caregiver instructs her. She waves to her mother as she goes out the door. The caregiver ties on Kira's bib. She plumps her hands on the high chair tray and smiles at the second caregiver, who has just come into her sight. She waves her hands in the air, smiles, pulls on her hair. When the caregiver puts some pieces of pancake on the tray, she holds one piece in her left hand while using her right hand to put pieces in her mouth. One piece drops to the floor. She looks over the side of the high chair, following the path of the fall until she locates the pancake on the floor. She shifts her gaze to the tray, takes another piece in one hand, and eats with the other. She watches the caregiver while she eats. Then she drops another piece where the first had fallen.

For infants and toddlers, feeding and eating certainly entail experiences of pleasure and satisfaction. Conversely, if problems exist, the eating itself may be uncomfortable, or a tense, unsatisfying time. Records will reveal the emotional impact of the situation over time and those characteristics that are singular to the child being observed.

However, for children under 3, eating and feeding are activities unto themselves. Being fed involves trusting an adult. It means that a certain synchronism exists between child and adult—making eye contact, molding of the infant body to that of the adult, conversational give-and-take. It also involves the coordination of eye and hand as the baby begins, for example, to reach for the spoon, and tactile investigation through mouth and hand of the varying textures of food. We also see the dawning, budding, and flowering of autonomy, and the beginnings of language. In sum, while eating and feeding may be categorized by adults as activities of certain characteristics, important to the child, they are probably perceived by children in a multitude of other ways.

It is for these reasons that we observe eating and feeding episodes. Through them we learn about many developments occurring in these young beings. When Gus, at 15 months, puts his remaining two drops of juice back into the pitcher, and then puts the cup itself into the pitcher, he is continuing his experimentation with reality as an extension of the eating situation. Pouring the juice back was an exercise of eye-hand coordination and a possible imitation of adults who do the pouring. Will the cup fit into the pitcher? Reality testing of space and size are taking place.

Looking thus beyond each observed action leads to the discovery that the world looks different through the eyes of the child than through the eyes of the adult.

*Napping.* While diapering/toileting and eating/feeding are routines that occur with some regularity and frequency, napping is a routine that is frequent but not always regular, depending on the nature and age of the baby. Some very young babies sleep long stretches between feedings, some take a series of "catnaps" with alert, or fussy, periods in between. Older babies may have consolidated their daytime sleeping to one or two naps. While some babies go off willingly to nap, looking forward to the restorative interlude, others are naysayers, if not in word then in deed—like the baby who refuses to lie down, but sits instead on the cot or in the crib, keeping eyes open at all cost; or the toddler who, shrieking and flailing about, keeps a distance from the rest space and sometimes, despite himself, falls asleep on a chair or on the floor late in the afternoon. Each baby has an individual style and a set of private feelings about sleep. Some are fearful and tense about sleeping in a place that is not home; others are content to sleep provided they have their favorite "cozy" from home; some are not used to sleeping alone without a parent or sibling; still others seem willing to lie down and sleep without any fanfare whatever.

Napping patterns sometimes change over time, however, from several naps to two, from two naps to one, from calm to tension-filled situations, from restless to relaxed. Recording over a period of time the baby's approach to the nap, the baby's response to the caregiver at this time, and the way in which the baby manages to fall asleep—and later to wake up—will reveal something about the baby's sense of trust in the caregiver, in the group, and in the environment in general. It will also show how willing the baby is to exchange the exciting, active, awake world for the passive world of sleep.

The following record of two children at nap time reveals their relaxed, natural, and trusting feelings about sleeping at their center:

> Nora, the caregiver, is holding Carmen's (32 months old) hand as they enter the nap room. Nora says to Sylvan (30 months), who is standing nearby, "Say good night to Carmen. She's going for her nap." Sylvan walks into the nap room with Nora and Carmen, watching as Carmen lies down and Nora covers her, patting her briefly on the back. "Have a good nap," says Nora as she and Sylvan leave the room, closing the door. Sylvan sits on the couch, while Nora fixes him a bottle of juice. Bringing the bottle to him, she sits on the couch and begins to take off his shoes. He leans against her, sucking on the bottle. "Shall we read a book?" she asks. "Yes." She begins to read *Goodnight Moon*. When it is finished, they walk into the nap room, and she covers him when he lies down. No words have been spoken, but an understanding of the routine and a pervading tenderness are apparent.

Records of the child asleep, if possible, as well as of the child waking up, may show another side of her personality. Attention to the following details will provide a rich record:

- Is the sleep restless and fidgety, or calm and quiet?
- On awakening, does the child cry, or call out, or pop out of bed and appear in the midst of activity?
  - » Is the child tense, or disoriented, or difficult to comfort?
  - » How does this behavior fit with the behavior you have seen in other situations?
- Do these reactions, to sleep and to awakening, have meanings for the baby? Can you surmise those meanings?

*Outings.* Getting ready for an outing, the outing itself, and the return to the center are all routine situations that afford an opportunity to understand the infant/toddler in more depth. Going out involves a transition from the known to the less known and means a separation from the classroom. If not all children are taken out at the same time, it also involves a separation from some adults and children. (In such a situation, it is worthwhile observing those children who do not go out, but who stay behind.) There are several observations that should be made.

- How does the child react to preparation for going out? (frightened, worried, matter of fact, with eager anticipation)
- Is the child able to contain excitement and attend to the necessities of dressing, or is the anticipation overwhelming, making dressing and organizing a difficult procedure?
- How does the style of the caregiver mesh with that of the child? A frantic caregiver, for example, might do little to help organize a toddler who is running about the room resisting wearing a coat or hat.
- How are negotiations between infants/toddlers and various caregivers carried out?
- What effect do the child's manner, requests, compliances, resistances, have on different adults? Some adults, for example, are charmed and bent to the will of a child who uses facial expressions and words with finesse, where others are offended by the use of such "wiles" and refuse to comply.

In the following record, Rashi, 34 months, wants to do things his way and the caregiver walks a careful line after making an initial error:

Rashi starts to go out the door to get his coat. The caregiver, Rich, says, "Wait, I have your coat here." Rashi begins to cry and wail. "Oh," says Rich, "I see that you want to get it yourself. I'll put it back on the hook." "No!" screams Rashi, grabbing the coat from Rich. He goes out to the hall and hangs it up himself. He returns to the room, stops, whirls himself in the opposite direction, and returns to the hall, grabs his coat off the hook, carries it into the room. He lays the coat on the floor in order to flip it over his head. He flips it, but it is upside down.

Casually, Rich says, "Rashi, your coat is upside down." Rashi ignores him. When Rich turns away to talk to another child, Rashi slips the coat off and tries again with an equal lack of success. He hands the coat to Rich without speaking, and Rich ties it around Rashi's waist by the sleeves. "No!" he shrieks as he pulls away. Rich quietly removes the coat and helps Rashi on with it. Rashi allows Rich to hold the coat while he puts his arms into the sleeves. He stares at Rich and commands him, "Zip it up!" Rich zips it, and they go out together, hand in hand.

Returning to the center after an outing involves, for the very young child, another transition that may ignite a range of feelings. If it is close to lunchtime, for instance, toddlers may experience hunger, or worry about an impending nap, or be just plain fatigued. How does this affect their behavior? What does it mean when the caregiver says, "Juan always cries when we get within a half block of the center," or "I have to watch Harry closely because as soon as he sees our doorway he begins to run"? What meaning does coming back to the center have for babies and toddlers, and what is each child's special way of communicating that meaning?

Look at Jonathan, 35 months, and Mara, 26 months, whose feelings on returning to the center from a short walk are much larger than their vocabularies.

> Coming into the classroom through the door, Mara and Jonathan both take hold of the doorknob at the same time. Both scream and jump up and down, trying to be the only one to hold the knob. Amid screams, Mara pokes Jonathan's eye. He continues to pull on the knob, while she screams, "No! No! Next time I close the door!" Betsy, the caregiver, reaches them at this point and says, evenly, "What's going on?" Mara shouts, "I close the door!" Betsy quietly asks, "Can I help you close the door?" Jonathan drops his hand from the knob and stands still, looking at Betsy. Mara continues to scream. Betsy asks her, "You want to do it yourself?" Mara looks at her and says yes. Jonathan watches quietly as Betsy stands still and Mara opens the door slightly and then closes it. The three of them, without speaking, turn and head toward the snack table.

Autonomy, a central developmental issue in 2-year-olds, is vigorously depicted in this anecdote. What contributed to the escalation of feeling will have to be surmised, or discovered by further recording. Records like these shed light on normal developmental situations and point the way to further study of the special individual characteristics of the children involved. Winnowing one from the other—developmental characteristics from individual behavior—is a task that requires continual recording.

## Playing and Exploring

It is surely through play that infants and toddlers learn their way about the world and exercise their burgeoning physical and intellectual skills. Their ceaseless tasting, smelling, poking, prodding, looking, and touching define them as scientists, forever wanting to find out "what" and "how." Who can say where play ends and learning begins, or where, at what point, random activity becomes abstract thought? Somewhere, and everywhere, in the activity of the under-3s lies the roots of thought, language, and conceptualization.

To record at random the play and exploration of infants and toddlers is to obtain and fully appreciate an intimate view of the young mind and body at work. Which behaviors, exactly, can truly be called play? Which can be called exploration? Which intentional? Which happenstance? Clearly, no specific behaviors in the very young can be labeled as such. It is beyond question that the total of the baby's activity is a composite of play, exploration, learning, and language development. These activities cannot be teased apart or preselected for observation. In fact, social interaction, language activities, perceptual-cognitive activities, and both large- and small-motor activities are included in a definition of babies' play. Thus, recording any behavior will most likely serve to reveal the young child playing, learning, and expressing feelings.

Here are situations that focus on babies and toddlers playing and exploring. In the first, the child is moving freely about his physical environment.

> Angelo (5 months) is lying on a small blanket on his stomach. Smoothly he rolls over on to his back and pats a toy that is next to him. He rolls again from his back to his stomach, props himself up on his arms, and smiles at Demaris the caregiver. He reaches out for a large snap bead that is in front of him, puts it in his mouth for a few seconds, drops the bead and rolls over onto his back again. Demaris offers him the snap bead, which he grasps and continues to chew on. He smiles broadly at her. His body is relaxed, and at times he moves his legs as he chews.

The second situation occurs when children are using any playthings, play equipment, or household items like pots and pans, boxes, and spoons.

> Marisol (9 months) is sitting on the floor. She spies one of her booties that has fallen off. She picks it up and begins to chew on it. She bangs

it several times on the wheel of a kiddie car. She drops the bootie, pulls the kiddie car over on its side, and squeals, "Ah da da da ba!" She pats the wheels and puts her hand under the car.

The third situation occurs when children are engaged with specific materials such as water, dough, blocks, paint, crayons, or food preparation.

Dana (18 months) stands at the water table tightly holding a small container that he has filled with water. He tips it carefully into a very large pot that is sitting in the water table. Looking directly at the stream of flowing water, he says in a loud and confident voice, "Dumpy!"

When collected, such observations will offer a view into the level of the child's curiosity and interest in objects, the development and control of eye-hand coordination and gross-motor ability, and the growing understanding of causes.

Within these records will be seen not only *what* the baby is learning but *how* the baby is learning it. Here is 19-month-old Ezra, who through imitation and random exploration is trying to understand the unknown properties of keys and keyholes, using his own familiar body as referent:

Isaac, 25 months, tries to open a cabinet door with a key he is holding. It doesn't work. Ezra watches Isaac and then tries the same motion on the door, but without the key. Ezra turns to Isaac and takes the key out of his hand. Isaac does not protest. Ezra shows the key to his father, who is sitting on the floor near the cabinet, waiting to take Ezra home. Ezra plops down on the floor next to his father. He lifts up his shirt and tries to put the key into his navel. Quietly, his father says, "Don't do that."

A world of difference exists between the 19-month-old toddler investigating the similarities of a keyhole and a navel, and an infant of 7 months who is beginning to teach herself that objects have a permanent existence.

Shao (7 months) is sitting in a high chair. She holds a rubber squeeze animal in both hands, joyously mouthing one of its ears. Suddenly it drops to the floor. She leans over, her eyes riveted on the fallen toy. Though the caregiver picks it up, Shao continues to look at the spot where the toy had been. The caregiver hands the animal to Shao, saying, "Here's your kitty, Shao." Shao pats the animal with one open palm, momentarily chews the ear, then examines it with her eyes as she turns it back and forth in her hand. Her expression is intent. She makes a series of "ah" sounds and returns to chewing seriously on the protruding ear.

With many more such experiences, plus maturation, Shao will develop a more certain sense of the existence and the qualities of things and people. In each anecdote above, the behavior observed was within a developmental range for each child at that age. But what if the behavior of the child raises questions for you? What if, for example, Shao were unable to hold and inspect the plaything, or were uninterested in, though capable of, doing so? All behavior must be evaluated and understood within an established framework of developmental progress and the observer must check any hints of possible developmental delay. Before any conclusion is made, however, records should be taken over a period of time to determine whether the behavior is merely a lapse, possibly due to illness or fatigue, or is, indeed, a matter for concerned attention.

One of the difficulties in recording play is that it frequently does not look like play. Often toddler activity looks like no activity. It looks like "fooling around" or "doing nothing." Here is Edwidge, 15 months old, engaged with a handful of plastic shapes that were designed for preschoolers. She, however, uses (plays with) them for her own purposes—grasping, clutching, collecting, feeling their texture, experiencing their weight, and above all, exercising her autonomy by doing with them what she will. No one intervenes in her explorations, so she has an opportunity to try out a range of actions.

Edwidge walks randomly about the room holding a few plastic shapes in her fists, plopping her feet as she goes, laughing and dropping some of the shapes on the floor. She momentarily puts her hand on the couch as she goes by, then climbs up on it, merrily announcing, "Eeh—ahh—ehh—da—dii—di." She puts a few of the shapes on the couch while still holding others in her hand. She turns her body so that she is on her tummy and, using her fists for support, clutches the shapes as she slides off the couch. She walks over to Joan, a caregiver, swinging her arms and shoulders. She passes Joan, smiling as she goes by, and climbs over a large hollow block, sits on it, all the while still clutching the plastic shapes. Sitting there, she puts one shape at a time in her mouth, giving them rapid little licks, then drops them next to her, on the block, saying, "Da" several times in a rising inflection. She retrieves the shapes from the block, walks to the slide, and places them on the steps. She raises her hand, saying, "Ga da" as she puts the shapes on the next higher step. She leaves the shapes there and walks away.

Around the age of 2, toddlers' random exploration and play begin to look more organized to the adult eye. The 2- to 2-and-a-half-year-old at a water basin engages in more recognizable actions with a sponge and bowl than does a 13-month-old, who might plop a crayon in the tub or venture a splash or two with an open hand.

Using materials like crayons or felt-nib markers takes on more complex dimensions as pure investigation is overlaid with symbolic meaning. Using crayons may stimulate in the 2-year-old a sense of pleasure in the colors themselves, as well as delight in mastery. A drawing by a child of 34 months, who carefully made, across the page, one vertical line after another, each of a separate color, evidences such delight in color.

On the other hand, observations of a 30-month-old, drawing picture after picture containing small, knotlike circles of different colors confined to the center of the paper, may point to another dimension. As he worked, his face was set, and his body was held stiffly erect in his chair. His teacher realized, both through observation and by collecting his drawings, that he did many such pictures during the first few weeks of school. Possibly he used these materials in an attempt to express his feelings about starting the new group experience.

For the 18- to 36-month-old, playing and exploring with materials allows the sheer pleasure of making a mark where there was none before, and of expressing deep feelings and ideas nonverbally. The use of such materials as paints, water, dough, and blocks also supports the budding human need to represent experience with the world. Can we say whether a drawing by Audette, at 35 months, of a large circle surrounded by many attached, perpendicular lines— which she calls a "sun"—is truly a spontaneous representation or a learned convention?

Close observation may reveal otherwise hidden developments. Two-year-old Louie indicates an awareness of print, but no one except the observer would know it.

Louie makes a large, blue oval shape on the paper. He says aloud (to no one in particular), "This is an *A*." He fills in the shape with red extending the original boundaries. He attaches a blue blob, paints over it in yellow. It becomes green. He swirls red across both shapes, puts the brush into the cup, and leaves the easel.

Surely, the beginnings of symbolic play, which flowers openly in the preschool years into complex role-taking, can be detected in the play of 2-year-olds. In the following record of vastly more elaborate action than is recorded in the previously described play of 19-month-old Ezra with the key, a symbolic reorganization of two salient features of the lives of these under-3s is seen. A few gestures and words represent their experience.

> Angel, 30 months, carries a block. As he strides along, he says, "I going to work. I going to work." Kristie, 26 months, walking with him, takes her lunch box from the shelf (these children bring their lunch to the center) and loudly announces, "We going to school." They walk along for a moment, and Angel spies a doll stroller, complete with doll. He pushes it as they continue to march around the room together, Kristie holding the lunch box, he still clutching the block. As they near the CD player, Kristie sits down to listen, and Angel moves to the table where the teacher is sitting.

Even more elaborate social play involving shared meaning is sometimes seen, especially if the toddlers have been in group care together for an extended period of time, as is the case below:

> Three children put one-inch-square colored cubes into small cups and pretend to drink. "This is my soda, this is Diet Coke. I like soda and Diet Coke. Here's the cake," says Tamar. She lines up several colored wooden cubes and each child puts a few cubes on a small plate. Jesse exclaims, "Happy birthday" and "blows out" the candles. Then they all blow and sing "Happy birthday to you." Lila gets three dolls, giving one to Tamar and one to Jesse. Each girl feeds cake to her doll using a small spoon.

To round out this prelude to a more developed use of expressive materials and imaginative play, look at Chapters 3 and 5, which explore the playing of 2- to 6-year-olds in depth.

### Interaction with Adults and Children

The phenomenon of infant and toddler social life has been richly described because there are so many opportunities to observe these very young children in groups (Balaban, 1992; Leavitt, 1994; Shonkoff & Phillips, 2000).

The social world of infants and toddlers is highlighted through anecdotes of interactions with both adults and other children. Records of the young child's interactions with adults may include exchanges with a wide range of people, from the familiar to the strange; from the baby's parents to the caregivers; from a student teacher to the cook; from a casual visitor to a regular delivery or service person. Including such a wide range of adults as material for observation widens the opportunity to appreciate the baby's repertoire for dealing with adults. Guidelines for these observations include the following:

- Exactly how does the child react to familiar people?
  » Is it always the same or does it vary?
  » Is it predictable?
- How does the child react to unfamiliar people?
  » Is there any difference in the child's reaction if the stranger is a man or a woman?
  » Have changes been seen in these reactions over time?
- Does the child initiate contacts with adults? How?
- What sorts of response does the child elicit from adults?
  » What are the range and variation of these responses?
- Is the child able to communicate his needs to the adult?
- Is the child able to attract attention to herself? How?

The quality of the interactions between an infant/toddler and adults is the single most significant aspect of that baby's life in group care. It is through these relationships that babies forge an opinion of the world and a concept of their own potentiality. Therefore, records of such transactions are crucial for understanding youngsters' view of their human environment. The implications for staff development are full of promise, for the records will address both the child's experience with adults and the adults' behavior.

> At the table where the toddlers are eating pancakes, the caregiver, Mark, holds Brittany (7 months) on his lap. He also holds a bottle of maple syrup. Brittany grasps the neck of the bottle and fingers the cap. When she lets go, Mark claps her hand against his. Brittany laughs. He turns her around to face him and gently bounces her on his knees. She laughs. She reaches out and touches the hair of the child who is sitting nearest to her, saying "AHH." At this moment another teacher brings in a huge pancake and all the children laugh at its size. Brittany laughs too.

Some children are skilled at eliciting responses from adults. Here is a record of Earl, 15 months, who has figured out a way to keep the universal game of peekaboo going, even after the caregiver thought it had ended:

> Ana Maria, the caregiver, is at one end of the fish tank and Earl is at the other. She initiates peekaboo by looking around the side of the tank and then popping her head back. Earl does the same, grinning from ear to ear. Then she catches his eye through the tank. She drops down out of sight. He giggles. She switches to the side again, and he looks for her there as she repeats the game. She leaves the fish tank for a moment, but sees him looking around the tank for her, so she returns to play the game again. He laughs and peeks around. This induces her to play yet again. She begins to put the blocks away, leaving the tank. He starts to put his bottle in the tank, but she bounds over just in time to stop him. He grins.

However, experiences with adults are not always such fun. Sometimes very young children become overwhelmed with thoughts of their absent parents and rely on adults to help them through difficult times. The availability of an empathic adult during a surge of strong feelings is a crucial factor in the child's positive perception of the social world. Here is 20-month-old Heather, at one moment listening placidly to a story, at the next sobbing for her mother:

> Cecilia is reading a story to Heather. Suddenly Heather begins to cry, and throws a small car. Soothingly, Cecilia says, "Your mommy will be back. She'll be back." Heather cries, "Mommy!" and runs to the door. She begins pounding on it. Cecilia puts her arms around Heather and says, "I'm going to pick you up and tell your bunny that I guess you're missing your mommy." Heather allows Cecilia to pick her up, they settle on the floor near the photo of her mother, and Cecilia says, "Mommy will come back. We'll tell her what you did today." She adds, "Dirt. Right?" Cecilia echoes, "Right. We went to see the tractor with the dirt." Cecilia puts her face close to Heather's, and they rub noses. Heather examines, with her fingers and her eyes, Cecilia's necklace and earrings. As she does so, Cecilia comments, "You are really interested in my earrings," and, pointing to the photo of Heather's mother, "Your mom has earrings, too." Suddenly, Heather pops out of Cecilia's lap and walks steadily to the other side of the room to watch some children who are sticking soft plastic shapes to the mirror.

Such a record helps magnify how rapidly Heather became flooded with frightening, lonely feelings and how she was able to use the ministrations of the adult to reorganize her briefly shattered self. The record also spotlights the caregiver's skill.

The meaningful, everyday, social milieu of the infant and toddler is also comprised of other children. The joy of two toddlers greeting each other as they enter a child care center often rivals that of the pleasure of 9-year-old "chums" seeing each other at the start of a school day.

Not only do such very young children enjoy one another's company but they also express preferences. It is not unusual to see a subdued toddler "come to life" with the arrival of a friend. Reactions occur not only to friends but to "enemies" as well. Some toddlers seem to have a truly active distaste for one another. Record-keeping in such instances gives staff members an opportunity to look deeply into both children's interpersonal relationships and their own role. Staff development can be continually replenished with new recorded observations. Such material feeds the wellsprings of teacher renewal.

What are some of the instances that include what we have termed infant/toddler interaction? They appear at almost any time during the day and require only the ear and eye of an aware adult—plus the ever-ready pad of paper and a pencil. Sam, at 18 months, is engaged in a true social exchange in the following record—first with 16-month-old Tina and then with his teacher:

> While eating dessert, Sam and Tina were sitting next to each other. They began to playfully feed each other. They both laughed and looked at each other as they took turns putting their spoons of applesauce into the mouth of the other. Sam smiled. He really enjoyed this game. He seemed to have had his fill of food and was obviously intent on the pleasure of this interaction.
>
> Sam ripped off his bib, wiped himself with a napkin, and then proceeded to spill and wipe milk on the table. With an expression of contentment and absorption, he wiped a little milk, spilled a little, and wiped a little more. The teacher stood quietly by for about 2 minutes, allowing Sam's play. Then she also wiped up the spill, took Sam's hand, and walked with him to wash his hands and get ready for rest.

Tina and Sam were experimenting with a very early form of mutual play. They were learning that age-mates are interesting people. Further, because Sam's teacher understood the toddler's need for experimentation, she was able to help him make the transition from lunch to rest pleasant and satisfying.

How much we can glean from even the tiniest views into toddler relations! Imitation, for example, is a main avenue that connects one toddler to another. Above we saw Sam and Tina engaged in mutual imitative feeding. Here are Bradley and Maryrose caught for a slight moment at the very edge of mutual play:

> Bradley, 18 months, climbs into an adult-sized rocking chair. He turns his body to sit down, legs splayed on the large seat, hands on the chair's arms. "Row, row," he sings in a loud voice. Maryrose, 17 months, walks up to him, holds the arm of the chair, and rocks it, saying, "Row, row." Bradley gets off the chair and walks away.

It is often in gross-motor play that the small beginnings of peer social life lie. Exchanges of looks; pokes or pushes; empathic pats for a crying comrade; offering, giving, or grabbing an object or food, are all actions that constitute early social interaction. Imitation is a form that is also seen in situations of more than two infant/toddlers and has a contagious aspect.

> The caregiver turns the rocking boat over so that it has three steps on either side of a platform. She sits next to it in a chair. Brian, 17 months, and Dom, 15 months, begin to climb the steps. Abby, 14 months, climbs behind them. When Brian sits on the platform, Dom sits, then Abby sits. Brian gets up and walks down the other side, holding the caregiver's hand. Then Abby does the same. They stand at the bottom, smiling.

As children grow closer to 2-and-a-half and 3 their imitative play displays more complexity, more use of language, perhaps more of what adults label "friendship." Such records can provide us with a short history of the ripening of a relationship. Wayne, 30 months, and Maria, 32 months, have discovered that jumping and falling on a mattress together is better than doing it alone.

> Wayne jumps up on the mattress, then lands on his bottom. He giggles. Maria, who has been standing by watching him, lies down on the mattress, watching him out of the corner of her eye. Wayne lies down next to her. They regard each other, smiling. Wayne, looking Maria in the eye, says, "Let's jump," with which they both jump up and fall down on their bottoms. They look at each other and laugh heartily. Then, without words, they both get up and repeat the action, laughing just as hard. Maria says to Wayne, "Watch!" as she jumps and falls. Then Wayne jumps and falls as Maria watches. Maria gets up and counts "One! Two! Three! Go down!" and falls. Then Wayne does the same. They do this several more times.

Interactions are not made only of pleasant stuff. Some involve fury, provocation, hostility, spite. A 17-month-old who often bit was captured in the following record, about to strike. Perhaps the other child's previous experience with her saved him.

> Twenty-month-old Steven is walking out of a small doorway in a large packing crate, at the same moment that Bonnie, 17 months, is walking in. They are squeezed body to body in this small space. She quietly places her teeth on his arm. He silently moves his arm away before she sinks her teeth in, and they continue moving in opposite directions.

Feelings of possessiveness are a frequent source of conflict to which a thoughtful caregiver can bring peace:

> Eric, 21 months, is standing quietly, holding a small toy boat, face impassive. His body is relaxed as he stands. Charlie walks over to Eric and lightly touches the boat with one finger. "My boat! My boat!" Eric screams, looking at Charlie. The caregiver comes over and says softly, "That boat is important to you, isn't it, Eric?" Eric relaxes again. Charlie wanders off.

Angry feelings are sometimes expressed by young babies, as seen in this "fight" between two 11-month-olds:

> Kathy is sitting on the playroom floor, happily gurgling, and shaking a multicolored teething ring up and down in her right hand. She is smiling up at the caregiver, who is sitting in the rocking chair holding a younger infant on her lap. There is one other baby, 11-month-old Randy, sitting by the doorway.
>
> A caregiver comes into the room carrying a diaper for Randy. She bends down to Randy, intending to pick him up and change him, but he resists so much that she lets the diaper drop next to him. As Kathy spots the diaper she makes an "aarr" sound and scoots over to the diaper. At this time, Randy is picking up the diaper and happily swinging it up and down. Kathy plops down next to him and snatches the diaper away with an impish grin on her face. Randy, with an indignant shriek, reaches for it and tries to pull it away. Kathy begins to cry angrily but does not relinquish the diaper, and a tug-of-war ensues.
>
> Kathy wins and takes off across the room in a speedy crawl with the diaper clutched tightly in her hand. Randy furiously crawls after her and overtakes her in the corner. Kathy, with an angry yet panicky expression on her face, looks to the caregiver for help as she cries and Randy determinedly reaches out for the diaper. Another tug-of-war—and this time Randy is the victor. He grunts and stuffs part of the diaper in his mouth,

then waves it in front of Kathy. She is sobbing in a hurt and angry tone and waves her arms frantically up and down, then rubs her right hand behind her ear. Randy is staring at her as she reaches out and grasps the diaper. She pulls it away with a triumphant look on her face and turns away from Randy to crawl up on a nearby platform. Once on the platform, she sits and smiles at the two caregivers and flings the diaper happily up and down; her mouth forms a wide grin and her tongue is peeking out at the corner.

Kathy then spots her bottle lying across the room and, abandoning the diaper, crawls over to the bottle, cooing softly. Randy has also apparently lost interest in the diaper and is playing with a large rubber ball. The diaper is now in shreds.

Continued recording of such incidents will turn up items that can be evaluated realistically within the total range of recorded interactions. Often teachers and caregivers think there is more conflict than there really is. This misconception occurs because conflict is more dramatic and, therefore, gains more adult attention. Loving relations are taken for granted. Records help put both sorts of transactions into proper perspective.

Since the relationships of babies and toddlers contain only the rudiments of later, fully formed relationships, they are often evanescent, rapidly developing, and of short duration. Yet the sum total of contacts, imitations, angers, and joys will reveal to the recorder a rich and varied social life.

## Language

The recording and study of infant and toddler language is an art of significant magnitude, which goes beyond the scope of this book. It is a field in which vast numbers of studies have been done. Scholars have devoted many years to unlocking the secrets of human speech by their painstaking gathering of verbatim language samples from the very young (e.g., Anisfeld, 1984; Nelson, 1989; Weir, 1962).

However, we who work with children under 3 cannot leave the total investigation of language development or child behavior to others. Teachers and caregivers need practice in the skill of collecting information in order to know firsthand how children learn to talk and to use language.

To this end, the collection of verbatim samples of language sounds, as well as words and sentences, will be a most rewarding undertaking. The coos and babbles of infancy can be recorded as well as the beginning words and phrases of toddlerhood. Such notations, which will be included as a matter of course in any observation, will reveal patterns of change and increasing complexity when scrutinized over as short a period as 2 or 3 months.

Toddlers' beginning language and concepts are fueled by the variety of sensory experiences that absorb their attention. In this record (adapted from Andersen, 1995) of Jane, the caregiver, walking outdoors with Oliver (28 months) and Pablo (16 months) on a bright fall day, how many words, memories, and ideas arise from sensory stimulation!

> As they step outside, a light breeze blows some leaves off a nearby tree. Oliver points excitedly at the leaves and cries out, "Bubbles?" Jane wonders if Oliver is making a connection between the way both the leaf and soap bubbles (his favorite activity) float gently on breezes. She says, "It does float like a bubble, doesn't it?" They walk to the corner where passengers are getting off and on a bus. Pablo cries out, "Bus, bus—Daddy, bus!" Jane replies, "Pablo, I'll bet you're thinking about coming to the center on the bus with your Daddy." As the bus pulls away, Jane and the children wait on the corner for the light to change. As Jane watches the street, Pablo looks up at the light and shadows moving across a building on the other side of the street. He pulls Jane's arm and points to the light, babbling some sounds with a questioning intonation. Jane comments, "Oh, you see the sunshine on the building." Pablo continues to study the play of light and shadow. As they walk across the street, Oliver spots his favorite neighborhood store—the one with a large display of sneakers in the window. He happily sings out, "Shoes, shoes, shoes."
>
> As they stop in front of the window, Oliver begins to carefully study the different sneakers. He looks at a particularly large pair and observes, "Daddy shoes." As Oliver studies the sneakers, Pablo moves his hand across the bricks on the lower part of the building. He discovers a hole in the mortar and spends several minutes poking his finger in and out of the hole. Suddenly the wind picks up and blows some clouds in front of the sun. Oliver looks at Jane and tucks his chin down to his chest, while Pablo snuggles against her leg. Oliver says, "Windy." Jane replies, "Yes, it's windy and chilly. Let's go back inside," and they head back to the center.

Words are not the only way caregivers and children connect to one another. Indeed, children's nonverbal language can engender a very special shared meaning (Stern, 1985), as a teacher recorded in the following (Hansen, 1995):

As Ana (24 months) approaches holding up a dripping scrub brush and sponge dishwashing wand, the teacher says, "I see, you have a scrub brush and a sponge." Ana smiles, turns her body, and gestures with the dishwashing wand toward the area where a large group of children are still scrubbing paint off the windows and deck. (p. 15)

The teacher went on to explain that

by pointing to the scene on the other side of the deck, Ana allowed me to see and experience the whole of how wonderful, scary, and exciting it was for her to be washing windows with a boisterous group of other toddlers. This is something she probably could not have conveyed to me with words. Compare what the effect of her possible words would be: "Look, we're washing windows." I hardly think that a sentence like that captures anything of what she was trying to share with me. (p. 15)

There are certain characteristics to notice as records are taken. The following suggestions are highlights for observational attention:

- Which situations seem to elicit the production of sounds in the infant? (a speaking adult, a moving toy, a music box, a small child)
- Does the presence or absence of the parent influence the infant's production of sounds? (the presence or absence of the caregiver, a stranger, other children)
- What new sounds appear in the infant's repertoire over a period of several days? Weeks?
- Does the baby, around 8 to 12 months of age, attempt to repeat words spoken directly to him? Which words?
- Does the baby babble? Under what circumstances?
- Does the toddler use sounds that are not understandable, but have the rhythm and cadence of English speech or the dominant language in her home?
- Does the toddler combine sounds into two or three syllables?
- Does the toddler produce recognizable words?
  » Does she combine any of these words to make two- or three-word sentences?
- What is the range of the baby or toddler's understanding of what is said to him?
- At what point does the child sing? Chant nonsense words? Repeat words for fun, rather than understanding?

Records like the following illustrate how much of a child's language is learned from and exercised with other children and how pleasurable imitation is for the very young. Mindy and Derrick, both 14 months, are sitting at a table with Ina, 24 months, eating apples and cheese:

> Mindy says, "Ba bee, ba bee."
> Derrick, imitating, says, "Ba bee." He then looks across the table at Mindy who says, "Bo."
> Derrick imitates again, "Bo."
> Ina says clearly, "I want more cheese."
> Derrick, pointing to the bowl on the counter where the cheese is kept, says, "Cheese." The caregiver hands the cheese to Derrick and Ina. Derrick chews the cheese, opens his mouth, and says, "Ah. Haa Ha," looking directly at Mindy, who laughs. Derrick throws back his head and makes a fake laugh. "Ah. Ha! Ha!" He repeats the motion and the sound three times. Then he laughs a genuine laugh and pushes the cheese into his mouth with his fingers. Ina, Mindy, and Derrick then together say, "Ba, ba, ba, ah, ha, ha." Mindy turns her face up to the ceiling and says, "Ah. Ha. Ha." She cackles.

Children use imitation and repetition for both learning and fun. There seems to be something inherently satisfying for them in this activity.

> Kelly, 25 months, peeks into the nap room, which is empty of children. "Nobody sleeping," he says to no one in particular. "Not Jonathan, not Sally, not Jamie, not Frannie, not Kelly. Nobody sleeping." He repeats his chant of nonsleeper's names, but this time he jumps in the air with each name.

As children near 3, language increasingly becomes a clarifying tool. As some of the children's ideas are recorded, we can understand in the smallest detail how truly full of mystery this confusing world is to children.

> At lunchtime, 30-month-old Nora was having trouble peeling her banana and asked the teacher for help. As the teacher peeled it, Nora told her, "My mommy put that peel on this morning."

Words are often interesting in and of themselves, and young children seem to enjoy their feeling on the tongue.

> When Joan, 24 months, asked her mother, "What's a budget cut?" we wonder what that phrase conjured up in her young mind.

Richard, 28 months, is sitting in the caregiver's lap, observing a group of children going out with another teacher to get their snack from the kitchen. Spontaneously, unrelated to ongoing events and to no one in particular, he says, "Spring water." "Do you drink spring water?" the teacher asks. He gives the teacher a blank look.

Records also show us just how much children love to play with language. It is a special kind of plaything.

When the teacher asks Antony what he is building, he says, "I'm building a traffic clack. A traffic clack. A traffic clack. A clacking sound makes a traffic clack."

There is no true end to the recording of infant/toddler language, social interaction, play, or behavior during caregiving routines. It is an ongoing, never-ending endeavor. Each day brings new change, new development, added skills, new feelings. In records lie a deep mine of treasures. The pen is the teacher's probe. The observer's tools—eyes, ears, and hands—are an unparalleled source of fresh and lively material that, when collected and sorted, assures constant refreshment in the practice of teaching.

# 12

# Recording the Behavior of Children for Whom There Are Special Concerns

Most teachers have at least one child in their group who causes them to wonder why each day is such a challenge for them and the child. We've all heard, or made, comments like these: "He just can't pay attention." "She seems to have no friends." "He is so very clumsy." "She's always a no-sayer." "He lets the other kids walk all over him."

Observation of children like these, whose behavior raises concerns, will not lead us to a conclusion or a diagnostic classification. However, observation can help teachers consider whether a child seems to be able to organize the continual stream of stimulation and information he takes in. Observation can help teachers become aware of how a child regulates and controls her behavior as well as her body's movements—with ease or with difficulty. Teachers can play a role, by sharing their records with the school director and staff, in the process of deciding how to help the child. In addition, it is imperative to consult a qualified professional if you suspect any developmental irregularity. A consultant may find these records helpful and use them along with relevant assessments to provide a diagnostic evaluation. Finally, several conferences with the parent(s) or family are required before referring the child to a specialist (Abbott & Gold, 1991). These conferences must be done with the utmost care and sensitivity because any news about a child's suspected difficulty is devastating to parents.

While it is common knowledge that there is an inseparable connection between mind and body, it is critical to remember that, for young children,

> until about the age of seven, the brain is primarily a *sensory processing machine*. . . . A young child . . . is concerned mainly with sensing [things] and moving his body in relationship to those sensations. His adaptive responses are more muscular, or *motor*, than mental. Thus the first seven

years of life are called the years of sensory motor development. (Ayres, 1979, p. 7, emphasis in original)

As adults we are so oriented to verbal expressions of thought and feeling that it is easy for us to overlook meaningful cues from children's body movements. Notice a child's confidence, or lack of confidence, in his body. Be aware of how much control, or lack of control, a child has of her body. Attend to how a child adapts his body to a wide range of situations—from playing games to sitting still. The child's relationship to her body is central because "the ability to fine-tune and regulate the body is the foundation upon which other regulatory abilities, including regulating thoughts and emotions are built" (Greenspan, 1989, p. 202).

As a rule, teachers become aware that a problem exists when a child exhibits bizarre or extreme forms of behavior—persistent unusual responses to other people and/or events, continual aggressiveness, excessive timidity, overdependence on adults, atypical, idiosyncratic, or limited language use. Yet less striking kinds of behavior such as poor large- or small-muscle coordination, inability to follow directions, difficulty in planning and organizing actions, trouble attending to the task at hand, and inhibiting impulses may also require special attention. Behaviors of this sort may be related to self-regulatory processes, or they might also be connected to cultural or linguistic differences.

Records will reveal whether certain behaviors that are of concern occur *frequently, persistently, and/or in consistent patterns* and *where, when, and under what circumstances.* Inattention, high activity level, and disruptiveness in young children, however,

> is not a predictor of lasting difficulties. These behaviors are normal and typical for [young children], who are just beginning to bring action under the control of thought. Instead the *severity and frequency* of these symptoms are critical in determining whether or not a [young] child is at risk for future problems. (Berk & Winsler, 1995, p. 90, emphasis in original)

Remember that *no single behavior is significant.* Only a combination of several that persist may signify the presence of a problem.

Observing and recording can support teachers as they look to Vygotsky's (1930/1978) teaching and discover what these children *can* do "independently and with the assistance of others" (p. 84) in the "zone of proximal development." Observation is a key to compassionate relationships with children whose behavior is puzzling or troublesome.

## SENSORY REACTIVITY AND SELF-REGULATION

It is through the sensory system that a person receives, interprets, and understands information about the environment.[1] How children organize, react to, and integrate this potpourri of sensory information influences their behavior, their affect, and their thought (Greenspan, 1992). This knowledge can direct teachers' attention to how the body and the brain act together in the social/emotional, physical, cognitive/communication/language, and play arenas of a child's life.

In this chapter we have separated these arenas for the purpose of more focused observation. Never forget, however, that these separate domains overlap and have strong mutual influences on one another. Physical difficulties, for example, can influence cognition—a child who is unable to crawl will receive a limited amount of information, perhaps affecting her thinking. The goal for children who are experiencing developmental difficulties is threefold: (1) to help them manage (self-regulate) their particular irregularities; (2) to help them integrate their social/emotional, physical, cognitive, and communicative selves (Greenspan, 1992); and (3) to discover their strengths and abilities.

### Social/Emotional Behaviors

We cannot begin to know all the causes of a child's difficult social or emotional behaviors, but we can describe what such behaviors are. These descriptions may provide clues to the nature of the teacher's response. For example, a child who seems unable to sequence his activities when he arrives at the classroom in the morning might be redirected in the following manner. The teacher could break down his tasks into small parts by giving instructions one at a time such as, "First, hang up your coat," then, after he does that, "Now put away your lunch box," and when he finishes that, "Now you can choose blocks or paint." This would be preferable to an all-in-one sequence such as, "Hang up your coat, put your lunch box away, and then choose an activity."

The following questions will guide your thinking about particular social/emotional behaviors of children for whom you have special

---

1. Sensory reactivity refers to processing—taking in and organizing stimuli—through the tactile, auditory, visual, olfactory, vestibular, and proprioceptive systems. Tactile refers to touch; auditory to hearing; visual to sight; olfactory to smell; and vestibular to the person's relation to gravity, affecting, through the inner ear, balance and stability in the world. Proprioceptive refers to knowing one's body in space: awareness of posture, movement, and changes in equilibrium; knowledge of position, weight, and resistance in relation to the body.

concerns. They will help organize your observations and influence your decisions about helpful adult responses.

- How does the child demonstrate her relationship to adults?
  - » Does she cling or touch adults excessively? Keep in mind that culturally related child-rearing practices need to be considered. It may be the first time the child has been left in the care of anyone other than the parent.
  - » Does she avoid adults? The child's age and experience are important to consider here—the younger the child the more dependent on adults. In the following anecdote, Theo is 5 years old and has attended the center for 3 years. The teacher provides a scaffold that enables him to organize his feelings and manage his difficulty in separating from his mother.

Theo enters the classroom leaning against his mother, tightly clasping her hand. He hides his head in her skirt. As she talks with the teacher, he releases her hand but tightly hangs on to one of her fingers. His mother guides him to a table where there are crayons and paper. He races the crayons back and forth across the paper, while she sits next to him. When she rises to leave, he drops the crayons, screws up his face, and grabs hold of her arm. The teacher says, "I'll walk with you and mommy to the outside door." When the teacher and Theo reenter the classroom, he is crying. She holds him on her lap. "I guess you miss Mom. Want to cuddle a little?" He puts his head against her. After a few moments he is able to control his crying. He moves from her lap to a table where he watches a Lotto game in progress.

- How confident is the child in regulating aggression? Does he require consistent help to control anger? Although we must rely on professional expertise to determine causes, it illuminates the importance of sensory processing to understand that some children who have difficulty with muscle tone (muscles that are too loose or too tight) or who confuse sights and sounds or have impairments in sight or sound also have difficulty with control of their behavior and their impulses. The teacher may be the first person to notice that the child has a sensory impairment because the demands of school are different from those at home. In the following record, we do not know the source of Bernard's difficulty, but we can see the result of the teacher's helpful response:

Bernard and Arturo, both 4, are in the classroom loft shouting, "Shut your mouth!" to each other. They grab pillows and begin slamming them against each other. The teacher below says, firmly, "The loft is for quiet playing." Arturo drops his pillow, but Bernard jumps on top of Arturo and bangs a pillow on him several more times. The teacher climbs into the loft and plies Bernard off. Arturo climbs down. The teacher sits for several minutes talking quietly to Bernard until he is able to reorganize himself and calmly climb down.

- Does the child fail to express emotion, either verbally or physically, in a situation that would ordinarily provoke it? In the following record, 3-year-old Michelle doesn't give any indication that the experience has affected her:

Michelle was riding a large tricycle on the roof playground. She fell over onto the brick floor, and the heavy tricycle toppled over on top of her. A teacher and another child rushed over to disentangle her from the tricycle. When Michelle and the tricycle were righted, she got back on without a sound and rode off. The other child observed in amazement, "Look at Michelle, teacher; she didn't even cry."

- How well does the child inhibit impulses? Impulsive behavior often distracts a child from the task at hand. These young children in the two anecdotes below are able to respond to the teacher's intervention.

Sitting at a table, Arelis (3 years, 8 months) is painting on a sheet of newsprint. Large brushes in four paint containers are next to her. Removing the brush from the blue paint, she pats the paper gently several times with the brush, creating a small blob. Then she takes all four brushes and puts them into the white paint cup. She picks up the container of yellow paint, now without its brush, and brings it to her mouth, pouting her lips forward as if she is about to sip it. Gently the teacher brings the cup down, saying, "Paint is not for drinking, Arelis." A few minutes later when she tries again to drink the paint, the teacher repeats her words, and Arelis puts the cup down.

Klion, age 5, slowly washed his hands. At the paper towel dispenser he pulled down the lever with great effort and tore off a towel. He continued to pull down the lever five or six times, tearing off a towel each time and dropping it into the wastebasket below the dispenser. As he began to pull down the lever again, the teacher said softly, "Klion, you have enough towels now. Let's dry your hands." Klion let go of the lever and dried his hands on the last towel.

- Does the child have persistent, strong fears such as of animals or of strangers when she is in a safe surrounding? Emotions such as fear, joy, sadness, sometimes get out of hand and their expression seems inappropriate.

At an age when we could expect him to begin to distinguish fantasy from reality and have some control over fears, Fred, 5-and-a-half, told the teacher that he was very scared on a recent plane trip because "The bees bite planes."

In the following record, a 6-year-old has a tantrum long past the tantrum age. The emotion, whatever it was, became more than he could regulate. However, children with communication disorders may resort to disruptive behavior as their only way of communicating their needs.

When the teacher, who was reading a story to the class, said she would fix the book because it was torn, Bruce (age 6) said he was going to shoot her. He lay prone on the floor, crying and kicking his legs. He sat up, continuing to cry and talking unintelligibly. After the teacher had mended the book with tape, he continued to cry, refused to listen to the story, and (referring to the tape) repeatedly yelled, "Take it off!"

- How does the child react when there is a change of routine or when he goes to new places? With anxiety? With fear? Calmly? With confidence?
- What is the child's tolerance for frustration? How does she react, for example, while waiting on line for a turn on the swing or when being presented with a difficult task?
- How does the child react to criticism or disapproval? What does he do when told no? In this record, Mary's behavior is unusual.

Most of the children in the 4-year-old group were seated at table waiting for clay. Mary was sitting between Meg and Hector. When she received her clay, she pounded it onto the board, and then tried to lift it. To her delight, she discovered that the board was stuck to the clay. She picked it up by the clay and banged it back down on the table several times. Hector asked her to stop, but she ignored him and continued banging. The the teacher called to her from the next table and asked her to stop. She yelled, "No!" repeatedly, then burst into tears.

- Does the child make eye contact with people? If she persistently avoids another's gaze, is this behavior culturally determined or a social difficulty?
- Can you tell from actions or words if the child is positive, self-deprecating, unsure of himself, overconfident? Does the child persistently punch himself, bang his head on the wall or floor repeatedly? The two children in these short records reveal something of their self-view that would bear continued observation.

  Jack (4) frequently called himself "stupid" and "dope."

  Alice (5) often crumpled up her painting or drawing, threw it in the trash, calling it a "shit picture."

- How does the child initiate interaction with adults and/or children? What characterizes those interactions? In the following record taken during a low-key time in the morning when parents and children are arriving at child care, Sura's style of confrontation with the adults seems out of sync with the circumstances.

  Sura (3-and-a-half) holds a leopard puppet that she thrusts menacingly at the teachers and parents who are in the room, loudly growling "RRRR." The adults feign alarm. She laughs raucously. She sidles up to Geraldo's dad, holding the puppet, and commands in a loud voice, "Take off your shirt!" Matter-of-factly, he replies, "Oh, I can't do that—I have to go to work." She laughs and hangs onto his leg, making his exit difficult. The teacher helps her move out of the way.

- Is the child excessively resistant to the teacher's suggestions and directions? For some reason, Omar finds the teacher's request totally unacceptable:

  Omar (5) has just eaten a snack and left the spoon on the table. As he starts across the room, the teacher requests, "Omar, please put your spoon in the sink." "NO!" he shouts, in a loud voice. She holds his hand. He resists and lies on the floor, pulling on her hand. She continues to hold his hand and quietly makes the request again. He lies on the floor for a few more minutes, glaring at her. Slowly he gets up, runs to the table, grabs the spoon, rushes across the room, and drops it in the sink. "Thank you, Omar," she says.

- How does the child respond to interference from other children? Does she welcome the overture? Reject it? Or give up materials or possessions to other children without objection as Isabella does?

> When Isabella (5-and-a-half) left her seat at the snack table, she announced in stentorian tones, "I'm going to the bathroom. So *don't* touch my chair!" As soon as she left, Ashley plunked herself on Isabella's chair. Returning from the bathroom, Isabella looked sheepishly at Ashley, cast her eyes down, and in a whisper said, "I'll sit here." She sat in Ashley's now vacant seat without protest.

Clues to a child's difficulties in the social/emotional arena can be gathered all through the day, during various activities. Routine activities such as eating, dressing, napping, lining up, may reveal the child's dependence on or independence of adults. Observation of play with blocks, paints, and water and dramatic play will uncover the character of a child's relationships with other children, his interest or lack of interest in others, and his tendency to sustain or confound these contacts.

It is important to have a good understanding of a child's cultural and linguistic background in order to avoid interpreting certain behavioral characteristics as emotional difficulties when they may in fact represent typical behavior within a particular culture. (For example, see the Final Summary record for Jai in Chapter 13.)

### Motor/Physical Functioning

How the child adapts his body movements to spatial requirements has social ramifications. A child's motor functioning has significant influence on her emotional, social, and cognitive behaviors. For example, difficulty negotiating space can have a negative impact on the development of a child's growing balance between independence and dependence (Greenspan, 1989). Colin's difficulty maneuvering in space is seen by other children as annoying, and he requires the teacher's intervention in order to repair the social damage.

> Five-year-old Colin was engaged in block building. Several times he knocked down the buildings of other children who were building near him, as he passed by. He was surprised each time it happened by the children's angry reactions. "It was an accident," the teacher explained when the children complained. "Let's fix it up." It was clearly not an intentional act.

Difficulties with motor planning may be related to a child's problems with self-control. Motor planning

> is integral to learning to crawl, sit, skip, button, or cut with scissors—in short, anything that involves sequencing a series of motor acts into a pattern. . . . Children who experience difficulty in motor planning need extra help in learning to negotiate successive stages in their emotional development—because each stage involves planning increasingly complicated motor activity: gesturing, talking, and interacting all involve the motor system. (Greenspan, 1989, p. 204)

Six-year-old Zack displays possible disorganized motor planning and lack of emotional control:

> While playing quietly with sand, Zack suddenly straightened his body and charged toward the light switch, shouting, "Put the light switch on!" He grabbed a chair, pushed it across the floor, bumping into two children and a table. He screamed at top volume in unison with the screeching noises made by the chair. Suddenly, he slapped himself hard on the head, dashed off to the teacher, and rubbed his head against her hand. She spoke to him calmly until he quieted.

A child who is constantly in motion or whose motion is purposeless and/or unrelated to a specific activity or situation or, conversely, one whose movements are sluggish or sleepy will face obstacles completing tasks, making friends, and paying attention. In the following examples, the children's movements seem unusual and striking in their lack of goal-directedness:

> Louisa walks around in circles, sometimes moves around the room repeatedly in the same order, from the block area to the easel to the book corner.

> Howie flaps his arms up and down when walking, unable to stop. There is no overt evidence that he is pretending to fly or be an airplane or a bird.

> Four-year-old Bernie turned the handle on the vise for a moment; took two small jumps, twice; stuck his hand in the empty aquarium; pointed at a variety of objects in succession; rocked back and forth from one leg to another, talking to himself all the time.

Aiden, 5 years old, has trouble sitting without twisting, turning, and squirming:

> Aiden is sitting in the circle during sharing time. His legs are folded crosswise. He pulls the waist string from his pants and slowly ties it in complex knots to the laces on his sneakers. After 5 or 10 minutes the waist string and the laces from both sneakers are knotted together, forming a "T" from waist to shoes. If he tried to stand up he would be unable to do so. The assistant teacher moves close to him and focuses his attention on the sharing-time comments. When sharing time is over, she quietly helps him untie the knots.

The questions that follow are meant as a guide for your observations of a child's gross motor functioning and are designed to bring your attention to certain significant aspects of a young child's motor patterns that might indicate a problem.

- What is the quality of the child's skills? (clumsy, inefficient, uncoordinated, smooth)
- What age-related skills does he do well? Which are difficult?
- What is the quality of the child's movements? (smooth, jerky, floppy, restricted, cautious, timid)
- What is the range of the child's age-related, self-help skills, such as putting on and removing clothing? Five-year-old Brandon took off his coat, but needed the teacher's help to put it on when it was time to go outside.
- How does the child manage stairs?
- What is her reaction to sudden movements and unexpected noise? Four-year-old Cathy's reaction seems extreme. Conversely, an absence of a reaction to unexpected noise can indicate a subtle hearing loss.

  > Cathy flinched and raised both hands in a protective movement when Larry bounced exuberantly into the room, landing solidly a good four or five feet away from her.

- Is he careless about his safety? In this record, Bert seems unaware of the danger.

  > Six-year-old Bert was about to step off a four-foot-high wall without looking when the teacher, who was standing next to him, put his arms around him to prevent the fall.

- Does the child use movement to express her ideas? Can she move like an animal? Like a train?
- Can the child use strength when needed?
- Does he stumble or fall often?
- What is the quality of her movements during rhythmical opportunities or when she jumps, runs, climbs, jumps rope, "pumps" while on a swing, uses a jungle gym, rides a trike or bike?
- Is he inclined to confine his activities to an unnecessarily small area, or does he tend to go beyond set or natural boundaries as does the child in the anecdote below?

  Six-year-old Gillian, playing Duck-Duck-Goose, ran around the circle of seated children several times, into a corner of the gym and back, before tapping another child on the head.

- Is the child able to judge the spatial relationship of objects to each other or to herself? For example, does she know whether there is enough space between two objects to move her wagon through? Dorine seems to have trouble in this arena:

  Four-year-old Dorine put a double-unit block across two uprights, forming a bridge. Her truck was too tall to fit through the opening, so she piled several more blocks on top of the cross piece, making the building, but not the opening, taller. She was upset that the truck still couldn't go through and called the teacher. The teacher focused her attention on the size of the space and the size of the truck. Dorine looked blank. The teacher moved the blocks off the top and showed Dorine how to make the opening larger.

A focus on visual/small motor coordination will help teachers see how young children attend to tasks, solve problems, and get along with others, and how comfortable they are in planning and carrying out many different types of activities. Remember that children with disabilities are vulnerable to stress (Williamson, 1988), so they may become easily overwhelmed. At the point of stress, a child might say about a collage project, "I don't want to do this," or become contentious, throwing the collage tray contents on the floor (Greenspan, 1989). Here the difficulty with a motor action takes on meaning in the social and emotional realm.

The following questions will focus your attention on some salient characteristics of children's capacity to perform skills requiring small-muscle coordination. What have you noticed about the children who cause you concern in this regard?

- Does a 2- to 3-year-old have difficulty stringing large beads?
- Is a 3- to 4-year-old able to hold a large crayon between thumb and fingers?
- Can a 3-year-old roll clay into balls or snakes, button or unbutton large buttons, pull a zipper up or down?
- Can a 4-year-old cut continuously with a scissors?
- Can a 5- to 6-year-old tie a bow on shoes?
- Can a 5- to 6-year-old hold a pencil like an adult? Is she completely left- or right-handed or clearly ambidextrous?
- Does the child, age appropriately, pick up or hold objects between thumb and index finger? What are his eating skills using fingers or utensils?
- How does she accomplish pouring from one container to another?
- How does he balance small blocks one atop another? How many? Does the ability seem appropriate to his age?
- With an age-appropriate puzzle, how does the child fit the pieces together? This 4-year-old finds the struggle to work the puzzle too great even with the teacher's help:

  Keily took the puzzle board and dumped out the five pieces on the table. He put the first piece in at random, then took a second piece and waved it around in an up-and-down motion. The teacher helped guide this piece into its proper place, leaving a space. She picked up a third piece and showed him where it fit. When he put it in, she said, "Good job!" As she picked up the next piece to help him, he got up and left the table.

- Does the child's gaze follow her reach in the activity in which she is engaged?
  » Does the child hold dolls, puzzles, or books less than 7 inches away from his eyes?
  » Does she hold things far away from the body in an attempt to see more clearly?

Whether mind (brain) and body function together determines how the child perceives and adapts to the world of people and things that surround him. There are some children for whom teachers have concern because these perceptions and adaptations are less than optimally integrated. Observation is key to knowing these children better.

## Cognitive Functioning, Language Skills, and Communication

Although there are many occasions in which we can observe the quality of children's thought, the extent and content of their knowledge can be observed very well during group discussions related to a story the teacher has just read, or when planning for or reviewing a trip, for example, to a neighborhood store or the fire station.

When we observe children involved in using materials such as paint, clay, water, or blocks or working at reading, writing, and math tasks, we need to notice the quality of their attention span. Is it equal to the task? Here is a series of questions to sharpen your awareness of a child's thinking, learning, and communicating when these cause concern.

- Does the child have difficulty making the choice of an activity?
  - » Does he usually finish it?
  - » Is he aware that he's done?
- Is she able to perceive similarities and differences—in shapes, colors, sizes, patterns?
- Does the child have a range of interests?
- Is the child's primary mode of learning limited to one modality, to the exclusion of other sensory modalities?
  - » For example, does the child rely on touch to the exclusion of sight, hearing, smell, or taste?
- Are the child's questions rooted in his experience? Do they make sense?
- Can she organize her explorations?
  - » Is there a forward-moving logic to her problem solving?
  - » Does it improve with failure?
- Can the child retain information that grows out of the life of the classroom, for example, does he remember names, the schedule of the day, what happened on a class trip a week ago?
- Is the child interested in what goes on around her? Does she often "tune out," as 3-year-old Sandy does in the record below?

  During the story reading, Sandy sits and plays with a small cup. She slides to the floor, lies down, and begins to masturbate. Gently the teacher helps her return to her chair.

- What is his ability to understand cause and effect? Sequencing? Categorizing? Can the child sustain goal-directedness despite distractions? In the following record,

7-year-old Todd is having trouble understanding a sorting task and is distracted by boys who are playing nearby:

Each child in the class has been given a package of pictures of various kinds of buildings to sort. Todd's pictures are scattered across his desk. He lets out an exaggerated pretend cry and beats his fists on the desk. He swings and kicks his feet under his chair and makes self-entertaining funny faces. He jumps up to join another boy who is working on the floor nearby. A tap on the shoulder by the teacher, and Todd returns to his desk to study his pictures. The teacher suggests that he put the pictures of the churches together in a pile and begins to help him organize his pictures. Twice he asks, "The same stuff goes together?" Later, he joins a group who are pasting their pictures in graph form, sorted into churches, homes, business buildings, and so forth. He shows a few pictures to the boy next to him, asking, "How about this?" Each time, he is told, "No, that's a home," or "No, that's a school."

- Does the child comprehend the sequence of events that make up the day?
  » Is she able to anticipate the next event? For example, does she know that every day after playtime, it is snacktime?
- How does she react to changes in the schedule, or changes in the classroom arrangement of furniture or materials?
- What is the child's understanding of rules, or codes of behavior?
  » Does he understand that some rules or codes of behavior change from place to place, from family to family, from person to person?
- What is the extent of the child's age-appropriate and culturally relevant general knowledge about the world and self, about work roles, animals, and natural processes such as birth, growth, death? In the following records, two five-year-olds seem quite confused about gender and birth.

Lillian waved her hand in the air when the teacher asked the *boys* to raise their hands.

Luca, whose mother was within days of giving birth, told the teacher that his mother was very fat because she had beer in her tummy. He said that the doctor would take it out by cutting her open.

- How coherent are the child's mental processes? In the following record, Martin, who is almost 6, appears to be thinking erratically:

Martin is making "stoneware" dishes out of clay. He tells a story about them to the teacher. "The title is 'Instructional Book.' Reflections of stoneware is very good. I want to go to outer space but I can't go."

"Why not?" asks the teacher.

"Because," he adds, "I have all this 'nail' [i.e., mail] business. You have to take the cracks and always make a serving dish and two cups and two bowls. And what you have to send away to [name of his school]. And people get what they want for free."

Children communicate with us and with one another in many ways—through their bodies; their facial expressions; their language; their sounds; their drawings, paintings, block buildings; their make-believe play. In all these ways, they tell us about their perceptions, their confusions, their wishes, their joys and sorrows, what they know and don't know, and what they wish to know. But it is not always a simple matter for teachers to get these messages when the children have difficulties in thinking, talking, playing, or in expressing their ideas.

- In what ways does the child communicate with others? Nonverbally (through body movement, gesture, and/or facial expressions) or verbally? When he is around other children, does he tend to speak very little, like 4-and-a-half-year-old Brad below?

Brad was engaged in a variety of activities with several children. They were stringing beads, playing a color-matching game, and "cooking" with play dough. He seldom spoke to any of the children; rather, he shook and nodded his head, indicating yes or no in response to their queries. During the color-matching game, he hit his head with his hands when the colored die did not turn up his color, smiling when it did.

- Does she tend to use verbal or nonverbal style more? Under what circumstances? With which people?
- What information and ideas does the child communicate?
- Can the child elaborate on communication? With other children? With adults?
- What is the quality of the child's receptive language? It can be difficult to assess receptive language abilities in children who are English language learners because they may not yet be able to expressively demonstrate what they know.

- » Does he have difficulty understanding what is said to him even though there is nothing wrong with his hearing?
  - » What is the range of his understanding?
  - » Can he follow a story at circle time?
- What is the quality of the child's expressive language?
  - » Is she able to say what she wants to say so that another person understands?
  - » If English is not her first language, can she say what she wants in her native language?
  - » Does she confuse words that are associated with one another, for example, saying "table" when she means "chair"?
- Does the child use pronouns such as *I, we, he, she,* and *they* as appropriate for his age? Pronoun use as a means of self-representation develops in the second and third years of life. In the following records, a 5- and a 4-year-old's manner of referring to themselves is cause for concern.

At age 5, Gilbert put on a white coat and said, "Me doctor."

Four-year-old Angie confuses *you* and *she* with *I.*

Angie says to the teacher, "Now it is morning. She gets up and has her breakfast."
  "What do you have for breakfast?" the teacher asks.
  Angie replies, "She has cereal. Then she has to get dressed and go to school. You [meaning "I"] want to ride the bike now."

- Is there evidence that the child's vocabulary is increasing over time? At an age when it is no longer expected, does the child substitute onomatopoeic sounds, such as "baaa, baaa" for sheep, "choo choo" for train?
- Does the child understand the turn-taking rules of communication?
- Is his speech intelligible?
- Does she use language to express emotions and feelings?
- Is he able to follow simple directions?
- Do you notice confusions like those that 4-year-old Linda, in the following anecdote, seems to have?

As the teacher tells the children to sit in a circle, Linda sits in the *center* of the circle. The teacher explains that she should sit on the tape, which had been put on the floor in the shape of a circle to help the children arrange themselves. Linda looks blank. Although the teacher suggests that she sit next to Loreen, Linda continues to sit in the center of the circle. She is the only child in the group who is unable to follow the directions.

- Does the child have difficulty understanding the meaning of various prepositions, such as *in, out, up, down, in front of, behind, next to*? Six-year-old Jay is unable to play a game that depends on knowing prepositions:

  In the game, the 1st-grade teacher tells the children to sit or stand behind, on, or in front of a chair, or she shows them what to do by placing a doll in those positions. Either Jay does incorrectly what was required, or he simply imitates the other children.

Opportunities to observe children thinking, speaking, and communicating exist all through the day—during routines, using materials, during story or circle times, or in the ordinary conversations that take place between teachers and children or children and children. And, of course, evidence of cognitive and communication capacities abounds when observing children at play.

### Play Skills and Play Themes

It is through observing children at play with objects and in make-believe play with one another and alone that teachers will find evidence of many of the behaviors highlighted in the sections above (Linder, 1990; Sheridan, Foley, & Radlinski, 1995). Some developmental irregularities may impact negatively on the child's skills in playing with others and interfere with the child's abilities in developing ideas and themes for play. More teacher intervention and scaffolding may be needed in such instances than with children who do not display behavioral difficulties (Berk & Winsler, 1995; Sheridan, Foley, & Radlinski, 1995).

Here are some questions to aid you in looking at a child's skill as a player and at her ability to evolve themes for play:

- Is the child comfortable with pretend play?
  - » Does the child enjoy play and find it a source of pleasure?
- Is the child able to make objects and people represent something or someone else, or does he always insist on realistic props?
  - » Can the child use a small box, for example, as a plane, or does he require the toy plane itself?

- Does the child organize her play well independently, or does she require external mediation from another child or the teacher? If so, how much and of what sort?
- Does he need to play in the proximity of an adult or can he play in a separate place?
- Does the child over age 3 still play mainly alone?
  - » When involved with others, is she able to coordinate pretend play?
  - » Can she maintain focus and attention during play?
- Is the child able to incorporate another child's ideas in play?
  - » Does he understand the "rules" of play like turn-taking or sticking to the theme, or does he find it difficult to compromise, like Janice below?

Five-year-old Janice joined two other children who were engaged in space play. "I'm the mommy!" she announced. "We're not playing that. You have to be a space ranger." "No, I'm the mommy. I'm the mommy," she begins to scream. "The children are playing space and want you to be a space ranger," the teacher explains. "No! No! I want to be the mommy." The teacher asks the others if they can use a mommy, but they all say no. "That's not going to work in this game," she tells Janice, "so let's try to find someone else who wants to play your game."

- Does the child have a range of themes and ideas for play, or is she stuck on certain ideas that she plays again and again?
- Is the child comfortable playing with a range of emotions?
  - » Is the play often a source of anxious feelings?
  - » Does he tend to get overexcited when involved in playing because of fear, overactivity, or overaggression? Here is 4-and-a-half-year-old Andy at play, displaying feelings that are overwhelming.

Andy sets up a line of chairs in the middle of the room and sits in the driver's seat—the first chair. He turns an imaginary wheel and says, "I'm the bus driver." As he continues to turn the wheel, he becomes excited, stands up, and whirls around and around. He drags his chair behind him across the floor, repeating, "I drive myself. I drive myself." Then he yells at top volume, "The bus is out of control, the bus is out of control!"

- Does the child identify with the "bad guy?"
  - » Does the play often end in disaster or destruction of the "good guy"?

» Is this a recurrent theme?
- Is the child often dictated to in play or regularly relegated to roles like the baby, the dog, or the cat?
- Is the child able to take on and elaborate a role such as family member, fire fighter, animal, TV character?
- In contrast, does the child often take on the role of an inanimate object?

Three-year-old Tyler, expressionless and standing still, said he was a "can opener." Later on he told the teacher he was a "rock."

Because play occurs with great frequency and seriousness in early childhood classrooms, it provides an unrivaled source for observation and record-taking of children for whom you have concerns. Unstructured playtime can be difficult for children with special needs. They may need help engaging in play with other children and may find some toys and materials difficult to handle. Children with sensory issues may be sensitive to the noise of free play. Some children may find the free flow of movement disorienting and/or chaotic, and may feel overwhelmed by the number of choices available to them. Some children with special needs may need help playing with other children as well as being taught how to play with certain toys. These children may need to avoid very large, open spaces, and protected spaces may be useful for them (Klein, Cook, & Richardson-Gibbs, 2001). It is also important to remember that there may be cultural differences in the way children play and the materials they have been exposed to.

## GENERAL IMPRESSION

An outstanding characteristic of children for whom one has special concerns, in addition to the specific kinds of behavior described above, that may indicate developmental irregularities, disturbances, and/or learning disabilities, is that they give the impression of being much younger than their chronological age. Jonah, for example, a 4-year-old, seemed like a 2- or very young 3-year-old. The babylike quality of his skin and hair contributed to this impression, as did his high-pitched voice, his babyish pronunciation of words (such as "apoo" for apple), his unawareness that his pants were constantly falling down, and the fact that he always played alone, never with other children. In other children, this impression may stem from other sources, such as a developmental lag in one or more aspects of functioning—physical, social, emotional, cognitive, language, and speech.

Remember, no single behavior listed above has significance by itself. A combination of several of them, however, especially if they occur frequently and persistently, may be indicative of a problem requiring intervention.

# 13

# Patterns—
# Summary—
# and Interpretation

We have taken individual children through their school or child care day now for many months. We caught their expressions as they arrived in the morning; we observed how they removed their outer clothes; we watched them at play, noting both their use of materials and their relationships with other children. We noticed how they conducted themselves at the table, how they took care of their bodily needs, how each responded to us, and how each behaved as a member of the group. As we observed, we learned something of what the children think about and how they feel they are getting along. Perhaps, too, we got clues as to what we could do to satisfy their particular needs for facing life now and in the future.

## PATTERNS

All this material from records collected over time must now be organized in such a way as to get at the nature of the children's responses more easily—their relations with adults, relations with children, use of materials, behavior during routines, their cognitive functioning and how they learn, their language development, and so on. Each child has a unique pattern of response in each of these areas. To find that pattern, we must turn to our records and pull out the episodes that together reveal the pattern.

Pulling out episodes in one area might look like a series of small summaries. Here is how one child's responses to adults would add up. The dates refer to the original records the teacher took. Each small summary refers to a whole record, of course.

Relations with adults

> 10/21: Khalid (age 5) looks to me for support when not wanting to get into game. I explain rules; he is reassured and agrees to play.
>
> 10/30: Khalid seeks me out to show me pipes through bricks, explaining what he sees. He brings car over and demonstrates its features. Talks a lot and shows evidence of different kinds of knowledge.
>
> 11/12: Khalid asks me if Darren is in charge of chairs at cleanup.
>
> 11/20: Khalid asks me what Liam and Paula have to do with each other.
>
> 12/1: I direct Khalid to let other children have turn on ropes. He follows directions, calls and asks me to watch him several times performing on ropes or tires.
>
> 12/15: Gym teacher gives Khalid directions which he follows. Khalid asks him a question later.
>
> 1/4: Khalid tells of discovery with a construction toy. Shares success with me.
>
> 1/10: Khalid enthusiastically shows me clay objects he made.

On the basis of the above digests of several episodes, the teacher was able to write up the pattern of Khalid's interactions with an adult as follows:

> Khalid feels comfortable with adults and sees them as resources for information and as people with whom to share discoveries and happy experiences. Khalid is at ease relying on adults when he needs them for support, for example, 10/21, on entering attribute game or to clarify questions; 11/20, in group meeting he asks what L. and P. have to do with each other when not sure. Khalid likes to have adults enjoy his activities and share his appreciation of objects and knowledge, but he doesn't have an overdependence on adults. He rarely seeks the teacher out for help, nor the student teacher if she is not actually near him. He is relatively self-sufficient. Khalid has positive relationships with adults and trusts them easily. He follows adult directions when in group or individual situations.

All the small summaries dealing with certain areas of functioning (routines, materials, play) will indicate a child's interaction with the environment. One can see what the patterns have been and what they have become. One will see growth, or perhaps lack of growth or even regression. The importance of any given area to the child will show up—the degree of interest and intensity—and whether these led to satisfaction or frustration. The child's behavior can be looked at in relation to that of others of the same age (they all seem able to take their clothes *off*, but not put them on again!), and to coming growth (he's finally gotten to the first rung of the jungle gym; he'll surely get to the top in the coming months). But conclusions must remain tentative (I think she'll come through . . . It looks as though . . . It seems to me . . .). All the conclusions about children's behavior need to be tested through further observation, action, and still further observation. At no time can we say about a dynamic, growing human being, "Aha, I've got him!" and be sure we are right.

Summaries of the physical functioning of a child and the overview of his adjustment to school or child care give us additional clues to use at some time in interpretation. Physical functioning can be deduced from records of the daily activity, which will show such persistent aspects of functioning as the following:

- Health and the secondary effects of illnesses, operations, and physical challenges
- Grace and coordination and their relation to emotional functioning
- Usual tempo
- Freedom or restraint of movement—expansive, abandoned, precise, vigorous, mild, lusty, strong, dainty, graceful, bouncy, earthbound, loose, disjointed, tense, relaxed, tight, restrained, uninhibited
- Amount of energy expended in relation to activity (how quickly does child become fatigued?)
- Evidence of qualities such as poised, restless, serene, earthbound, airy, stolid
- Attitude toward use of the body in relation to large muscular movements, such as running or climbing (eagerness, caution, fear, pleasure)
- Attitude toward use of the body in relation to fine body movements, such as writing or sewing (relaxed, tense, enjoys, tries too hard)
- Usual facial expression (frowns, smiles, looks serene)

Adjustment to school or child care is something else that cannot be set to absolute standards and in its specifics will be different for different children. Yet we can get an overall picture of a child's functioning if we do not feel too rigid about standards ourselves.

We might think of children as adjusted to school when they come into the classroom readily without their parents or caregivers and know school routines, group rules, and normal daily procedures; where materials are, who people are, what is expected of them, and what they can expect of others. Incidentally, early records that show the child's first responses to a new situation are helpful in assessing the changes that take place over time. The "feeling" that a teacher has about a child's being well adjusted to school should be bolstered by tangible, concrete evidence that this is really so. One might see two levels of adjustments: (1) separation from parent(s) or caregivers—reactions to routines, knowledge of where things are, and so on—and (2) when a child is really herself, natural and spontaneous.

## FEATURES OF THE FINAL SUMMARY

There comes a time when we are interested in a final summary of the child's behavior over time. It may be for the school files and next year's teacher, for consultation with the school psychologist, or for a conference with the parent. In any case, we need to put our material together in such a way that we can get a fairly complete picture of a child's behavior at school or child care.

In the final summary, we include digests of the patterns of behavior at routines, with materials, with children, with adults, and so on, and a survey of intellectual functioning and language. We could also include observations that show what frustrates a child and what gives satisfaction. We might include information gleaned otherwise than through observation, such as items from the admittance file, the nurse's files, or conferences with parents. We include a description of the environment.

All this evidence is then looked at objectively to see which parts in one area of functioning seem to have a bearing on other parts elsewhere. For example, a summary of use of outdoor equipment (which we have not included by itself) might show a consistent picture of nonuse. The child looks sturdy enough, but he does not hang by his legs on the parallel bars, climb to heights, or slide down the high slide. He plays outside with apparent contentment, but only with the wagons, the sand, chalk, balls, and water. Anything more than 2 feet high is seemingly not for him. Is there anything in his play elsewhere that seems related to his behavior on the equipment? Is there anything in the information on his health and physical background that throws light on his behavior in the yard? Is the child's behavior on equipment connected with his age? Is there anything in his choice of stories or activities in music and movement that offers a clue? Is there anything he said in discussion (or did not say when everyone else was clamoring to say the same thing)? Does the child behave with caution in a wide range of contexts or in very particular ones? Does he show tension in other situations of height (for example, at the head of the stairs)? Does the child seem generally contented? In other words, how does any one piece of behavior fit in relation to whatever else we know about the child? By itself, nonuse of high equipment can be open to a variety of inept interpretations, depending on the fancy of the observer. But in relation to other aspects of a child's behavior, it takes on the specific meaning it has for *this child*, and that can be anything from simple inexperience and normal caution to undeveloped muscles, malnutrition, or fear of heights.

Let us take other possible relationships. A child has certain attitudes toward other children. Is there anything in her attitude toward adults that seems to be of a piece? Is her attitude toward herself and her accomplishments with materials involved here? Does her capacity to take frustration, as evidenced in numerous situations, relate to her getting along with children?

What behavior at routines is related to behavior with adults? What behavior at play is related to behavior with adults? What behavior at the table is related to behavior with children? Is there a common thread running throughout? The same happy-go-lucky attitudes at routines, at play, and with adults? The same inability to find satisfaction? The same even keel? The same passionate outbursts?

## Trends

The final record includes *trends* of behavior.

Apparently Simon is outgrowing his need to suck his thumb. Over the months he has left off perpetual sucking for brief returns at naptime.

Alfonso stops now for a good look when someone comes toward him fast. Instead of screaming, he sizes up the situation. He turns and runs without looking back.

Tammy sits with books and really seems to be enjoying them. She sits through a short story too, apparently able to follow it. Last week she asked a question about the character in the story. Tammy is learning to concentrate on happenings outside herself.

## Problems

Perhaps if we recognize that the growing-up process is not accomplished with smoothness and evenness by anyone, we can use the word *problems* in its proper context. Every child at some time or other has a problem or hurdle to overcome and conquer if he is to grow. These problems, or hurdles, might also be indicated in the final summary:

> Six-year-old Jai has a strong awareness of what I consider "appropriate" classroom behavior and can be relied upon to follow the classroom rules. But he struggles with expressive language, attributable at least in part to the fact that English is his second language, and still seems uncomfortable expressing his ideas during whole-group discussions. His most successful verbal interactions occur one-on-one, especially with me and other teachers. Yet he is very adept at working independently and does not seek adult support. I believe that he will really benefit by forming a strong relationship with me in school in order to build his confidence so that he is more willing to speak to the whole group.

## Evaluating Growth

The trends and problems merge into an evaluation of growth. "He has grown so much" has real meaning when it is qualified: "He has learned to . . . ; he used to . . . , but now . . . ; he uses so many colors, so many materials, so many ideas and words; he makes, he says, he does." It is all in the record. And how easily we forget what children did 3 months ago if we do not write it down!

## Predictions

We can guess what the future holds for a child's growth and can recommend what that child should have for the best chances for growth. We can make recommendations to the next teacher and perhaps to the parents.

> Based on my analysis of observations taken over time, I have some recommendations for Fernando's 1st-grade teacher. Because Fernando sometimes has difficulty adjusting to new situations, it is important that he be given time to get used to the new classroom environment and not be "pushed" to participate in everything right away. He needs time to find his own place and his own voice and I can imagine that he might

initially feel overwhelmed by the prospect of getting to know many new children. He needs time *and* flexibility. Because of evidence of a strong intra-personal intelligence, Fernando can be relied on to know what he needs in order to begin to feel comfortable. It may take the form of his initially sitting outside the meeting circle or when given a choice, repeatedly choosing art over other activities during the first weeks of school. He may also need special preparation when going somewhere new or meeting a new person in the classroom. Teachers should also be aware of his occasional anxiety about being sick and be patient and understanding if he seems worried.

## Extremes

In the final record we would note *extremes* of behavior, such as overdependence, overall immaturity with materials, complete rejection of routines, or overall extraordinary competence. Every child can be expected to show some inconsistency, but extremes of behavior may mean real trouble or special talent and should be noted. Along the same lines are such special problems as stuttering, excessive thumb-sucking, accident-proneness, persistent reluctance to become involved, frequent expression of fear, passivity. These behaviors are normal to young children but cause us concern when they take up so much of a child's energy that there is little left for wholesome play.

## The Whole Child

We must also note the special quality of the personality as we see it—dramatic, sociable, gentle, sturdy, inquisitive. After recording minutiae, we have the right to give our own sensory impression! Not every child calls forth the one apt word, but many do, and we need not hesitate to include it in the final summary. We may well begin or end a summary of a child's behavior with "He strikes me as an imp," "She appears to be in perpetual motion," "She seems to me to be such an utterly competent person." On their own, these words and phrases are open to question. But with evidence piled up in the summary of many aspects of behavior, the teacher is justified in adding this wholly understandable personal reaction.

Nate's most outstanding characteristic is his most positive strength—his creativity, which appears again and again in art and ballet. In a society such as ours, where creativity is sorely needed (but often misunderstood), hopefully Nate will go far with his talents if he is allowed to develop them further. He is motivated in these areas, he likes to perform. He thrives in his classroom environment because his teacher places a high value on self-expression and creativity. He is a sociable creature—gets along with others, is well liked, and considered a benefit to the class. He is very intelligent.

## The Environment

Describing the situation in which the child lives his or her daily life brings deeper insight to our study. What are the main features of the child's *neighborhood? School? Classroom?*

In the description of the classroom, include such details as the number and ages of the children; the daily schedule; number of adults and their roles; range and condition of the equipment; room arrangement, including quiet spaces for children; the placement of children's and teacher's desks and how this affects teacher-child interaction.

In the following sample description of 6-year-old Cleo's urban environment, the wealth of detail provides a compelling picture of the child's daily surroundings. It is for the observer to surmise how this particular environment makes an impact on the child.

> *The Neighborhood.* The street is tree-lined. To the east of the school is a 22–story white brick apartment building; to the west is a red brick church with a small school attached to it. Opposite the school is a row of five-story walk-ups and a 14-story red brick, doorman-attended apartment building. Next door is a five-story building; its ground-floor store front bears a sign reading "Tarot Card Reading." On the corner is a small candy/cigarette store with a large awning that reads "Lotto." Near the school is a large hospital, which employs many of the residents living in the vicinity of the school.
>
> The people on the street are of all ages and ethnicities. Cleo's parents bring her to school by public transportation.
>
> *The School.* The school is 91 years old, red brick, five stories tall. One must walk up a flight of steps to the building, enter the "IN" door, ascend another flight of stairs, go through another door where a security guard sits at a desk. Children's painted self-portraits hang on the walls on either side of the staircase. The hallway is decorated with photographs of each class, a display case of student-made weavings and clay pinch pots, and a large mural titled "Winter in the City." The walls are painted greenish-blue; on the ceiling are fluorescent lights. The cafeteria

is on the first floor. The acoustics are terrible when a large number of children are present. The third, fourth, and fifth floors contain classrooms. There is a water fountain and a bathroom in working order on each floor.

*The Classroom.* There are 27 children in Cleo's class. In the front of the room is a large rectangular charcoal-gray rug, which is used for class discussions and meetings. Every day the blackboard displays the problem of the day, the morning message, the calendar, the schedule, and the attendance chart. Two charts hang above the blackboard: "Rules for the work group" and "Class community rules." On the far side of the blackboard is a closet for coats.

There are three laminate-top round tables and two rectangular ones. The teacher has her own chair, but no desk. There are distinctly marked math and reading areas. All materials are labeled and accessible to the children. The reading area includes the class library, which has a small carpet, several pillows, and shelves stocked with dictionaries and picture and chapter books. There are shelves filled with such things as pencils, glue, markers, and paper. The walls are decorated with the children's sketches related to their study of the neighborhood.

From such detailed descriptions of the child's environment we can begin to see the child in context. We can begin to surmise what messages about school and learning reach the child; what is communicated about the goals of the educational program; what is communicated about the value of motivation, creativity, self-initiation, social behavior. In addition, if the home/community environment is accessible and can be described, an even more textured setting will help reveal the child.

## INTERPRETATION

By this time we seem to know our child well. There does not seem to be much that we have missed. The next question the teachers usually ask is, why? Why does the child do as he does? Is it because the child was "spoiled"? Is it because of a loving or a rejecting mother, grandmother, brother, or sister? Is it because she feels inadequate, overconfident? Is it . . . Is it . . . ? Of course we want to know. We work closely with children and do many things for and with them. It is impossible not to hypothesize about the causes of their behavior.

Whether we are right or wrong can make an important difference to a child's growth and happiness. It is dangerous to interpret incorrectly. Any interpretation at all must not only be tentative and subject to change if new facts emerge, but must definitely relate to a background of information.

Behavior has so many different causes that teachers need information about the child's physical being and an understanding of the relationship among physical, emotional, and intellectual states. We need to evaluate what determines our expectations about a child's behavior at any given age and be aware of how children grow and learn in the mainstream culture as well as in many nonmainstream cultures. We need to know whether every neighborhood places a premium on the same kind of behavior; whether every family conforms to neighborhood expectations; to what extent community standards and values play a part in parent and child behavior; and what views of the world have been passed on to this child. Teachers must also be cognizant of specific events and stresses that have affected the child.

Interpretation is difficult because it involves knowing so much. It involves feelings, too, *our* feelings. Can we put ourselves in a child's place? Can we do it and remain objectively adult? Or do we respond to what we like or don't like, agree with or disagree with, as we interpret? Are we competing with the parents when we find fault with the child? Are we boosting our own morale when we say the child has made superior progress at school?

Interpreting causes of behavior is dangerous unless we tread carefully. Can we verify every statement we make? Do we have evidence for our hunches and our guesses? Is the child more important to us than being right? Are we willing to give up a pet theory because it really does not fit the child? Here is what one teacher commented about the process of observing and recording:

> It is hard to be an observer. All the time you are recording, you are also responding, directly or indirectly, to what you see and hear. We can't step out of being human. This is why the child you observe becomes closer to you. They can sense your response directed at them and respond back.

The same behavior can mean different things in different children. Children hit out of anger, fear, resentment, jealousy, panic, defiance. They can withdraw into silence out of anger, fear, resentment, jealousy, panic, defiance. A child will not necessarily do what we do, although some will. We must learn to study children in general in order to find the answers for the individual child about whom we are concerned. We must also study individuals and extend our understanding to all. Each human being is unique, as we ourselves are. Each human being wants to be understood for his unique self, as we ourselves do. Let us be just to the children we teach, and guard their precious individualities and their cultural heritage. If we would understand them, let us learn to gather accurately the evidence that will give us the clues we need. To our clues we must bring the illumination offered by knowledge of human behavior and the understanding of the role of children's social communities.

## FINAL SUMMARY

The following is a final summary, a putting-together of all the separate summaries, prepared at the end of the school year by a teacher of 3-year-old D'Andre.

> It seems that D'Andre possess a "slow-to-warm-up" temperament, spending time looking before he acts. This has an impact on how he relates to new situations and activities, holding back at first but then becoming very focused once he becomes involved. His emotional stance seems to be predominantly calm and even. He is a great experimenter when he uses expressive materials. He seems to be particularly enthralled by painting activities, experimenting thoroughly with brush, paper, and paint. Yet with other materials that do not call for creative expression, he is less experimental, such as the time he was observed trying to connect magnetic trains but then quickly giving up.
>
> A striking feature of D'Andre's behavior is the difference between his interactions with his peers and his interactions with adults. While it may be considered age-appropriate for D'Andre to seek out and relate to adults more than children, there is a significant absence of direct attempts on his part to initiate interactions with his peers in contrast to his clear ability to do so with adults. This does not, however, indicate a general disregard for or disinterest in other children. For example, he was observed throwing his head back and laughing when another child near him laughed. Another time while he was working alone in the block area, he stopped abruptly when he heard children pouring Legos out of the bin onto the floor. He walked slowly toward the spot where the other children were using the Legos, but stopped

halfway and stared, then turned slowly around and walked back to the block area. Thus, he seems to exhibit the intention and desire to interact but appears at times unsure or apprehensive about how to initiate contact.

D'Andre demonstrates a broad vocabulary and ability to construct full sentences when he talks to adults. He often initiates conversations with them, asking for help or expressing his needs, wants, and ideas. In contrast, the language he uses with peers is simpler and consists mainly of one-word utterances or phrases that are akin to the way they speak. Perhaps he is just more comfortable with adults, being an only child in a two-parent family. He appears to be very attached to his mother as evidenced by his hesitance in separating from her at the beginning of each day. At times his mother seems to have high expectations for him as evidenced by her choosing to read a book to him that was above his level and her expressed concern that he might regress when he started in a new school. Perhaps this contributes to a lack of confidence on his part as when he stands passively when she puts on his coat or requires a lot of help from adults in putting on his socks.

It will be invaluable for D'Andre's future teachers to keep in mind that his slow-to-warm-up temperament contributes to his tendency to stand back and observe before acting. Combined with his calm demeanor and ability to stay focused once he becomes involved in an activity, this might make it easy for teachers to lose sight of him. Yet he will need their support at times, particularly in new situations and in making social connections with other children. Helping his mother recognize and appreciate his strengths may ease her anxieties about his school performance.

Children are complicated creatures, as all human beings are. But because they are still openly revealing their feelings and thoughts and are uninhibited in reaching out to life, sensitive adults can get to know them well enough to gauge their needs with a fair degree of accuracy.

Each child is a unique combination of inherited unknowns interacting with particular family and cultural influences. As such, each child is unlike anyone else. Each child is also representative of a stage of development in the life of a human being, and as such shares many characteristics with other children at the same stage. And finally, each child at school is a member of a society of peers in which the struggle both to be oneself and to belong to the group calls forth particular responses to the demands of all the others who are equally engaged in balancing out their separate, individual needs with the satisfactions of belonging to the whole group.

Although there is much we can learn about children, no teacher can ever know any child so well that there will be no surprises. The very nature of children's ongoing growth implies change, and that requires a constant state of open-mindedness from a teacher. We can only make educated guesses today as to how a child responds to life. Tomorrow we start all over again, because every growing child's tomorrow is a little different from that child's today.

# References

Abbott, C. F., & Gold, S. (1991). Conferring with parents when you're concerned that their child needs special services. *Young Children, 46*(4), 10–14.

Andersen, K. (1995). Beyond playgrounds: Outdoor experiences for toddlers. Unpublished paper, Bank Street Graduate School of Education, New York.

Anisfeld, M. (1984). *Language development from birth to three.* Hillsdale, NJ: Erlbaum.

Ayres, A. J. (1979). *Sensory integration and the child.* Los Angeles: Western Psychological Services.

Balaban, N. (1992). Mainstreamed, mixed-age groups of infants and toddlers at the Bank Street Family Center. In S. Provence, J. Pawl, & E. Fenichel (Eds.), *The zero to three anthology, 1984–1992* (pp. 23–28). Arlington, VA: Zero to Three/National Center for Clinical Infant Programs.

Berk, L. E. (1985). Why children talk to themselves. *Young Children, 40*(5), 46–52.

Berk, L. E. (1994, November). Why children talk to themselves. *Scientific American,* pp. 78–83.

Berk, L., & Winsler, A. (1995). *Scaffolding children's learning: Vygotsky and early childhood education.* Washington, DC: National Association for the Education of Young Children.

Bowman, B. T., & Stott, F. (1994). Understanding development in a cultural context: The challenge for teachers. In B. L. Mallory & R. S. New (Eds.), *Diversity and developmentally appropriate practices: Challenges for early childhood education* (pp. 119–135). New York: Teachers College Press.

Bram, J. (1955). *Language and society.* New York: Random House.

Brown-Murray, G. (2006). Unpublished student journal, Bank Street College of Education.

Brownell, C. A. (1990). Social skills in toddlers: Competencies and constraints illustrated by same-age and mixed-age interaction. *Child Development, 61,* 838–848.

Carew, J. V., Chan, I., & Halfar, C. (1976). *Observing intelligence in young children.* Englewood Cliffs, NJ: Prentice-Hall.

Cazden, C., John, V. P., & Hymes, D. (Eds.). (1972). *Functions of language in the classroom.* New York: Teachers College Press.

Clay, M. (1975). *What did I write?* Auckland, New Zealand: Heinemann.

Clay, M. (1991). *Becoming literate: The construction of inner control.* Portsmouth, NH: Heinemann.

Clay, M. (2002). *An observation survey of early literacy achievement.* Portsmouth, NH: Heinemann.

Cohen, D. (1971). The young child . . . Learning to observe and observing to learn. In G. Engstrom (Ed.), *The significance of the young child's motor development* (pp. 35–44). Washington, DC: National Association for the Education of Young Children.

Cohen, D. H., Stern, V., & Balaban, N. (1997). *Observing and recording the behavior of young children* (4th ed.). New York: Teachers College Press.

Cole, M., & Cole, S. R. (2005). *The development of children* (5th ed.). New York: Worth.

Cuffaro, H. K. (1996). Dramatic play—The experience of block building. In E. S. Hirsch (Ed.), *The block book* (3rd ed., pp. 75–102). Washington, DC: National Association for the Education of Young Children.

Delpit, L. (1995). *Other people's children: Cultural conflict in the classroom.* New York: New Press.

Delpit, L. (2002). What should teachers do? Ebonics and culturally responsive instruction. In B. M. Power & R. S. Hubbard (Eds.), *Language development: A reader for teachers* (2nd ed., pp. 124–128). Upper Saddle River, NJ: Pearson.

Derman-Sparks, L., & the A. B. C. Task Force. (1989). *Anti-bias curriculum: Tools for empowering young children.* Washington, DC: National Association for the Education of Young Children.

Donaldson, M. (1978). *Children's minds.* London: Fontana.

Gardner, H. (1999). *Intelligence reframed.* New York: Basic Books.

Gibson, L. (1989). *Literacy learning in the early years: Through children's eyes.* New York: Teachers College Press.

Goldstein, B. A. (2004). *Bilingual language development and disorders in Spanish-English speakers.* Baltimore, MD: Brooks.

Goswami, U. (1998). *Cognition in children.* Hove, East Sussex, UK: Psychology Press.

Greenspan, S. I. (1989). *The essential partnership: How parents and children can meet the emotional challenges of infancy and childhood.* New York: Viking Penguin.

Greenspan, S. I. (1992). *Infancy and early childhood: The practice of clinical assessment and intervention with emotional and developmental challenges.*

Madison, CT: International Universities Press.

Gumperz, J. J., & Hernandez-Chavez, E. (1972). Bilingualism, bidialectalism, and classroom interaction. In C. Cazden, V. P. John, & D. Hymes (Eds.), *Functions of language in the classroom* (pp. 84–108). New York: Teachers College Press.

Haight, W. L., & Miller, P. J. (1993). *Pretending at home: Early development in a sociocultural context.* Albany: State University of New York Press.

Hansen, N. (1995). A developmental study. Unpublished paper, Bank Street College of Education, New York.

Hayes, K. (1993). Supporting emergent literacy in a 4/5's classroom. Unpublished master's thesis, Bank Street College of Education, New York.

Hayes, L. (1990). From scribbling to writing: Smoothing the way. *Young Children, 45*(3), 62–69.

Heath, S. B. (1982). What no bedtime story means: Narrative skills at home and school. *Language in Society, 11,* 49–76.

Heath, S. B. (1983). *Ways with words: Language, life, and work in communities and classrooms.* Cambridge: Cambridge University Press.

Hirsch, E. S. (Ed.). (1996). *The block book* (3rd ed.). Washington, DC: National Association for the Education of Young Children.

Hurley, S. R., & Tinajero, J. V. (Eds.). (2001). *Literacy assessment of second language learners.* Boston: Allyn & Bacon.

Jersild, A. T. (1955). *When teachers face themselves.* New York: Bureau of Publications, Teachers College, Columbia University.

Kang, K. C. (1990, September 8). Koreans have a reason not to smile. *New York Times,* p. 23.

Keenan, E. O., & Klein, E. (1975). Coherency in children's discourse. *Journal of Psycholinguistic Research, 40*(4), 365–380.

Klein, M., Cook, R., & Richardson-Gibbs, A. M. (2001). *Strategies for including children with special needs in early childhood settings.* Albany, NY: Delmar.

Kritchevsky, S., Prescott, E., & Walling, L. (1969). *Planning environments for young children: Physical space.* Washington, DC: National Association for the Education of Young Children.

Leavitt, R. L. (1994). *Power and emotion in infant-toddler day care.* Albany: State University of New York Press.

Linder, T. W. (1990). *Transdisciplinary play-based assessment: A functional approach to working with young children.* Baltimore, MD: Brookes.

Lubeck, S. (1994). The politics of developmentally appropriate practice: Exploring issues of culture, class, and curriculum. In B. L. Mallory & R. S. New (Eds.), *Diversity and developmentally appropriate practices: Challenges for early childhood education* (pp. 17–43). New York: Teachers College Press.

Mallory, B. L., & New, R. S. (Eds.). (1994). *Diversity and developmentally appropriate practices: Challenges for early childhood education.* New York: Teachers College Press.

Mann, T., Steward, M., Eggbeer, L., & Norton, D. (2007). Zero to Three's Task Force on culture and development: Learning to walk the talk. *Zero to Three, 27*(5), 7–15.

Martin, N. (1987). On the move. In D. Goswani & P. R. Stillman (Eds.), *Reclaiming the classroom* (pp. 20–28). Upper Montclair, NJ: Boynton/ Cook.

Meece, J. (2002). *Child and adolescent development for educators.* New York: McGraw-Hill.

Michaels, S. (1981). "Sharing time": Children's narrative styles and differential access to literacy. *Language in Society, 10,* 423–442.

Monighan Nourot, P., & Van Hoorn, J. L. (1991). Symbolic play in preschool and primary settings. *Young Children, 46*(6), 40–50.

National Association for the Education of Young Children. (2006). Early Childhood Program Standards and Accreditation Criteria. Available at www.naeyc.org/accreditation/criteria/

National Association for the Education of Young Children & the National Association of Early Childhood Specialists in State Departments of Education (NAEYC & NAECS/SDE). (1991). Guidelines for appropriate curriculum content and assessment in programs serving children ages 3 through 8. *Young Children, 46*(3), 21–38.

National Association for the Education of Young Children & the National Association of Early Childhood Specialists in State Departments of Education (NAEYC & NAECS/SDE). (2003). Early Childhood Curriculum Assessment and Program Evaluation: Building an Effective, Accountable System in Programs for Children Birth through Age 8. Available at www.naeyc.org/positions/pdf/CAPEexpand.pdf

Nelson, K. (1989). *Narratives from the crib.* Cambridge, MA: Harvard University Press.

New, R. S. (1994). Culture, child development, and developmentally appropriate practices: Teachers as collaborative researchers. In B. L. Mallory & R. S. New (Eds.), *Diversity and developmentally appropriate practices: Challenges for early childhood education* (pp. 65–83). New York: Teachers College Press.

Owens, R. (2001). *Language development: An introduction* (5th ed.). Boston, MA: Allyn and Bacon.

Paley, V. G. (1984). *Boys & girls: Superheroes in the doll corner.* Chicago, IL: University of Chicago Press.

Perez, B., & Torres-Guzman, M. E. (1992). *Learning in two worlds: An integrated Spanish/English biliteracy approach.* New York: Longmans.

Piaget, J. (1962a). *The language and thought of the child.* London: Kegan Paul, Trench, and Trubner.

Piaget, J. (1962b). *Play, dreams and imitation in childhood.* New York: W. W. Norton.

Piaget, J. (1965). *The moral judgement of the child.* New York: Free Press.

Piaget, J., & Inhelder, B. (1969). *The psychology of the child.* New York: Basic Books.

Powell, D. (1994, June 22). Supporting parents, during the formative years. Speech, Bank Street College of Education, New York.

Project Healthy Choices. (n.d.). *Stories from East Harlem.* New York: Bank Street College of Education.

Resch, R. C. (1977). On separating as a developmental phenomenon: A natural study. *Psychoanalytic Contemporary Science* (pp. 207–269).

Rogoff, B. (1990). *Apprenticeship in thinking: Cognitive development in social context.* New York: Oxford University Press.

Rogoff, B., Mistry, J., Goncu, A., & Mosier, C. (1993). Guided participation in cultural activity by toddlers and caregivers. *Monograph of the society for research in child development, 58*(8, Serial No. 236).

Roopnarine, J. L., Johnson, J. E., & Hooper, F. H. (1994). *Children's play in diverse cultures.* Albany: State University of New York Press.

Schön, D. A. (1983). *The reflective practitioner.* New York: Basic Books.

Sheridan, M. K., Foley, G. M., & Radlinski, S. H. (1995). *Using the supportive play model: Individualized intervention in early childhood practice.* New York: Teachers College Press.

Shinn, M. W. (1985). *The biography of a baby.* Reading, MA: Addison-Wesley. (Original work published 1900)

Shonkoff, J. & Phillips, D. (Eds.). (2000). *From neurons to neighborhoods: The science of early childhood development.* Committee on integrating the science of early childhood development. Washington, DC: Academy Press.

Singer, D. G., & Singer, J. L. (1990). *The house of make-believe: Play and the development of imagination.* Cambridge, MA: Harvard University Press.

Stern, D. N. (1985). *The interpersonal world of the infant.* New York: Basic Books.

Tabors, P. O. (1997). *One child, two languages: A guide for preschool educators of children learning English as a second language.* Baltimore, MD: Brookes.

Thomas, A., & Chess, S. (1977). *Temperament and development.* New York: Brunner/Mazel.

Vygotsky, L. (1962). *Thought and language.* Cambridge, MA: MIT Press. (Original work published 1934)

Vygotsky, L. S. (1976). Play and its role in the mental development of the child. In J. S. Bruner, A. Jolly, & K. Sylva (Eds.), *Play—Its role in development and evolution* (pp. 536–554). New York: Basic Books. (Original work published 1933)

Vygotsky, L. S. (1978). *Mind in society: The development of higher psychological processes* (M. Cole, V. John Steiner, S. Scribner, & E. Souberman, Eds.). Cambridge, MA: Harvard University Press. (Original work published 1930)

Weir, R. (1962). *Language in the crib.* The Hague: Mouton.

Williamson, G. G. (1988). Motor control as a resource for adaptive coping. *Zero to three: Bulletin of National Center for Clinical Infant Programs, 9*(1), 1–7.

Wood, D. (1988). *How children think and learn: The social contexts of cognitive development.* Cambridge, MA: Basil Blackwell.

Wood, D., Bruner, J., & Ross, G. (1976). The role of tutoring in problem solving. *Journal of Child Psychology and Psychiatry, 17*(2), 89–100.

# Index

# About
# the Authors

**Dorothy H. Cohen**, at the time of her death, was senior faculty in Graduate Programs at Bank Street College, where she had taught for many years. She received her doctorate from New York University, having also done graduate work at both Bank Street and Teachers College. At the time of this book's first edition, she taught at Patterson State Teachers College and Long Island University as well. A well-known speaker, author of many articles and *The Learning Child*, she also co-authored *Kindergarten: A Year of Learning* (later titled *Kindergarten and Early Schooling*) with Marguerita Rudolph.

**Virginia Stern** was a longtime Associate in the Research Division of Bank Street College before her death. Although she was engaged in varied research projects there, of particular interest was her involvement in a study of 2-year-olds and her special attention to dramatic play. Receiving an undergraduate degree in psychology and economics from Antioch College, she earned her graduate degree from Bank Street. In addition to lecturing and writing on early childhood, she was a successful sculptor and a teacher of classical piano.

**Nancy Balaban** is a faculty member and former Director of the Infant and Parent Development and Early Intervention Program at Bank Street Graduate School of Education. A graduate of Wellesley College, she received her master's degree from Bank Street College and doctorate from New York University. She has an extensive background as an early childhood teacher and teacher educator. A speaker and writer, she is author of *Everyday Goodbyes: Starting School* and *Early Care: A Guide to the Separation Process* in addition to journal articles and book chapters.

**Nancy Gropper** is a faculty member and former Director of the Student Teaching Program in Early Childhood & Childhood Education at Bank Street Graduate School of Education. She received both her doctorate and master's degree from Teachers College and her bachelor's degree from the University of Delaware. She was a faculty member at Brooklyn College and at the State University of New York at New Paltz, where she served as Chair of the Department of Elementary Education. She was formerly an early childhood classroom teacher. Dr. Gropper has extensive experience as an evaluator of educational programs, and among her publications are articles focused on gender issues.